AF540990

# Contents

# Preface

Library Management System is essentially meant of collections. It is a multi-user version and can take care of all the fundamental functions of a Library like Cataloguing, Circulation, Accessioning and Housekeeping. Modern libraries are not made up of just Books but CD ROM's, Articles, Project Reports, Bound volumes are substantial part of the holding, Managing the holdings manually is a not a simple job. In modern library system scientific management requires complete mental revolution on the part of workers and management. In the age of IT revolution, library system has also undergone drastic changes. Modern libraries often publish lists of accessions and may maintain a readers' advisory service. Interlibrary loan services, lecture series, public book reviews, and the maintenance of special juvenile collections are other important recent developments.

The concept of *Modern Library System* is categorically narrated in this book. Academics and professionals in the field will find this work an authentic reference tool.

***—Author***

# 1

# Library Manual

## INTRODUCTION

Library manual is a source of information, a constitution which lists out all departments, sections and their functions, procedures and policies within the library. It is a source that library staff will consult whenever there is any confusion about any function or procedure. Lot of efforts goes into the preparation of the manual. It goes through a series of meetings with all stake holders where the procedures and functions and policies are deliberated in detail, over and again to draft the final policy. Hence, a Library Manual goes throu]gh a validation process before it is finally accepted as a policy document.

## ROLE OF LIBRARY

Library plays a very critical role in supporting the academic programmes of the institute. It identifies, evaluates, procures, processes and then makes these learning resources available to the faculty and students for their teaching, learning and research assignments. Thet is why, DR.S.R. Ranganathan, facther of library Science development in India has famously said that the Library is the trinity of Learning Resources, Faculty/Students and the Library Staff.

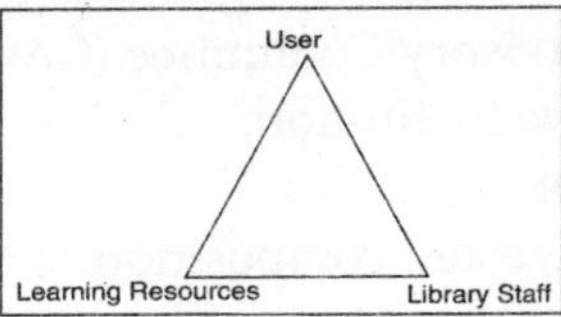


**Fig.** 1.1

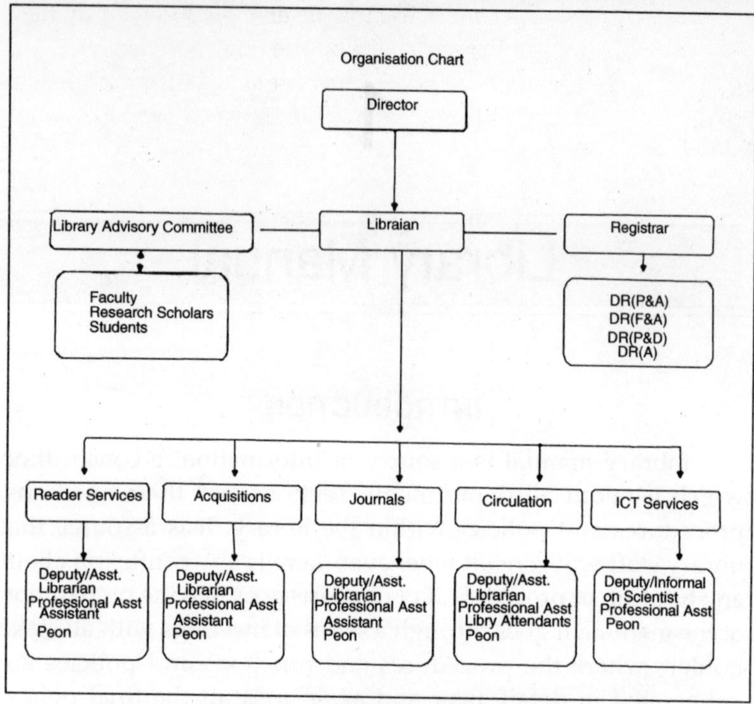


**Fig.** 1.2. Organization Chart.

## LIBRARY ADVISORY COMMITTEE (LAC)

The function of the Library Advisory Committee is to support the functioning of the library so that it can facilitate the library development plans by advocating the library development activities with the management. The purpose of the Library Advisory Committee is to act as a channel of communication and dialogue between the University Library and its users. The Committee's main objective is to aid in the establishment a bridge between the Library and the academic fraternity and the institute management.

The Library Advisory Committee (LAC) is to be appointed by the Director of the Institution:

* *Composition:*
  - The suggested composition of this Committee is as follows:

a. *Chairperson:* Director/or any person nominated by the Director will be the chairperson
b. *Members:* One faculty each from Schools/ Independent Centers (Librarian to propose panel names)
c. *Secretary:* Librarian Shall be the Secretary of LAC
d. All officers of the Library shall participate in the meeting to provide required inputs

* *Meeting Frequency:* The LAC would meet at least once in every quarter to review the library affairs
* *Tenure*: The committee shall be reconstituted once in two years. Director can recommend a replacement for a member who withdraws from the LAC. No member shall serve the Committee for more than two consecutive terms. For the sake of continuation one third of members from previous committee need to continue
* *Meeting Minutes:* Meeting minutes shall be recorded and circulated to all members for consideration. In the next meeting, the minutes shall be confirmed by the members.
* Terms of Reference for LAC:
  - To provide general direction to the Library
  - To review the functioning of the library with regards to its support to the academic programmes of the institute.
  - To advise the management on matters of policy relating to development of library.
  - To outline the library collection development policy as and when required, for its implementation.
  - To monitor and evaluate, from time to time, trends and developments in information technologies, networking, library automation, library cooperation etc., and to direct the library in their adoption.
  - To suggest ways and means to generate revenue from library resources.
  - To formulate action plan for the development of library infrastructure, facilities, products and services.

- Evaluate the suggestions made by the library users
- To formulate the policy for library use and procedure to be framed
- To assist library in providing need based information services
- To review the requirements of the new programmes being introduced and advise library about financial assistance.
- Evaluating the books procurement school wise and allocation of budget accordingly.
- Any other function as assigned by Director

## LIBRARY BUDGET/FINANCES

Library budget means the financial allocation to procure documents and provide access to the information resources.

The present annual library budget of the library has the following components:

* UGC Plan Grants
* Allocation from Institute Maintenance Grants (Journals)
* School/Centre Grants(Like DRS Projects, etc)
* Programme Specific Grants (Like JTCDM, SRTT Grants, etc.)
* Trust/endowment Grants (Tata Excellence Grants)

### Allocation from Projects being Carried Out at TISS

Several projects are being carried out at institute. Most of them depend upon to a great extent on library infrastructure for the learning resources and internet access. However, not all projects have a separate allocation to be given to library for using the library facility. Library will grow only when it is supported by all who make use of its resources. In this case, each project, should earmark at least 8% of its total project cost towards library expenditure. And this should be indicated to the library, so that all the learning resources needed by the project and their faculties are procured using their own project funds.

Annual Reports, directories, Year Books, India Reference Annuals and those having no archival importance (such as India-a reference annual, Handbook of universities, Swami's handbook, etc.) may be procured under noncapital budget sub head. Budget must have contingency funds for Binding and other stationery needed to process and maintain the Books/Journals

## Library: Different from Stores

As indicated in the GoI. M.F. OM 23(7)- EII(A)/83 dated 7th Feburary 1984, (GFR 116(2)(1) (1978)), "the position of library books, etc., is different from that of stores".

The above OM is reproduced below:

* "Librarian subject to the powers delegated under Delegation of Financial powers Rules, 1978, may purchase books, etc., from the reputed and standard book sellers on the prevalent terms and conditions. Tenders need not be called for this purpose."

## Resources with Ephemeral Value and those whose Revised Editions are Frequently Published

Annuals, directories, yearbooks, Swamy's handbooks, etc., do not carry long lasting value, and therefore be purchased from contingent expenditure budgets only which also would facilitate easy weeding out of these items. The categorization of the documents for its ephemeral value or otherwise be decided by the library committee.

# PROCUREMENT OF LEARNING RESOURCES

Procurement of learning resource constitutes the primary responsibility of library. Library makes a systematic effort in building up the collection development by identifying, evaluating, selecting, processing and making it available to the users. Whether it's a book, journal or an online database, any learning resource that gets added goes through a rigorous selection process. And since this collection building requires huge sums of money and has long-lasting repercussions, it is very much essential that libraries have a well thought out collection development policy.

## PROCUREMENT OF BOOKS/REPORTS

* Faculty can recommend the books to be procured for

their courses and research

* Students/Research Scholars can also recommend the books for procurement provided their recommendation is endorsed by a faculty member
* All faculty indents will be routed through Finance/ Accounts Department for the approval of Registrar and Director for making financial arrangement.
* The ordering can be done by print, online, e-mail, etc., depending upon the convenience of the library with standard terms and conditions
* Purchase Orders will be Issued by the Librarian
* Appoint a Panel of Vendors based on their performance like response to the queries, speed of supply, adherence to the terms and conditions, etc.
* Updating vendor panel from time to time based on their performance is a continuous activity and this should be done by ordering books to test vendors.
* A panel should have at least 8 Vendors
* There are also cases where the documents/books can be obtained only from specific sources, standard agencies – who are not on the panel.

## Terms and Conditions for Vendors

* Supply of publications at current catalogue prices.
* Foreign Exchange rates to be charged according to Good Offices Committee Report Rates (GOC)
* Minimum 10% discount to be fixed for all
* In the case of short/no discount titles or titles procured from abroad against specific orders (like institutional/ society publications), the supplier may charge 15% on the net landed cost of the publication. The invoice of publication may be worked out as follows:
  - Published price minus (-) discount earned plus (+) 15% handling charges of the overseas agent if any. To this is to be added the actual freight, clearance, bank and postal charges; documentary evidence is to be given to library for such charges on demand.

* No discount for Central and State Government publications
* Wherever advance payment is required, the same may be made and a record thereof should be maintained
* Certificates on bills by Library
  - Only latest editions have been supplied (b)
  - Prices have been correctly charged in accordance with the publisher's latest catalogue.
* Unless otherwise mentioned on the books, all bills to carry the price proof (like photocopy of publishers catalogue, print out from publishers online catalogue, distributors invoice the vendor)
* The Purchase Order issued will be valid for only 90 days unless otherwise mentioned.

## Procurement Process

* *Initiation of Acquisition:*
  - Receiving Recommendations by Indent Forms, E-mails, Noting Sheets, Publisher Catalogues marked and singned
  - Find out the Exact details of the Title recommended
  - Duplicate Checking
  - Correspond with Suppliers/vendors for checking Availability Status
  - Put up for Approval( A/c Dept, Registrar and Director)
  - Prepare and Issue Purchase Orders
* *Accessioning:*
  - *Accessioning*: Enter the details of the Invoice and Books in Accession Register.
  - Assign Accession Numbers to Titles in Computer Purchase Bills.
  - Pass entries in Bill Register and forward bills.
  - Maintain Bill File.
  - Maintain Bill Register Data in EXCEL Sheet for reporting.
* *Invoice Processing:*
  - Receive Books from Suppliers/Vendors,

- Crosschecking with Purchase Orders,
- Foreign Exchange Rate Verification as per Good Offices Committee Report rates,
- Price Proof Verification for Foreign Publications and for books on which price is not mentioned ( Photocopy of the Publisher catalogue, Print out from the Publisher's Website, photocopy of the invoice received by the supplier from the distributor),
- Prepare Book Received Report (BRR) on SLIM database,
- Prepare Purchase Bill (PB) on SLIM database,

* *Classifying:*

- Classify Books/Thesis/Dissertations as per the Dewey Decimal Classification (DDC) Schedule,
- Assign Cutter Numbers,
- Write the Class No, Cutter No and Collation on the back of Title page,

* *Cataloguing:*

- Bibliographic Details of each book is entered into Cataloguing Module database according to AACR2 Standards.
- Assigning Keywords: Minimum three keywords are assigned to each title.
- *Data Validation*: Regular editing of various access points in database like Author, Title, Class No, etc.
- Making Analytical Entries, wherever needed.

* *Processing Books:*

- *Stamping*: Library Stamp to be put on the back of Title page, on Secret page and on the Last page.
- Paste bar Codes on the Front Page and on the Title page and laminate it with Cello tape.
- Insert 3M Security Tattle Tape.
- Prepare Book cards using SLIM.
- Send the completely ready to use new arrivals to New Additions Rack, Reference Section or Reserve Shelf, as the case may be.

* Institute Material like Dissertation/Thesis/Reports and the Books received as Gift:

- These items to be treated like books for processing, etc.
- If the book/Report is already available in Main Library, then it will be sent to Rural Campus.

* *Financial Planning/Budgeting:*
  - *Monthly Utilization Report:* Grants/Account wise.
  - Inform Faculty/Project In charge about the status of funds every two months.
  - Initiate utilization of funds in advance so that funds are utilized before the deadlines set in.
  - Prepare proposals/ requests for mobilizing funds for the acquisition.
* *Reports to be generated (Monthly):*
  - No. of Requests Received from Faculty.
  - No. of Titles Recommended.
  - Status of the recommended titles( Already Library has, Out of Print, Untraced).
  - No. of Titles Ordered.
  - No. of Titles received( Success rate).
  - No. of Titles received as Gifts/Donations.
  - "New Additions Bulletin" (Monthly).
  - Book Received information to recommending faculty ( Fortnightly).
* *Vendor Follow Up:*
  - Titles Not Supplied.
  - Reminders to Suppliers fortnightly.
  - After checking the inability of one supplier, redirecting the Order to another supplier.

## SUBSCRIPTIONS OF JOURNALS

### Availability of Funds

* Ensure that adequate recurring/annual funds are available for the Journals Subscription/renewals etc. as required.

### Procedure for Preparing a Panel of Vendors

Library should have a panel of vendors for different kinds

of documents with following criteria:

* Registration number obtained under shop act, age of the organization
* *Performance:* Response to the correspondence, speed of supply, adherence to the terms and conditions
* Experience by the peers
* PAN/TAN, Sales/ VAT tax number
* Publishers that a vendor supports
* Vendors turnover having at least 10 times of the value of the order (for the journals subscriptions)
* Updating panel from time to time based on the performance of the vendor is a continuous activity and this should be done by ordering books to test vendors.
* Based on the performance, the panel should have least number of vendors

**Terms and Conditions**

* Supply of periodicals at current catalogue prices.
* Sign an Agreement with the vendors in case of Foreign Journals
* Proof of GOC exchange rates having prices in foreign currencies as on the date/month of invoice for the remittance journal subscriptions
* Wherever advance payment is required, the same may be made and a record thereof should be maintained
* Normally there is no discount on the journals
* Certificates on bills: prices have been correctly charged in accordance with the publisher's latest catalogue.
* Library should not subscribe journals against 'personal subscriptions'. However, Journals received against institutional membership are acceptable.
* Journal subscription payments: The payment towards the journal subscriptions could be made
  - Directly to the publisher or
  - Through the subscription agent(s)/ vendor(s).

Following options are also available:

- All subscriptions should be made through the

Library only and the amount paid to the publishers/vendors by the vendors against firm orders after receiving one of the following documentary proofs:

a. After direct confirmation from publishers/ vendors that the journals are subscribed in the name of the Institute.

b. Proof for Remittance:

   i. Invoice/Bill in duplicate should be provide by the publisher/vendor.

   ii. Publishers' Renewal Letter/Notice mentioning the subscription price/cost (*e.g.* Indian journals).

   iii. Even print out of the from the Publishers'/ journal's official website can also be considered wherein the proper invoice/bill etc. not received by the publisher/s.

   iv. A copy of the letter sent to the publisher giving details of the journals for which remittance has been made and.

   v. Copy of demand draft issued by bank attested by the bank or a letter from the bank giving details of remittance (if the payment is made by foreign currency draft obtained from the bank).

- Publisher's acknowledgement of receipt of payment or letter from bank as a proof regarding the final remittance to the publisher (if the payment is made from vendor's foreign currency account).
- Advance payment against bank guarantee. The bank guarantee can be released only after receiving any of the above documents/proofs as spelt above.

* *Missing Issues:* Replace original missing issues or publishers certified and reproduced copy or extend the subscription period equivalent to corresponding period or refund either in the form of credit note or Demand Draft or Cheque.

* *Claims:* Missing issues/delayed supply of the journal issues can be claimed on quarterly basis.
* *Online Access:* Negotiate with the publishers/vendors and arrive at win-win situation regarding electronic version of the print subscriptions and get access to such materials.
* Try to enforce terms to the publishers/vendors in form of the pricing, access to the back volumes, locking period, perpetual access, archival rights, governing laws, training and awareness programmes, immunity, access to the walk-in-users, usage statistics, simultaneous access, etc.
* There are no standard/uniformly acceptable terms that are yet to be established in this area, as this is almost virgin and challenging field. Hence go on with mutually benefiting terms and conditions while dealing with the vendors which can be revised time to time.
* *Consortium:* Since the Institute has access to the 'UGC-Infonet e-Consortium' care should be taken to check for duplication before placing any order.
* *Trial Access:* Many a times publishers propose for trial access to their respective journals collections which can be made accessible through the Institute's IP numbers to supplement the existing journals collection whenever possible.

## Ordering Journals

* Compile priority list with the approval of library advisory committee and the Director
* Adhere to the Terms and Conditions of the Library
* Budget estimate based on the costs, currency conversion
* Place orders from available options as indicated in terms and conditions
* Payment against the original and proper invoice/bill/renewal notice etc.

## Receipt of and Access to the Materials

*Check-in System:*

* Ensure that the items received are as per the order/

access is enabled to the desired resource

* Manual (Kardex) and computerized record of receipts of the journal issues
* Article/s entry into the in-house database in response to the set user profile
* Timely display of the Loose Issues of the periodicals on the respective display racks.
* Linking to the online content wherever applicable
* Accessioning the virtual resources should not be done since they do not exist in physical form.
* Accompanying materials such as CDs/DVDs etc are being preserved at the INFLIBNET Centre of the Library. Other than CDs/DVDs are kept with the Periodicals Section.

*Certification/ notification against advance payments:*

* The invoices/bills and documentary proofs be duly scrutinized by library. The invoices/bills duly certified by the Head of the library or his/her designated authority be sent to F&A Section for payment.
* In case of advance payment, after the receipt of the document the necessary entry should be made in records to close down the outstanding balance.
* A proper Bill Register to be maintained to record all the payments sought/made

## Gratis and Exchange Periodicals

* The documents relevant to the scope of the Institute's study and research areas be added and accessioned in the collection
* Try to get the free/discounted subscription/s to the periodical/s wherever possible.
* Gratis may be accepted from the Institute's faculty, scholars, or outside institutes and organisations of similar interest.
* Avoid duplication unless essential
* Find good place for the documents that are not relevant to the Institute
* No need to maintain a separate collection/s

* There should be a proper record of gratis items and can be acknowledged appropriately
* Journals under Exchange mode are being handled by the Manager, Publications Unit, and the Library is at the receiving end only.
* Claims regarding the non-receipts of Exchange Journals will be addressed to the Manager, Publications Unit, TISS, Mumbai.
* Journals under 'Exchange and Free Subscription' can be treated as regular subscriptions and article entry is advised to be done in the Library Database and the completed volumes will be bound and accessioned and archived.

## Archiving and Weeding Out

In order to provide better access to the frequently consulted literature, back volumes are archived in a less active storage area. Though the library gets access to the back volumes online from the publisher's websites, etc., the print volumes of these journals also be considered for archiving in less active storage area. Adequate space should be provided for archival storage to Library if not available.

The following categories of materials can be considered for weeding out:

* Ephemeral material (*e.g.* newsletters, progress reports, pamphlets) including those materials that lose value after a certain period of time such as: annual reports, directories, yearbooks, etc. These are weeded out annually.
* Duplicate issues of the journals may not necessarily be weeded out even the volumes are bound. They can be passed on to the Rural Campus or any institute/ organisation's Library to seek the prospect readers.

## Other Resources Managed

### *Other than Journals*

A variety of other information resources are received and

displayed for use in the Periodicals Section which are being received free of charge, namely:

* Complimentary Loose issues of Journals
* Annual Reports
* Working Papers
* Occasional Papers
* Discussion Papers
* Technical/Trend Reports
* Brochures
* Prospectus etc.

And, the receipt should be acknowledged timely and oblige.

### *Non-Book Materials*

A small collection of Non-Book Materials such as Audio Cassettes, Video Cassettes/VHSs, Microfilms, Microfiche, 35mm films, Psychological Tests, Booklets, Posters etc is being maintained at the Periodicals Section and enlisted in a computer file (MS-Excel). These materials are open to all our Library users.

### Maintenance of Records

The transactions of all the activities/procedures/etc. in the Periodicals Section should be carefully and properly recorded for the relevant information and documentation.

In this regard apart from the automated system, the section maintains the following documents for keeping the records:

* Periodicals Record Registers
* Bills Register
* Gratis Journals Record Register
* Kardex
* Card Catalogue for Bound Volumes and
* Various Files

## PROCUREMENT OF E-RESOURCES

* Large opportunities exist in this area for negotiation with the publishers/ resource providers and arrive at win-win situation. Ejournals, e-books, databases, etc., are the resources available in electronic form and one can have virtual access to these.

* There exist many pricing models. The libraries can adopt the model depending on various factors. The libraries have to decide based on the estimated usage and cost to go for any of the access.
* Experiences indicate that the young generation of users are for the e-access and therefore there is a need to have a major shift of our print resources to e-resources. This would also resolve other management issues.
* One can enforce terms to the publishers/vendors in form of the pricing, access to the back volumes, locking period, perpetual access, archival rights, governing laws, training and awareness programmes, immunity, access to the walk-in-users, usage statistics, simultaneous access, etc.
* There are no standard/ uniformly acceptable terms that are yet to be established in this area, as this is almost virgin and challenging field.
* Since the UGC Infonet e-journals consortium is providing access to large number of resources to Universities, care needs to be taken that institute gets maximum number of e journals from that consortia.
* In case of termination of the agreement or on expiry of the agreement, the licensor shall provide the full-text of the e-journals entered into agreement and for the period of agreement on the prevalent state of art formats *i.e.* DVDs, CDs, etc., with the retrieval software.
* E-books are becoming a common reality. Like journals it is essential that the access to these resources be provided taking in to account current pricing models and trends in usage.

## CIRCULATION SECTION

Circulation Section handles the Front Desk operations of the library and is very important because it is the first contact point for faculty and users to the library. Efficient functioning Circulation Desk leaves a lasting impression on the user and hence it is very important section of the library.

Major Activities of the Section are:

* Issue and returns of Learning Resources(Primarily Books)
* Attending the Users' query for effective interpretation of library rules and regulations
* Registration of new Members and issue of barcode Generated ID Card for Users
* Inter Library Loan Service
* Operation of "Circulation Module" of Library Management Software SLIM ++. Maintenance and updatation of all data related to users at Circulation desk in SLIM ++ software
* Sending Reminders to overdue documents users
* Display of Books during Seminars/Workshops
* Maintenance of Compendiums
* Correspondence and No Due issuing
* Library Orientations/Information Literacy
* Assisting the users for accessing OPAC and Reference
* Assigning Library Staff duties for Sturdays/Sundays

## ISSUE/RETURN PROCEDURE

Issue/Return of library materials is the routine operation of any library.

Proper flowchart/sequence of activities to be followed to issue and receive the library books is defined as followed:

* While Issuing Book:
  - Quickly glance the book for any damage
  - Ensure that the User writes the details of book in passbook and signs on the Book card
  - Enter details into Issue Database
  - Discharge the books as per 3M Security
  - Prepare gate pass
  - Handover the books/Passbook to the user
* While Receiving the Books:
  - Quickly glance the book for any damage
  - Check Due dates for necessary action
  - Cancel the entries in Pass Book
  - Cancel the entries from user Account in SLIM
  - Charge books as per 3M security System
  - Send them to Stack for Shelving

## LOAN CRITERIA/BORROWING ENTITLEMENTS FOR FACULTY/STUDENTS/ADMIN

Clearly define the number of items that and user is eligible to borrow:

| Category of User | General Shelf Books | | Reserve Shelf Books | |
|---|---|---|---|---|
| | No. of Books | Issue Period | No. of Books | Issue Period |
| Faculty/ Adhoc Faculty | 20 Books | 30 Days | 2 | 2 Days |
| Visiting Faculty | 2 | 15 | | |
| Days Administrative Staff | 5 | 15 | | |
| Days Part Time Ph.D. Scholars | 5 | 30 Days | | |
| M.Phil/Ph.D.Scholars | 10 | 15 Days | 1 | 2 Days |
| Students | 5 | 15 Days | 1 | 2 Days |
| Short Term Courses (DPM, DHA, CSW, EE, etc. | 4 | 15 Days | 1 | 2 Days |
| Research/ Project Assistant | 2 | 15 Days | | |
| Alumni | 1 | 30 Days | | |
| Institutional Membership | 3 | 30 Days | | |

## DOCUMENTS THAT CAN AND CANNOT BE BORROWED

*Books that can be borrowed:*

* Books from the general shelf can be borrowed.
* Reserve Shelf Books can be borrowed only for a day
* CD ROMS, DVDs and audio video cassettes can be borrowed for a period of one week

*Books that cannot be borrowed:*

* Journals Bound Volumes, Loose issues of journals and the latest available issue of the magazines are to be referred within library premises and are not available for issuing out.
* Dissertations/Project Works submitted by TISS Students are not issuable.

*Renewals/Reservations and Over Due/Fines:*

* Books can be renewed for another term of 15 days if there is no demand on them. The renewal must be made on or before the due date
* There will be a over due charge ₹.1/- per day per book

*Loss or Mutilation of documents by Students:*

* Library materials are to be handled with care.
* If a book is lost or mutilated beyond usable condition, then the book has to be replaced with the same or latest edition of that book.
* If the book is out of print, then three times the cost of the book has to be paid to the library.
* If the book is reported (in writing) as lost/ misplaced, the overdue charges are not levied in such case from the date of report until the same is replaced(it must be resolved within two months)

*Day Membership/Visitors Access:*

* All students/researchers from outside TISS who wants to utilize the library are allowed to utilize the library services if they produce valid identity cards and register as day members by paying library fee of ₹.15.00

*Theft/Misuse of Library resources:*

* The theft or abuse of Library resources like books, journal issues, reports, and dissertations will be viewed very seriously.
* Each case will be examined to ascertain its genuineness and the matter will be reported to the LAC/Director for further action.

*Issue of Library Use Certificates:*

* Circulation Desk Shall issue Library use/Attendance certificate to research scholars who request for it. They must apply for it by using the prescribed form of library and produce an introduction letter from the Librarian of their institute/college.

## COLLECTION DEVELOPMENT

All academic and research libraries have a common objective to provide its users the information they want. The effectiveness of this function is directly related to collection development and organization information services. Collection development being the most important of these primary functions, a written acquisition policy outlining the various procedures and methods necessary for collection development is prepared.

### STRENGTH AND WEAKNESS OF THE EXISTING COLLECTION

Institute is starting several new courses. From the seven programmes, now TISS offers 14 post graduate programmes. In relation to these new programmes, Library must make special provision in the budget to strengthen the new programmes with minimal learning resources. Based on the observations, an effort should be done to add books, journals and e-Resources in the area of the new programme.

### FOLLOW UP WITH FUNDING AGENCIES

Library should follow up with funding agencies like UGC, Trusts/endowments for augmenting finances to strengthen the collection development process.

### FOLLOW UP WITH UGC INFONET (CONSORTIUM)

Library must continuously follow up with consortium agencies like UGC infonet for inclusion and addition of new journals and databases to support the new academic programmes

## SHIFT TOWARDS E-RESOURCES

Because of the conveniences like multiple access and anywhere, anytime access, there is a considerable demand for online databases, ejournals and e-books. TISS also has excellent access infrastructure like Cyber Library, 2mbps broadband internet, Wi-fi connectivity in the campus. These e-resources can also be accessed from all new campuses like Hyderabad, Tuljapur, etc. Hence, emphasis may be given more towards e-resources.

## STACK ROOM/DISPLAY AREA MANAGEMENT

Collection Organization plays a very important role in ensuring the optimum utilization of the books, journals kept in the library.

Presently, the learning resources are stacked/displayed in the following categories:

* General Stack Area (Spread across three floors for books/bound Volumes)
* Reserve Shelf Collection(consisting of books in high demand, Thesis/Dissertations, TISS project Reports)
* Reference Section (Consisting of Encyclopedias, Dictionaries, Manuals, etc)
* News paper/Magazine Display Area (Ground Floor)
* Journal Display Racks ( Second Floor)

It is essential that all efforts are carried out by the library for pleasant display and quick retrieval of books/journals by the users.

Library must ensure that:

* All the books removed from the stacks are replaced back in their shelves at least twice a day
* Each unit of Stack to have a designated Library Attendant
* Shelf Reading must be done continuously to look for misplaced books
* Books reported untraced by users be traced in the quickest possible time with documentation like when the request was received and when it was solved
* The stacks should be properly labeled with subject guides and Class Number Guides

## STOCK VERIFICATION AND PROCEDURE TO WITHDRAW BOOKS

### STOCK VERIFICATION

Physical verification of the library stocks has to be carried out to identify the losses, identifying misplaced documents, identifying documents that need repair, etc. Depending upon the size of the library following periodicity is fixed:

| Size of library | Periodicity |
|---|---|
| Up to 20,000 volumes including journal back volumes | 100% physical verification at 3 year intervals |
| Above 20,000 and up to 50,000 volumes including the journal back volumes | 100% physical verification at 5 year intervals |
| Above 50,000 volumes and up to 1,00,000 volumes including the journal back volumes | Sample (20% of the total stock) physical verification at intervals of not more than 5 years. If such a sample verification reveals losses up to 10% of the sample chosen, complete verification is required to be done |
| Above 1,00,000 volumes including the journal back volumes | (10% of the total stock) physical verification at intervals of not Sample more than 5 years. If such a sample verification reveals losses up to 10% of the sample chosen, complete verification is required to be done |

The sample can be of random generation of numbers. The verification has to be carried out by a team of members appointed by the LAC and the library staff will assist the verification team.

### LOSS OF PUBLICATIONS

* Some loss of publications is inevitable especially in the context of open access practice in libraries. The librarian has a role as information manager and not just a custodian. Therefore he/she should not be held

responsible for the losses.

* Loss of 5 volumes per 1000 volumes issued and/or consulted in a year may be taken as reasonable.
* Loss of a book of the value exceeding ₹.2000.00 for books published in India and ₹.10,000.00 for books published abroad and books of special nature and rarity shall invariably be investigated and consequential action taken. The Director will write off all such losses. The base values suggested for Indian and foreign books shall be reviewed every five years.
* A publication may be considered as lost only when it is found missing in two successive stock verifications and thereafter only action be taken to write off the publications by competent authority.
* If the loss of book is more than the permissible extent, the causes of such loss may be investigated by the competent authority and the remedial measures be strengthened.
* Occasional loss/damage of issues of periodicals is inevitable during postal transit. If the payment is made directly to the publisher, then sometimes it is not possible to get the replacement. In such cases, the nonreceipts/ damages be considered as loss for write-off.
* Librarian may write off the loss of books, volumes, etc. mentioned in the proceeding paragraph provided the total value of all such books, etc. does not exceed the monetary limit prescribed the Delegation of Financial Powers Rules, 1978 for Head of a Department in respect of deficiencies and depreciations in the value of stores included in the stock and other accounts. In the event of the total value exceeding the monetary limit specified above, the loss of books shall be written off by the competent authority as specified in the Delegation of Financial Power Rules, 1978's.
* There may be no objection to the Librarian disposing of mutilated/ damaged/ obsolete volumes to the best

interest of the library. However, the disposal of such volumes should be made on the recommendations of a Library Advisory Committee to be appointed by the competent authority which shall decide whether the books mutilated/damaged/obsolete are not fit for further use.

## PROCEDURE FOR WRITE-OFF

* List the documents not found during stock verification
* Library staff to make all possible efforts to locate the document not found during stock verification (the process can go up to six months but not as an exclusive task)
* Prepare pre-final list of the documents not found and publicize
* Compile a final list of documents not found
* Compare with the list of earlier stock verification to identify common entries
* Compare losses with borrowing/ consulting/ photo-copying statistics
* Put up the list of common entries to the Director along with justification for the losses (open access, limited staff, inadequate security system, large number of students visiting library, losses within permissible limits, etc.)
* Get approval from the Director
* Issue OM
* Make necessary entries in the accession register, write-off register, assets register, etc
* Remove records from databases
* Close file.
* Improve the system with additional precautionary measures

## PREVENTIVE MEASURES

Some preventive measures are listed below:

* Follow closed access to the rare books and specialized collections.
* The exit/entry to the library be monitored
* Sealing of windows with wire mesh, installation of

wicket gate, adequate vigilance in the stack room(s), provision of adequate lighting, use of electronic or magnetic gadgets for detection of the theft, closed-circuit television monitoring system, introduction of identity/membership cards for identification of users, etc., can be adopted.

* Inadequate staff in the library is also one of the reasons for the losses.

## USER SERVICES

### REFERENCE SERVICE

Library houses all important reference sources like Encyclopaedias, Dictionaries, handbooks and Manuals, Statistics, Yearbooks. The collection ranges from general to subject specific sources. All the reference sources are housed in the Ground floor Reference section. Users can also contact staff on duty for any assistance. Library also has access to online reference sources which may be accessed from the library website.

### INFORMATION LITERACY/LIBRARY ORIENTATION

Library will conduct Information Literacy/User Education/Orientation programmes to all in the beginning of the academic year. Besides this, these awareness programmes should be conducted when requested by users from time to time.

### INTER–LIBRARY LOAN

Library maintains an inter –library loan arrangement with leading local libraries like IIT Mumbai, Homi Bhabha Centre for Science Education and Research TIFR), Mumbai University, SNDT University, IGIDR, etc. Apart from this library also has membership with DELNET. Hence, all possible efforts must be made to make available the learning resources needed for the faculty and students.

### PHOTOCOPYING SERVICES

Presently library maintains two heavy duty photocopying

machines. Two operators are appointed to provide photocopying service in shift basis.

## ICT SERVICES DIVISION

### UGC-INFONET SERVICES

The SDTM Library is one of the members of INFLIBNET UGC-Infonet Digital Library Consortium since 2003. UGC has set up this programme to promote use of electronic databases and full text access to e-journals by the research and Academic community of the country.

Online databases are accessible via the Library Homepage, which provide access to full-text scholarly research articles beyond the physical wall of the library:

* Access to more than 7000 full text scholarly journals online
* Nine online databases in the field of social science: Project Muse (389 journals); Oxford University Press (202 journals); JSTOR (729 journals); Springer Link (1236 journals); Taylor and Francis (1076 journals); JCCC (Gateway Portal); ISID; Cambridge Journals Online (279 journals); Wiley Interscience (502 journals) available under the UGC-Infonet services
* Library subscribe to Sage Online Journals (240 journals); Emerald Management Xtra (160 journals); ABI/INFORM Complete™ (2950 journals); indiastat.com (statistical database); World Bank Databases (GDF+WDI+e-Library)
* IP Based access to all e-Resources
* Statistical usage reports of e-resources

### DOCUMENT DELIVERY SERVICES

TISS Library has been recognized as one of the Twenty Two Document Delivery Centres established by UGC-INFLIBNET, Ahmedabad. The Centre will deliver, on demand, the copies of research papers from 4000 and odd print journals subscribed by these 22 centres apart from 7000 and odd full text e-journals, conference proceedings and other materials. Access to all these journals has been provided through JCCC gateway portal. Users can also submit an online request in JCCC for the article from both print and e-journals.

## DIGITAL LIBRARY SERVICES

A State-of-art Digital Library provides seamless access to various CD-ROM Databases, Electronic Theses and Dissertations, In-house Bibliographic and full text Databases, Institutional Repository, MK Tata Centre Archive etc.

Major CD-ROM database collections includes ProQuest, Wilson Social Science Abstract, Popline, ABI/INFORM etc:

* Access to Electronic version of Indian Journal of Social Work and Sociological Bulletin on Library intranet
* Digitisation of library materials including Rare and Out of Print books but in demand
* Digitisation of Theses and Dissertations submitted to the institute
* External Digitisation projects
* Scanning and printing facility for the students

## CYBER LIBRARY

The SDTM Library has set up Cyber Library with over 100 Pentium computers working in a networked environment through connectivity provided by ERNET India using 2 Mbps High Bandwidth Leased Line. It was inaugurated and thrown open to the students on 12th November, 2008 during the ILA International Conference from 12-15 November, 2008 organised by the library in collaboration with Indian Library Association. The Online databases like Project Muse, Springer Link, JSTOR, Blackwell will provide access to full text journals through UGCInfonet E-Journals Consortia. In addition, SPSS and SAS computing facilities will also be accessible to the scholars.

Salient features of SDTM Cyber Library:

* Cyber library in a networked environment with 100 computers using a dedicated 2 Mbps leased line
* Open 24 × 7 and 365 days a year

* Both reading and computing facilities
* Laser printing facility
* Access to full text online journals through UGC-Infonet E-Journals Consortia and other library e-resources.
* IP based Web Cameras for surveillance to enhance security of the library resources

Cyber Library-Acceptable Use and Code of Conduct:

* Do Not Connect Your Mobile To Computers.
* Do Not Install Any Software Without Prior Permission Of IT Team.
* Do Not Download Movies OR Songs.
* Do Not Remove LAN Cord, Keyboard And Mouse From The Computers.
* Do Not Save Any Document On The Desktop.
* Kindly Scan Your Pen Drive, CDs OR DVDs Before use.
* Keep Your Mobile On Silent Mode.
* Eatables are not allowed inside the Cyber Library.
* Take Care Of Your Own Belongings.
* Turn Off The Computer After Your Work Is Completed.
* All Drives Will Be Formatted After Every 15 Days by IT team Without Any Intimation.
* IT Team Will Not be Responsible For Any Data Loss
* Kindly Co-operate With IT Team For Minimum Downtime Of The Computers.
* Please Inform To IT Team In Case Of Any Computers Problem.
* Please Keep The Cyber Library Clean.
* Keep Silence In Cyber Library.

## LICENSES AND FAIR USE OF E-RESOURCES

The INFLIBNET Consortium subscribes to thousands of electronic journals including full-text electronic resources and bibliographic databases for its member institutions. All electronic resources available through the Consortium are governed by license agreements.

The terms and conditions for using these resources are spelled out in license agreements that are signed with each publisher by the INFLIBNET Consortium on behalf of its member institutions.

The licenses for electronic resources impose two types of restrictions on its usage, namely:

* Who can use these resources; and
* How the resources can be used.

The first restriction defines authorized users for e-resources, which generally includes students, faculty, staff and onsite visitors of a subscribing institution. The second restriction deals with how these resources can be used. It is the responsibility of individual users to ensure that e-resources are used for personal, educational and research purposes only. Most of the agreements entered into by the Consortium and publishers specify items that users are prohibited to do.

Some of them are as follows:

* Systematic or programmatic downloading, retention, and printing are prohibited. For example, you cannot download entire issue of a journal or print out several copies of the same article.
* Electronic distribution of content is also restricted although the specific restrictions vary from publisher to publisher. It may be permissible to forward an article to another colleague in your own institution by e-mail, however, transmitting an article to someone outside of the institution, or to a large group of recipients, a mailing list, or an electronic bulletin board, is not allowed.
* If you are teaching a class, you can print out a copy of an article from an electronic journal and include it in your course pack. However, do not make multiple copies for circulation. Copyright laws protect published material in any format so that it cannot be copied except in accordance with fair use. Providing access to material for educational purposes falls within the realm of fair use.
* Please ensure that the resource is used for educational and research purposes and not for commercial purposes.

* Providing electronic links on your course web pages to the Library's licensed resources is permitted but you cannot post the PDF of an article on your website. The publishers' main concern is that people outside of your campus network should not be able to access resources licensed by your institution. However, a researcher can post-a pre-print of an article written by himself.
* As with any kind of scholarly communication, a researcher can use phrases or quotes from other articles and cite the source of information. However, a researcher is prohibited from using large chunk of information from an article or from a chapter in a book.

### What Happens if the Licence is Violated

Publishers track the use of their electronic resources in terms of number of downloads made by subscribing institution. Misuse, if any, is notified to the subscribing institution with details of kinds of violations and institution is expected to take action.

The publisher also suspends the access to e-resource pending suitable action by subscribing institution. The access is stopped not only for journals where license agreement was violated but for all journals by the same publisher. Moreover, the access is suspended not only for the individual violator but for the entire institution.

### Conditions of Use and Licensing Restrictions for Electronic Resources

The Consortium subscribes to thousands of electronic journals and bibliographic databases for use by authorized users in member institutions. The terms and conditions for using these resources are spelled out in electronic resource license agreements with each publisher. It is the responsibility of individual users to ensure that the use of electronic resources does not breach the terms and conditions specified in the license agreements.

Licences vary from publisher to publisher; however, the general principles are as follows:

* Permitted:
  - Viewing, downloading, copying, printing and saving a copy of search results
  - Viewing, downloading, copying, printing and saving individual articles
  - Using e-resources for scholarly, educational or scientific research, teaching, private study and clinical purposes
  - Sending a copy of an article to another authorized user (*i.e.* current faculty, students or staff)
  - Posting the URL to the publisher's version of the article on a class website (publisher links will allow only authorized users access)
* Not Permitted:
  - Use of robots or intelligent agents to do systematic, bulk or automatic downloading is not permitted
  - Systematic downloading or printing of entire journal issues or volumes, or large portions of other e-resources is not permitted
  - Using e-resources for commercial gain is not permitted (*i.e.* reselling, redistributing or republishing licensed content)
  - Transmitting, disseminating or otherwise making online content available to unauthorized users (*i.e.* sending to mailing lists or electronic bulletin boards) is not permitted
  - Posting the publisher's version or PDF of an article to an open class website is not permitted (instead, post the URL to the article which will allow only authorized users access)

Breaches of the license agreement with publishers could result in the suspension of access to the resources for the member institutions. Generic license agreements for all publishers specifying all the terms and conditions of the following databases are available at their respective website.

e-Resources under UGC-Infonet Digital Consortium:

* Project Muse (389 journals)
* Oxford University Press (202 journals)
* JSTOR (729 journals)
* Springer Link (1236 journals)
* Taylor and Francis (1076 journals)
* JCCC (Gateway Portal)
* ISID (Industrial Development Bibliographic Database)
* Cambridge Journals Online (279 journals)
* Wiley Interscience (502 journals)

e-Resources Subscribed by SDTM Library:

* Sage Publications (240 journals)
* Emerald Management Xtra (160 journals)
* ABI/INFORM Complete™ (2950 journals)
* indiastat.com (statistical database)
* World Bank Databases (GDF+WDI+e-Library)

## Computer Access-Acceptable Use and Code of Conduct

Only registered members of the Library are authorized to use the Computers, Internet facility or to access e-Resources. Prior to such authorization, the students must sign and return the Library Registration Form acknowledging their responsibilities and the consequences of violation. Students are expected to observe network etiquette by being polite. Students are prohibited from pretending to be someone else; transmitting obscene messages or pictures; revealing personal addresses or telephone numbers-either their own or another person's; or using the network in a way that would disrupt use by others. The following policy for acceptable use of computers, networks, and system resources, including the Internet and e-resources, shall apply to all TISS administrators, faculty, staff, and students. All technology equipment shall be used under the supervision of the site administrator. Any user who violates any condition of this policy is subject to disciplinary action or administrative sanctions.

In addition to any other disciplinary action taken, the Technology Department reserves the right to terminate access to system resources for any user who violates these guidelines:

* Every user in whose name a system account is issued will be responsible at all times for its proper use.
* Users shall not let other persons use their name, logon, password, or files for any reason
* Users shall not use others' system accounts or try to discover another user's password.
* Users shall not erase, rename, or make unusable anyone else's computer files, programmes or disks.
* Users shall not use computers for any non-instructional or non-administrative purpose, including, instant messaging, online shopping, or personal use of streaming media such as online radio stations or video broadcasts.
* Users may not install, download, copy, or distribute copyrighted materials such as software, audio or video, files, graphics, and text without the written permission of the administrator.
* Users shall not use the computers for illegal purposes, in support of illegal activities, or for any other activity prohibited.
* Users shall not write, produce, generate, copy, propagate, or attempt to introduce any computer code designed to self-replicate, damage, or otherwise hinder the performance of any computer's memory, file system, or software. Such software is often called a bug, virus, worm, Trojan Horse, or other name.
* Users shall not use computers to purposefully distribute, create, or copy messages or materials that are abusive, obscene, sexually oriented, threatening, harassing, damaging to another's reputation, or illegal.
* Users shall not use computers to purposefully access materials that are abusive, obscene, sexually oriented, threatening, harassing, damaging to another's reputation, or illegal. In the event that accidental access to prohibited materials occurs, users are expected to immediately discontinue such access and report the incident either to Library staff or to the administrator.
* Users shall not intentionally damage the system,

damage information belonging to others, misuse system resources, or allow others to misuse system resources.

* Users shall not alter or vandalize computers, networks, printers, or other associated equipment and system resources. Alteration or vandalism includes, but is not limited to: removal of parts, intentional destruction of equipment, altering system settings or software, installing unauthorized or unlicensed software or programmes, attempting to degrade or disrupt system performance, or attempting to make system resources unusable.
* Users shall not use computers for the forgery or attempted forgery of e-mail messages. Attempts to read, delete, copy, or modify the e-mail of other system users, deliberate interference with the ability of other users to send/receive e-mail, or the use of another person's e-mail account is prohibited.
* Users should not use library network for sending and receiving a large number of personal messages, including using group e-mail distribution lists to send non-administrative or non-instructional messages to other users.

## NATIONAL CENTRE FOR SOCIAL SCIENCES INFORMATION AND DOCUMENTATION

The TISS library with its valuable collections both in terms of quality and quantity in the field of social sciences, social work, health sciences act as a nodal centre of major source of information in the field of social sciences in India as well as abroad. This Centre's vision is to bring world class information services to the academic community of India in the field of social science. The main mandate is to provide full range of documentation and information services in the area of social sciences apart from the core subject of Social Work, which will accept request from other user libraries via post, telephone, e-mail or fax and delivers the information. The centre is also providing 50 research students space for retrieving information, analysing data with all IT infrastructure from India and abroad with residential facility from the institute.

Salient features of the Centre are:

* Provide seamless, network access to worldwide scholarly information resources of relevance to the academic community, facilitating improved learning, teaching, research, collaboration and information sharing
* Provide orientation and training to the academic community in making effective use of electronic information sources, tools and services
* Dedicated Data Centre for e-journals, full text CD-ROM databases in the field of social sciences
* Training Centre for Research Scholars from NGO's, Institutions who are involved in Social Science Research and dissemination of information

## PHYSICAL AMBIENCES

* *Cleanliness:* Library is a central resource department that is the backbone of all academic programmes of the institute. Students and faculty would be spending their considerable time in library premises pursuing their research and studies. Hence, it is very much essential that library has a checking system in place to monitor the cleanliness and hygiene of the library premises like regular sweeping, cleaning and mopping of all floors, and washrooms.
* *Electricity and Water and Ventilation:* Library will ensure that these essential things are working at all times and users would not be put to any inconvenience.
* *Floor Plan and Direction/Guideposts:* Library shall have floor plans designed and proper directions/guideposts for people to move around the library looking for resources/services.

## MANAGING THE PERFORMANCE OF LIBRARY TEAM

TISS library is managed by a professionally qualified and competent team. It is suggested that the performance of the team can be optimized by taking the following measures.

## CLEARLY DEFINED JOB DESCRIPTIONS AT ALL LEVELS

Each member of the library team shall have a clearly defined, unambiguous job description that facilitates and gels with the library's and then Institute's Mission and Vision Statements. The organization chart with a clear reporting structure be developed for having effective span of control within the library.

## QUARTERLY WORK PLAN AND PREDEFINED, AGREED TARGETS FOR ACHIEVEMENT

Each section in the library shall have a Quarterly Work Plan. Here, the works to be carried in the next quarter and the predetermined, agreed targets for achievements will be decided. There will be a review process after the every quarterly for assessment.

## GENERAL CONDUCT

Every member of library team shall exhibit the highest level of professional conduct in discharging their duties. Staffs are expected to be in their sections unless otherwise their work takes them away from the desk. Providing polite and efficient service shall be the motto of the library.

## DEPARTMENT PERFORMANCE AUDIT BY YEARLY USER FEEDBACK SURVEYS

Library will initiate a annual department performance audit wherein the performance of each section of library will be evaluated based on the feedback surveys, user satisfaction surveys. This feedback and evaluation will certainly help library to overcome any lacunae in the facilities and services being provided.

## BIMONTHLY REPORTS ABOUT LIBRARY FUNCTIONING

Library shall compile, analyse and submit a performance report every two months. IN this, the performance and productivity of each section of the library shall be reported with descriptions as to how many targets were achieved, difficulties faced and how they were overcame.

## GENERAL RULES AND REGULATIONS

* All the students/scholars and outsiders entering the Library shall deposit their bags and other belongings at the entrance and sign in the Register at the checkpoint. Only notebooks and the Library books to be returned will be allowed inside. Do not to leave any valuables at the Check Point. Library is not responsible for any loss of personal belongings. All files, books and notebooks must be presented to the security guard at the checkpoint for inspection while leaving the Library. Library does not permit any exception in the observance of this rule.
* Identity Card is compulsory for getting access to the library.
* Books removed from the shelves by students, if not required for reference, should be kept on the book trolley or on table nearest to them. Please do not try to shelve them yourself. *Please remember that a book misplaced is a book lost.*
* The newspaper(s) should be folded properly after reading and kept back in the designated place.
* Readers should not deface, mark, cut, mutilate or damage library resources in any way. If anyone is found doing so, he will be charged the full replacement cost of the resource. Books Borrowed should be protected from RAIN, DUST, INSECT, etc.
* All the students/scholars are required to bring three copies of their recent photographs (Passport Size) along with the Fee Receipt while applying for Library membership.
* All the students are advised to bring their own Reading Cards while using the Library.
* The Reserve Shelf book must be returned on the due date between 9.00 am to 10.00 am. And General Shelf books on or before the due date. General Shelf books are issued upto 8.00 pm.
* Claim for Reserve Shelf books should be made in the

Register maintained at the counter between 8.30 am to 2.00 pm and they should be collected between 3.30 pm to 7.00 pm.

* Books are issued to students for overnight during the examination time only.
* Compendiums should be issued on reserve shelf card only.
* Those students who do not return the books, issued for overnight use, in time, will not be issued any book for a period of 7 days.
* *All the students who want to return the books issued on their names are advised to wait until the books are shown as cancelled against their names.*
* The "PASS OUT" slip should be handed over to the security guard at the checkpoint before taking out the issued book/s.
* There will be a fine of ₹ 1.00 per General Shelf book and Reserve shelf book, ₹ 2.00.
* For the loss of Readers Ticket, a fine of ₹.10 each will be charged.
* Students are advised not to issue Books to others on their names.
* A fine of ₹ 75 will be charged for the loss of compendium, files and such other reading materials. For book three times of the original price charged.
* Coupon for Xeroxing is available at the cash counter in the A/C Section up to 3.00 P.M. The Xeroxing charge per exposure is 0.50 p. After 3.00 P.M. payment can be made by cash in the library.
* Conversation and discussion disturbs library ambience. Therefore, all are requested to maintain dignified silence. If discussion is necessary, the common room should be utilized for the same.
* Smoking is not permitted in the Library.
* All users are requested to keep their mobiles switched off or in silent mode in the Library.
* Beverages and Eatables are not allowed inside the library.

* No visitor or guest is permitted to use the Library without the prior permission of the Librarian. He/She is required to produce a proper introduction letter from the concerned Institution/Organization to which he/she is attached. A fee of ₹.15 per day is charged for a visitor who wishes to use the Library facility.
* No photograph of the Library shall be taken without the prior permission of the Librarian.
* Library reserves the right to call back any issued book/item at any time.
* All research scholars are advised not to keep Library books/journals (loose and bound) inside their cupboard without getting them issued.
* Librarian reserves the right to check the Ph.D. and M.Phil tables and cupboards, whenever necessary.
* All students are advised to come to the Library in decent dress as they are in the classrooms.
* Demand and suggestion slips are available at the circulation desk for your use.

## REQUISITION FORMS USED IN LIBRARY

* Library Membership Form
* Day Membership/Visitor Membership Form
* Book Recommendation Form
* Journal Recommendation Form
* Book Reservation Form
* Misplaced Book Trace Request Form
* Photocopying Services Request Form
* Inter Library Loan Request Form
* Group Visit Facilitation Form

# 2

# Board and Director: Roles and Responsibilities

## UNDERSTANDING THE ROLE OF THE LIBRARY BOARD OF TRUSTEES

In Indiana alone, there are more than 1,700 public library trustees representing 238 libraries. As you know, each library has its own board of trustees, usually comprised of a president, vice president, treasurer and members at large. But what you may not know is the variety of duties performed by trustees. Tasked with setting policies, hiring the director, planning for the future of the library, monitoring and evaluating the overall effectiveness of the library, and advocating for the library in the community as well as for the community itself, the board of trustees is ultimately responsible for the successes and failures of the library. And while the board rarely involves itself in day-to-day issues—rather delegating most tasks to the library director, at which point a task may be further delegated to staff — the board of trustees must nonetheless set the framework for the success of the library and its policies.

Often this involves developing a long-range plan with the library director responsible for the development of a short-range (1-year) plan created to carry out the long-term vision of the board. It is the role of the board of trustees to approve the annual budget (typically provided by the library director), as well as to monitor the performance of the library and library director, and evaluate progress the library has made towards achieving set goals. One such way the trustees can monitor the director's performance without following him or her around all day is by creating a clear, specific job description for the director and by building a strong working relationship between the director and board of trustees. By doing so, the board is able to effectively evaluate the director's performance.

Likewise, the trustees must also build a strong working relationship with each other and evaluate themselves individually and as a team. As far as who does what, it is important to note that while the board of trustees has the final authority over the library, the director is in charge of virtually all day-to-day matters of routine management. Because of this, it is of utmost importance that the trustees, library director and library staff work together as a team towards a common goal. Currently, hot-button advocacy issues facing most library trustees include budget reductions and how libraries can survive them while protecting jobs and continuing to provide services to communities that often need these services more than ever before, but each community has its own special needs and the board of trustees for each library must advocate for these needs as well.

## BOARD AND DIRECTOR'S RESPONSIBILITIES

If there is a mantra for governing boards of library trustees it is: "The board sets policy, the director operates the library with the assistance of staff." What does this really mean, and what are the differences? Because I have worn the hats of both a librarian and a trustee, I was asked to offer some thoughts on this topic.

Sometimes the line between policy and operation is very thin and the differences are subtle. Basically, the board of trustees and the library director must work as a team, just as the director must construct a team with staff. In order to work successfully, it must be a process of two-way communication, consultation and trust building.

### BUILDING A BOARD, DIRECTOR, AND STAFF TEAM

In addition to regular board meetings, an annual planning retreat with the director and selected staff is an opportunity to build communications and plan for the library future. Although the library vision and mission statements do not change very often, they should be reviewed along with the library strategic or long-range plan and annual plans. A retreat offers the time to discuss in depth, and to clarify directions, goals and strategies for the coming year.

These meetings are, by law, open public meetings that the public may attend so opportunities for citizen input can be incorporated into the retreat agenda. Indeed, ongoing ways should be found to obtain input from residents of the library community. The board should meet following the retreat and include on its agenda a discussion of appropriate policies and plans for the library.

## COMMUNITY INVOLVEMENT

If the trustees and director are to fulfill their responsibilities, both must be active in the community. Both must know the community to develop those policies and practices that bring the best possible library service their community. Any five- or seven-person library board is likely to represent a variety of community connections. These connections can provide avenues to knowing and understanding the community and to advocacy for the library. Trustees have a responsibility to stay informed–to regularly attend board meetings and to read and understand information presented to them about the library and its operation.

They also have a responsibility to actively listen to community residents. It is equally important that they advocate for the library with community residents and with local, state, and federal governmental representatives. In order to do this, trustees will need to answer questions and to explain library policies and practices. They need to work as a team with the library director, because some questions, especially about library practice, are best directed to the library director. The director and staff must also be prepared to explain library policies and actively advocate for the library.

## DEVELOPING POLICIES

There are several levels of decision-making involved in policy-making. There are many times when the board will ask the library director to analyse impacts before it establishes a policy, and there will be times when the director will consult the board before proceeding with a specific course of action. Often the director will call the board's attention to need for policy in a specific area and may draft language for the board to consider.

In other instances the board may identify need for a policy and will either ask the director to draft language for board discussion and action or they may jointly develop specific language. Sometimes the director will make decisions related to library operations and will simply inform the board of her or his actions, or perhaps ask for their concurrence for a proposed course of action.

This latter course of action is probably wise in situations where it is not initially clear whether additional policy decisions will need to be made or where the distinction between practice and policy is not entirely clear. Discussion can usually clarify the issues and decisions can be made, often by consensus. Certain kinds of decisions may be delegated to the director.

## EXAMPLES OF DIRECTOR AND BOARD ROLES AND RESPONSIBILITIES

Let me elaborate on the respective roles and responsibilities of trustees and director with several examples. Especially in large libraries, some of the tasks or decisions that I've identified as the director's will likely be delegated to managerial or supervisory library staff.

### Mission/Roles of the Library in the Community

It is the governing board's responsibility to determine the mission and roles of the library after a planning process that includes a great deal of input from residents of the community, and in coordination with the library director. These fundamental decisions need to be articulated in a mission statement and supported by policy and planning. Once those fundamental decisions are made, it is the board's responsibility to hire a director who is in agreement with and can support the chosen roles.

In the case of the newly formed Stevens County Rural Library District, the roles were actually established before the director was hired and the board needed to assure that the new director supported the roles. A more specific example of how this works: Board policy or the library mission states that the library is to be user friendly and a place where people feel welcome. It is the library director's responsibility to make it happen. It will involve setting expectations regarding attitudes of staff towards the library customers, training for staff, and establishing library practices and procedures that make users feel welcome and satisfy their needs. These are all responsibilities of the director.

## Budgets, Contracts, and Grants

The board approves the library budget, as drawn up and recommended by the director, but it is based on goals set by the board. The budget corresponds to the annual work plan for the director and staff. The board may suggest general policy directions for the budget, but the director in consultation with staff decides what is possible within budget constraints, and how best to meet the entire gamut of needs. The director expends money within approved budget parameters and keeps the board informed. While trustees may review and approve vouchers each month, they should not approve individual expenditures. The board should be informed by the director of any major changes needed in the budget and the proposed changes must have board concurrence. Trustees should not be involved in adjustments made to budgets as long as those adjustments are within general budget parameters as approved by the board.

A contract or grant must also correspond to the goals of the library. The board must approve all contracts with contracting cities, consultants, and the like but the contract or grant specifics will be drawn up and recommended by the director. Trustees must certainly be kept informed of potential contracts or grants, and should provide input regarding the content or parameters of impending contracts or grant documents. Whether to apply for a particular grant or enter into a contract with a specific entity may be a policy matter, and thus the board will make the final decision. There may be instances where the board determines that it is appropriate to delegate to the director the responsibility for signing agreements on behalf of the library.

## Buildings and Property

The board, in consultation with the director, may determine in policy whether to own buildings or rent space, whether to buy land for buildings, the general locations of new buildings, etc. On the other hand, the board may also establish a broad goal that will guide the director and staff in making these decisions. This broad approval usually happens when there are multiple decisions to be made as a result of a substantial bond issue. The governing board may also set policies such as whether to allocate a certain percentage of a building's cost for art works. The director makes recommendations on these matters and implements the decisions. The director decides, without further board action, on specifics such as colour scheme and décor, furniture, computer system requirements and design of the building. The director will keep the board informed and trustees may offer opinions, but these are operational decisions that should be made by the director.

## Personnel

The board establishes overall personnel policies such as guidelines for salary and benefits, hiring practices, and other personnel actions unless the library is part of a city and must follow municipal policy. The director implements personnel policies. Trustees should not become involved unless personnel policy changes are called for. Unless the library is part of a municipal system that maintains authority to hire the director, the board hires the library director and sets salary and benefits. In this process, the board may seek input from library staff and/ or community residents, but the ultimate decision rests with the board.

In turn, the director hires library staff and the board is not involved in interviewing or selection. Unless the salary schedule is established by the city, the board approves the salary schedule as drawn up and recommended by the director. It is the director's responsibility to decide where a job classification will be placed on that salary schedule. If library staff belong to a labour union, the library trustees should not take an active part in labour negotiations.

The board might, however, approve the hiring of a consultant to assist the director by carrying out negotiations. When an agreement is reached and recommended by the director, the board will approve the labour contract. The board does an annual performance review for the library director. As a result of the review the board and director should jointly set goals and expectations for the coming year. The annual performance review of the director will be based on how well those goals and expectations have been achieved. The director will carry out annual performance reviews of library staff, set goals for staff performance, and determine staff training needs. The board approves policies for staff training, attendance at conferences, workshops or classes, travel reimbursement and the like, but they are not involved in staff review. Staff development policy statements will likely be drawn up by the director, based on staff needs and available budget, and recommended to the board.

Such "working policies" are really largely procedural and, as such, the responsibility of the director. If underlying policy statements are needed, the director informs the board of the need and recommends content or draws up language for board consideration. Disciplinary actions related to library staff are a responsibility of the library director. Although the board sets disciplinary policy as part of overall personnel policy, unless it is mandated by their city government, board members should not become involved in specific disciplinary actions. Complaints made directly to board members must be referred back to the director for action.

The director should always consult the library attorney on any disciplinary actions that may reach the point of hearings before a human rights commission or a lawsuit. Trustees must certainly be kept informed and will probably need to approve expenditures for attorney fees. Disciplinary action or firing of a library director is, of course, a governing board responsibility.

## Collections, Hours, and Services

These are "working policies" or operational procedures and largely the responsibility of the library director. The board of trustees sets the goals in its adopted plan and defines strategies for collections, access and services, but it is up to the library director and staff to implement the actions that meet the goals. Although a board member may have a special interest in a particular collection, or personally see a need for certain services, a board member must make it very clear that their personal suggestions are not endorsed by the authority of the board. The director and staff must always remain free to consider board member suggestions, just as they would any citizen suggestions, but staff are ultimately responsible for judging how best to develop the collection and library services.

The board may adopt a goal that addresses the issue of access to the library, thereby setting an expectation for the number of hours open or other services. The director, however, must decide how many and what hours are feasible within the budget, and balance available staff resources with the expertise needed by the facility. The director should keep the board informed of what has been put into practice. A similar process will govern decision about services such as story times for children, computers for public access, outreach services to nursing or retirement homes, and others.

## Community Relations and Publicity

The library board might establish a goal stating that the library will support and encourage partnerships and cooperative ventures with community organizations whenever feasible. The director is then clearly enabled to create working agreements with such organizations. However, this is an example of a situation where the director may appropriately decide that such relationships are good library practice and simply proceed to implement cooperative actions while keeping the board informed.

An example might be that the library agrees to house the materials of a local genealogical or historical society. This action may, or may not, require a formal agreement that the board should approve. The board might establish a goal that says the library will use all means possible to keep residents of the community informed about the library, its services, and activities. The details of how this is to be done and by whom are for the director to decide. However, it is wise for the trustees and director to work together and decide which activities are appropriate for board members to undertake and which are director or staff functions. The words of wisdom are "Just be sure everyone is delivering the same message."

### Wrapping Up

The director must do her or his best to carry out the governing board goals and policy directions. It is imperative that the board backs the director's decisions. It is not always crystal clear where policy stops and practice starts. However, we are all in this library business together. People become librarians because they believe in the value of libraries to communities. People become library trustees for the very same reason. By clarifying our respective roles and responsibilities, by building trust and good communication, and by working together as a team, we can all be more effective in bringing the best possible library service to the people of our communities.

## GOVERNING AND ADVISORY LIBRARY BOARD RELATIONSHIPS

Library boards exist in political environments, regardless if they are advisory or governing. Relationships between library boards and their appointing authorities can be collegial or fractious, depending upon the issues at hand. A board's effectiveness is influenced by its breadth of representation from key community constituents among its members and its active involvement in community life. In all library settings, success is influenced by a clear understanding of and commitment to the library's mission and an appreciation for the political dynamics.

### Contracting or Annexed Cities and Towns

Library boards in cities and towns that contract for library services or are annexed to a rural or intercounty library district are advisory. They are a special interest standing committee whose mission is to advocate for the library for such purposes as building improvements in cities where library services are in city owned facilities. They may also be an advisory committee to the rural or intercounty library district whose role is to provide library personnel, programmes, services, materials and various policies for their use in the city or town.

### City or Town Libraries

Library boards in cities that support an independent public library may be advisory to the city or may be responsible for the management of the library. In cities that elected to be an Optional Municipal Code city to broaden the city's power of self-government, the library board is advisory. The public library is considered a department of the city. The breadth of responsibilities of the advisory board may vary according to local tradition and expectation.

For instance, policies affecting the public's use of the library–meeting rooms, circulation, collection development, unattended children, rules of conduct–may be delegated to the library board for adoption or may be enacted by the city council as ordinances. In cities that are not an Optional Municipal Code city, the library board is responsible for the management and control of the library. These responsibilities include employing library staff, controlling finances and setting policies for the governance of the library, but they exist within the context of a city.

### Library Districts and Regional Libraries

Library boards for rural county, intercounty, island, partial-county library districts and regional libraries are the governing bodies for these municipal corporations. Their responsibilities include levying tax, entering into contracts, employing staff, controlling finances, leasing and purchasing real estate, and setting policies for the governance of the library. Even though county commissioners and/or city councils appoint them, they are not advisory to them. Their responsibility is foremost for the operations and integrity of their library.

## LIBRARY BOARD MEETING MINUTES

*Responsibilities:*

* Adopt appropriate written policies to govern the operation and services of the Library.
* Secure adequate funding to carry out library programmes and services.
* Adopt an annual budget.
* Custody and responsibility for all property of the Library, including the building.
* Become familiar with appropriate local and state laws; actively represent Library interests to the City Council.
* Reflect community needs and interests when considering Library services and programmes.
* Communicate information about Library programmes, services and needs to the community.
* Attend all board meetings, workshops and training activities.
* Foster cooperation with other area libraries to maximize use of available resources.
* Maintain relationships with the Colville Library Improvement Club.

*Preferred Qualifications:*

* Interest in public library services, in the community, and in the public library's relationship to the community.
* Recognition of the public library's importance as a center of information, of community culture, continuing education, and recreation.
* Willingness to serve as an advocate for public libraries.
* Previous governing or advisory board experience.
* Open mindedness, intellectual curiosity, and respect for the opinions of others.
* Ability to work effectively with others; trustees, director, staff and the public.
* Ability to think critically in planning and problem solving.
* Willingness to devote the necessary time and effort to carry out the trusteeship responsibilities.

*Time Requirements:*

* Five-year commitment.
* Attend quarterly scheduled board meetings.
* Attend any scheduled briefings on services and programmes, any special meetings.
* Read background materials sent prior to each meeting.
* Attend relevant continuing education functions, usually no more than one per year.
* Occasional attendance at community and library meetings and activities.

## LIBRARY BOARD OF TRUSTEES

The management and control of a library shall be vested in a board of trustees. In cities and counties, the board shall consist of five members except that in cities of the second class, it shall consist of seven members. In the event a contract for library service is made pursuant to subsection of KRS 173.310, the board may consist of equal representation from the contracting parties with the total membership not to exceed twelve. In a library region, there shall be five members, except if the number of counties exceeds five, there shall be one trustee from each county in the region.

Within thirty days after the establishment of a library has been authorized by any of the methods authorized by KRS 173.310, a library board shall be appointed. In cities the trustees shall be appointed by the mayor and in counties they shall be appointed by the county judge/executive. There shall be established a board of trustees in each regional library district for purposes of coordinating library programmes and effecting economies and efficiencies of the member county library systems. In each regional library district, the trustees shall be appointed by the joint action of the judges/executive of the respective counties or as may be agreed upon by contract.

In any region in which there are four or less counties, provision shall be made in the contract for rotation of members and an equitable adjustment of terms. If a region consists of an even number of counties, the trustees appointed by the judges/ executive of the respective counties shall appoint an additional trustee whose term of office shall be four years and whose successor shall be appointed by the trustees in office at the time of expiration of such term. Trustees shall be appointed from the governmental unit at large with special reference to their fitness for such office. Upon initial establishment of the board, members of the board shall be appointed to terms as follows: two members for two years, one member for three years, and two members for four years respectively, and thereafter trustees shall be appointed to serve terms of four years. Trustees may serve for two consecutive terms after which they shall not succeed themselves.

They may be reappointed no earlier than twelve months following the end of their last service. Vacancies shall be filled for the unexpired terms as soon as possible in the same manner as the original appointments. In the event that vacancies have existed for a period of at least six months, the Governor of the Commonwealth of Kentucky, upon the recommendation of the state librarian, may make such necessary appointments. After absence of a trustee from four regular monthly meetings of the board during any one year of the trustee's term, the trustee shall be considered to have automatically resigned from the board. An advisory board may be appointed and serve as specified in bylaws of the public library board of trustees.

Library trustees shall not receive a salary or other compensation for their services, but may be reimbursed for actual expenses necessarily incurred in the performance of their duties, upon approval by the board. Before entering upon the duties of his office, a trustee shall take oath that he will faithfully discharge his duties.

No board shall employ as a member of its library staff any member of the board or any person related closer than a second cousin to any member of the board. No person is eligible to this office that is directly or indirectly interested in the sale to the library of books, magazines, supplies, equipment, materials, insurance or services for which library funds are expended. A library trustee may be removed only by vote of the legislative body of the respective governmental unit from which he was appointed.

* *Effective:* July 13, 1990
* History:
  - Amended 1990 Ky. Acts ch. 58, sec. 1, effective July 13, 1990. –
  - Amended 1982 Ky. Acts ch. 245, sec. 9, effective July 15, 1982. –
  - Amended 1976 Ky. Acts ch. 367, sec. 2. –
  - Amended 1974 Ky. Acts ch. 8, sec. 4. –
  - Amended 1970 Ky. Acts ch. 109, sec. 1. –
  - Created 1944 Ky. Acts ch. 160, sec. 5.

## LIBRARY EMPLOYEES' CODE OF ETHICS

Jefferson-Madison Regional Library encourages employees to strive for the highest level of ethical conduct, and to that end employees will:

* Provide the highest level of service to all library users through appropriate and usefully organized resources, equitable service policies, equitable access, and accurate, unbiased, and courteous responses to all requests.
* Uphold the principles of intellectual freedom and resist all efforts to censor library resources.
* Protect each library user's right to privacy and confidentiality with respect to information sought or received and resources consulted, borrowed, acquired or transmitted.
* Make a good faith effort to recognize and respect intellectual property rights.
* Treat co-workers and other colleagues with respect and fairness, and advocate conditions of employment that safeguard the rights and welfare of all employees.
* Distinguish clearly in their actions and statements between their personal convictions and philosophies and their professional duties and do not allow personal beliefs to interfere with fair representation of the aims of the library or the provision of access to library resources.

* Avoid situations in which personal interests might be advanced or financial benefits gained at the expense of the library patrons, colleagues, or Jefferson-Madison Regional Library.
* Strive for excellence by maintaining and enhancing knowledge and skills, by encouraging the professional development of co-workers, and by fostering the aspirations of potential members of the library profession.

# 3

# Digital Library System

## A MODERN DIGITAL LIBRARY SYSTEM

Invenio is an integrated digital library system originally developed at CERN to run the CERN Document Server, currently one of the largest institutional repositories worldwide. It was started over 15 years ago and has been matured through many release cycles. Invenio is a GPL2 Open Source project based on Apache/WSGI + Python + MySQL architecture. Its modular design enables it to serve a wide variety of usages, from a multimedia digital object repository, to a web journal, to a fully functional digital library.

The development strategy used to implement Invenio ensures it is flexible in any layer. Being based on open standards such as MARCXML and OAI-PMH 2.0 its interoperability with other digital libraries is guaranteed. Being originally designed to cope with the CERN requirements for digital object management, Invenio is suitable for middle-to-large scale digital repositories. Records can be of any nature. This presentation will introduce the different features of Invenio, their usage in the CERN context and how other institutions and projects are also driving some of its development.

### USAGE

Besides being used to run the CERN Document Server, Invenio has also been chosen by several other big institutions or projects. Among them it is about to be used to serve the SPIRES High Energy Physics information through the recently launched

INSPIRE service, that will become the repository of reference for high energy physics. It is used by the EPFL. ADS has expressed interest to move to an Invenio-based platform, while starting a collaboration at the data level between astrophysics and high energy physics worlds. For example in Spain Invenio is already used by the *Dipòsit Digital de Documents* (DDD) and by the "Repositorio Digital de la Universidad de Zaragoza". Recently the European Commission has chosen Invenio to become part of two important projects D4ScienceII, and OpenAIRE, with the latter having the goal to set up a portal where all the EC funded research project documents will be available.

## FEATURES

Let us demonstrate the key Invenio features by following the lifetime of a record in the system, from ingestion to dissemination. As an integrated digital library, Invenio is built to allow the management of digital objects and the meta-data associated with them. Meta-data are stored in the MARCXML format, which has the flexibility to store any kind of information and which can be easily converted, thanks to XML style-sheets to any other meta-data format.

## INGESTING RECORDS

Data and Meta-data can enter into Invenio powered repositories through different ways. They can be manually deposited by an author, through custom and fully configurable web interfaces, backed by an equally configurable work-flow architecture, that lets the submission administrator set up any kind of procedure triggered by a deposition. Meta-data and data can as well be harvested regularly from OAI-PMH compatible repositories. Data can also be input into the system from any non-standard format by writing ad-hoc conversion scripts either in XSLT or in the proprietary BibConvert's language. Users also have the possibility to upload records by sending e-mails that will be parsed automatically. The system can be configured to accept submission by robots thanks to the availability of a simple web API.

## DIGITAL OBJECT MANIPULATION

Fully fledged tools to integrate and manipulate digital objects are available. In particular Invenio can manage multiple formats for the same document, multiple revisions, automatic conversions between formats, automatic stamping of PDF documents with watermarks, creating icons, automatic text extraction to allow for full-text searching, automatic meta-data extraction and many more. Data consistency is also ensured by MD5 checksum being continuously verified.

## INDEXING AND RANKING

All the new records ingested into the system and their modifications are indexed by a very fast indexing engine that has been developed in-house. All the indexing stages are configurable; which metadata fields to index, how to extract tokens, which language is expected in order to apply stemming and removing stop words, and so on. A plug-in based ranking engine takes care of creating special indexes to be used at search time for sorting results based on word similarity, citations, download statistics, and to present citation networks.

## CURATING RECORDS

Curators have powerful web-based tools to manipulate records, whilst maintaining change histories, auto-completion of fields based on fully configurable knowledge bases, multi-record modification, assisted duplicate record finding and an efficient AJAX-based record merging tool, and so on. Curators can also exploit flexible tools to perform meta-data compliance checks against configurable rules. Automatic tools are also available to extract citations and references from scientific papers and to extract keywords based on a given ontology, to enrich the available meta-data. Distributed curation activities can be instantiated through integration of Invenio with RT, one of the most famous open source ticketing systems.

## DISPLAYING RECORDS

Bibliographic records can be displayed in any format, thanks to an easy and fully-configurable formatting layer, which allows creation of record-based rules to choose which representation of a record to use, while each representation can be fine tuned to fit any particular need. Thus any kind of content can be hosted and properly displayed, such as multimedia documents, books, address book contacts, and so on. Records can be organized in a flexible hierarchical structure using real and virtual collections. Each collection can in turn be customised to choose the look and feel and the kind of features enabled. The whole web appearance of Invenio can be fully customised thanks to an integrated templating system, thus facilitating integration of Invenio into an existing institutional portal. Since Invenio is being developed in an international environment it supports internationalization and comes translated already in 25 different languages.

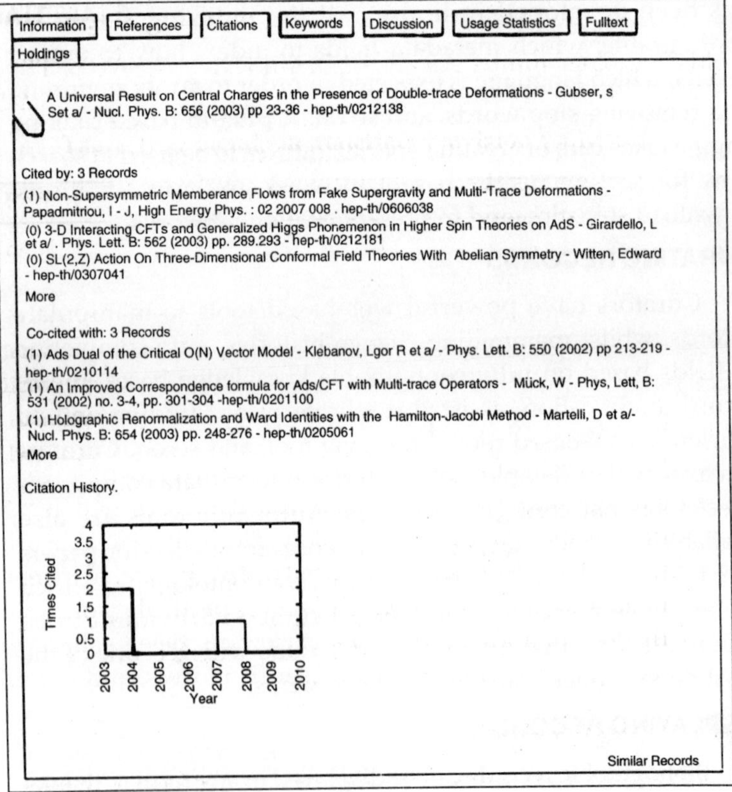


**Fig.** 3.1

## SEARCHING AND BROWSING RECORDS

A powerful search engine resides at the core of Invenio Fig. 3.1. Supporting a Google-like syntax, it can be used to dig into the repositories in a very easy way, while allowing the more experienced users to take advantage of many advanced features such as regular expressions, range queries, selection of meta-data, and many more. Results can be clustered by collections and ranked with respect to word similarity, number of citations, downloads based rankings, and any other pluggable algorithm. Any search query can automatically turned into an RSS feed to add to a personal news aggregator. Thanks to integrated support for MODS and UnAPI standards, search results can be stored in Zotero, a powerful Firefox plug-in useful to organize a personal digital library. The system offers users powerful citation and author analyses.

## COLLABORATIVE TOOLS

Invenio integrates several collaborative and typical web 2.0 tools such as baskets, to store and share records or external resources with other users, personal e-mail notification alerts, record commenting and reviewing, internal web-based messaging tools, approval/reviewing work-flows.

## EXPORTING RECORDS

Data and meta-data can be exported in several ways, the most important being through OAI-PHM protocol and by means of a pluggable exporting module.

## AUTHENTICATION AND AUTHORIZATION

While offering for free local accounts management, Invenio can be integrated with institutional user databases to delegate the authentication phase and to exploit externally available user details. Using the *role based access control* (RBAC) model of Invenio one can define a list of roles, attach users to particular roles, and grant rights to perform actions such as view-restricted-collections based on user group membership, user IP address, and more.

## CIRCULATION

Invenio supports the operation of a physical library by integrating a circulation module, as well as by supporting inter library loans. Users can submit loan requests, and follow the request status, the librarians have a web interface to accept/reject loan requests, to send overdue letters, to set up sub-libraries, etc.

## CREATING JOURNALS

As an example of an application that has been built on top of the core Invenio, the web journal module lets repository administrators create online web journals with regular issues built from articles stored in the repository itself. A specific appearance can be set up in order to have a layout providing journal-like reading experience. This is currently used today for producing the official CERN Bulletin, which is issued every two weeks.

# MANAGING ACCESS TO THE WEB-BASED DIGITAL RESOURCES: ISSUES AND IMPLICATIONS

The invention of the printing press in the 15th century was a landmark in the history of scholarly communication. It was possible to produce large number of documents with the help of printing press. Moreover, the libraries, in the real sense of the term, came into existence only after the invention of the printing press. But now with the emergence of *information and communication technologies* (ICTs), the LI profession is finding itself into a paradoxical situation. The web, which has no head and tail, is both blessing and curse for the stakeholders. As there is no competition for space in the web, a lot of junk is being made available by the information elite. The non-elite members of the society are being left behind in the emerging information society. As such, the existing gap between the 'info-rich' and the 'info-poor' is widening further at a warp speed. Therefore, there is a strong need that we take cognizance of this phenomena and develop certain policies and strategies to separate web-based junk from the quality information, as well as to bridge the widening gap, between the 'haves' and the 'have nots'.

## RESOURCE SHARING

We are surrounded by rapid economic, educational, political, cultural, and technological changes. Declining library budgets, growing user expectations, shifting priorities of governments, commercialization of education, consumerism, and digitization of documents are forcing the LI professionals to devise new ways and means to survive and thrive in the networked environments.

There is a shift from just- in-case to just-in-time approach for managing access to right information. It is not possible for a stand alone library to meet all the information needs of its end-users. Resource sharing via networking is the only alternative. There is a trend towards library and information networks. LANs, MANs, WANs, Intranets, and Extranets are manifestations of this trend. The Internet is a striking development of our times. It is a vast storehouse of information and a perpetual discourse of human minds is going on it. Moreover it has dramatically changed the whole process of scholarly communication. Conceptual access to tacit knowledge has been improved significantly.

The traditional pattern of authorship is also changing. Validation and creditation of intellectual property is becoming more difficult as there is no stability on the Internet. Moreover many people contribute to discussions via virtual conferences, seminars, discussion lists, newsgroups, and bulletin boards. As such the traditional competencies are falling short to manage access to the web-based digital resources.

*It is very important for the professionals to know:*

* What information is available;
* Where it is located; and
* How to access it.

All this can not be done in a piece meal manner. We must develop systems thinking and follow a holistic approach. Following are a few ways and means to do this.

## STRATEGIES FOR ACCESS MANAGEMENT

As has already been pointed out that there is a trend towards managing access rather than ownership of information. The first and foremost requirement is to enhance awareness of the authorities, professionals and end-users of the web-based resources. Electronic journals, virtual reference desks, opacs, digital databases, scholarly discussion lists, mailing lists, electronic newsletters, bulletin boards, community telecentres, etc are the new resources and services on the web which must be managed to satisfy the info-literate end-users. It is essential now to get commitment from the higher authorities for providing the Internet connectivity. This is the basic requirement to get benefits of the web.

## REDESIGNING THE LIS COURSES

The Library and Information Science courses must be redesigned to incorporate the IT components. Only this way we can provide competent manpower to the LI profession. There should also be a provision for continuing education and training programmes. ILA, IASLIC, IATLIS, SIS, INFLIBNET, NISSAT, UGC, universities and other organizations such as INSDOC, NASSDOC, and DRTC can contribute a lot in this regard. These bodies are already very active, but still there is a strong need for regularizing and coordinating their efforts.

## EMPOWERMENT OF THE STAKEHOLDERS

The LI professionals and the end-users are the main stakeholders who are going to be directly affected by the widening gap between the stand alone and networked libraries. As such there is a strong need to empower the LI professionals and the end-users. LI professionals must be provided with opportunities to update their knowledge base and develop their skills. Efforts must be made to change their mind-set to overcome their resistance to integration of web-based resources in libraries. Critical thinking, and thorough understanding of the networked environment must be cultivated among them. Similarly, it is now possible to empower the end-users also. With the emergence of user friendly 'drag and drop' and 'point and click' systems it is possible for the end-users to find pertinent information in many cases. Information literacy is a way to empower the end-users.

## INFORMATION LITERACY

It includes basic computer and network literacy. Besides, the end-user must be enabled to search right information as well as make its judicious use in a timely manner. LI professionals have a pivotal role to play in this regard. They should not only act as facilitators and tutors but also as motivators.

## QUALITY INFORMATION MANAGEMENT

As there is no competition for space in the web, it has become very difficult to retrieve relevant information in time. In case of general information web returns thousands of entries, and in case of esoteric information sometimes not even a single relevant reference is available. The end result of this phenomenon is a frustrated end-user.

We must make efforts to help the end-users to come out of such a demoralizing and demotivating situation. LI professionals must search the web on regular basis and customise the retrieved information according to the interests of the end-users. Only this way we can manage access to the web based resources. LI professionals have an ethical commitment to serve as gatekeepers. Quality information must be sifted from the information deluge which is engulfing the emerging information society.

## WRAPPING UP

There are certain issues which must be addressed immediately. These relate to implementation of the National Policy on Library and Information System, enhancing end-users' awareness of the web-based resources and services, empowering the LI professionals, getting commitment from the purse holders for the Internet connectivity, managing access to digital documents, customizing digital resources to the needs of the end-users, and developing and mounting indigenous databases on the web. Inflibnet and Delnet are doing a good job in this regard. Library associations, universities, R&D organizations, the UGC, Nissat, Insdoc, Nassdoc, DRTC, etc should provide leadership to the LI professionals for bridging the existing gap between the 'haves' and 'have nots' at least in India.

This is not an easy task. It has wide implications for the LI professionals. As suggested, have to develop suitable policies and strategies, adequate infrastructure, and competent LI professionals. Besides, there must be a provision for continuous maintenance of the LI infrastructure as the ICTs will never be stable. We are living in an era, where uncertainty is the only certainty, instability is the only stability, and change is the only constant.

We must learn to create and manage change. Only this way we can survive and thrive in the networked environment, and provide delight to the end-users. We must automate our library and information systems, but not our thinking. Our biggest challenge is to provide access to multimedia information. Biggest challenge it is because information today has become fluid and transcendental. Managing access to digital information is just like hunting a moving object. Only competent LI professionals with thorough understanding of the web-based environment will be in a position to manage access to web-based digital resources.

## METAMORPHISM OF LIBRARIES

During the movement of library system, developmental changes such as, closed access to open access, the role of library from a store-house to active information service organization and reading place to center of recreation have been seen. Now digital media is being used to store, process and retrieve information that causes Metamorphosis in the very form and function of library, though the philosophy of librarianship is still the same.

## METAPHORISM OF LIBRARY TO DIGITAL LIBRARY

Metamorphism of library means that, the library has passed through certain amount of pressure and environmental change to be addressed, in today's electronic age, as digital library. Basically the term Metamorphism is borrowed from geology and according to Webster's Dictionary it is "a pronounced change effected by pressure, heat, and water that results in a more compact and more highly crystalline condition."

### Technology

Technology has influenced libraries in many aspects:

#### *Media*

Electronic storage forms have changed through magnetic

tapes, floppies, CDROM and now DVDs. The very storage capacity of CD-ROM made 20 volumes of The Oxford English Dictionary available only on one CD. The newly developed DVD technology stores 4.7 GB-17GB data, depending upon the specifications. These powerful storage devices have compressed the size of Library in Digitized form.

### *Cost*

Cheaper and reliable technologies have reduced the cost of products resulting in increased storage capacity of libraries in less cost. The cost of CDs has come down very fast in last two years. But new technology like that of DVD is still costly, but may come down after wider use. Compared to traditional books or other materials, the digitized products are cheaper from the library point of view.

The 20 volumes of normal OED cost £ 1800 and in leather jacket cost £ 3750, while in CDROM cost £ 175 and updation is £ 51.06. Duplication through computer is cheap. Practically one can copy any amount of data within short time. Besides, documents lose fidelity in traditional environment and offset printing is too costly. Digitized duplication does not lose single per cent fidelity. But copyright issue is not to be overlooked.

### *Access*

In online digital environment information can be accessed at any time. Such facility can be extended to user's home or office. Besides, there is no danger of nonavailability of document due to circulation.

### Publication

Technology has no doubt changed the trend of publication. Lots of products are available on Internet and in electronic form. Though most of the products are of low quality, content or presentation wise, but the advantage with these products is, ease of accessibility. So, such products force standard products to go online in order to keep them-self in market. For example, Encyclopedia Britannica couldn't cope the challenge posed by inexpensive, CD-ROM encyclopedia and thus it had to be published electronically. In case of e-publishing, there is scope for improvement in performance, because such publications can be well reviewed by many persons. Better version of the work can come very fast compared to paper form. This particular characteristic is making digital or electronic publishing common and more feasible than the traditional one.

### Barrier for Use

Studies show that as the distance to library increases, users become more unwilling to go to library. A study shows that in Penn State, USA, the idea of offsite repository was disliked by users for all journals published before 1973, which where less used, though it takes only one day to retrieve an article from the off-site collection. The frequency of use of off- site collection was only 4 items per person per year among the total users in institute numbering 1050.

### Usage of Electronic Information

It is hard to measure online activities but studies show that usage of electronic information is increasing almost at the rate of 100%. For example, take the data of Library of Congress:

**Table 3.1. Library of Congress Statistics.**

| Month | GB | Request (million) |
|---|---|---|
| Feb 1995 | 14.0 | 1.1 |
| Feb 1996 | 31.2 | 3.9 |
| Feb 1997 | 109.4 | 15.1 |
| Feb 1998 | 282.0 | 36.0 |
| Feb 1999 | 535.0 | 48.6 |
| Feb 2000 | 741.1 | 61.3 |

Usage of theses and dissertations is not restricted to institute. Now there are Internet based digital libraries, which provide full text access to theses and dissertations. The Brazilian SciELO (Scientific electronic Library Online) project started out in early 1958. The number of pages transmitted from Brazilian SciELO project grew from 4943 in January 1999 to 63,695 an year after.

Similarly, data from Firstmonday shows that in early 1999, full paper download growth ranged from 50,000 to 60,000 per month, which went to 110,000 - 120,000 per month in early 2000. That shows how fast electronic form is picking up.

## WHAT IS IT

In digital libraries information is stored in digital form *i.e.* on computer or CD-ROM or magnetic tapes and is retrieved through digital information access tools.

## MODELLING THE DIGITAL LIBRARY

Development of digital library involves several issues. It may extend from administrative level to accessibility of information. The development of digital library can be taken as a project in the traditional library.

### Digitisation

This is the heart of the project. Following questions must be answered before digitization:

* What element of the original to be captureed?
* How to capture?
* Copyright permission

The exposition of recorded knowledge takes place in four forms:

* Image.
* Text.
* Audio.
* Video.

### Cataloguing

Library catalogue, as we know, gives the information about the holdings of library. In Digital library, there are two ways of doing the work:

#### *Creation of Catalogue*

Catalogue pages can easily be created in HTML format, having the information about title, author, publisher, place and so on. Or even library automation packages, having OPAC module, can be used for the same, provided they have facility of web interface.

### Metadata

The term metadata stands for data about the data. There are many popular metadata approaches and the most popular, particularly for the Internet resources, is Dublin Core. It contains the following 15 elements:

| Content | Intellectual Property | Instantiation |
|---|---|---|
| Title | Creator (Author) | Date |
| Subject | Publisher | Type |
| Description | Contributor (Other agent) | Format (Form) |
| Source | Rights | Identifier |
| Relation | | |
| Language | | |
| Coverage | | |

There are two different approaches of using metadata.

*Approach 1*

* Metatags can be embedded in the HTML documents. For example,
* <meta name = "DC.Author" content = "S.R. Ranganathan">
* <meta name = "DC.Title" content = "Prolegomena to Library Classification">
* <meta name = "DC.OtherAgent" role = "Assisted by" content = "M.A. Gopinath">
* This tag resides in the <head> and before <title>.
* *Disadvantages:*
  - <meta> tags is being used for many things like reloading a page or directing a page to some other URL.
  - It doesn't give flexibility. For example, there are well defined set of tags, which gives robustness to document structure.

## Approach 2

*Warwick framework: Resource Description Framework*:

* Warwick framework supports the existing metadata. Basically it uses the "Container Package model". That means, there is a Container, inside which there are packages of different nature. Packages can be of different types:
  - *Primitive Package:* Contains one or more elements of metadata. Each of them has a type. Ex: MARC package, Dublin Core package, etc.
  - Indirect package: Basically these are links, giving direction to the other information resource.
  - *Containers Package:* A package itself can be a container.

*Resource Description Framework (RDF):*

* This was instantiated by W3C. A project called *Platform for Internet Content Selection* (PICS), to rate the webpages was started by W3C.. Later on, the scope of this project increased and one can set its own parameters to rate the webpages. The second approach leads to description of resource and thus *Resource Description Framework* (RDF) was born.

*RDF Model:*

* Resource is an object that is uniquely identified by a *Universal Resource Identifier* (URI). Resource has Properties. Properties have Property types. And these Property types have Values.

If we generate an RDF model, resources are at nodes, property types are links and values are in quotes.

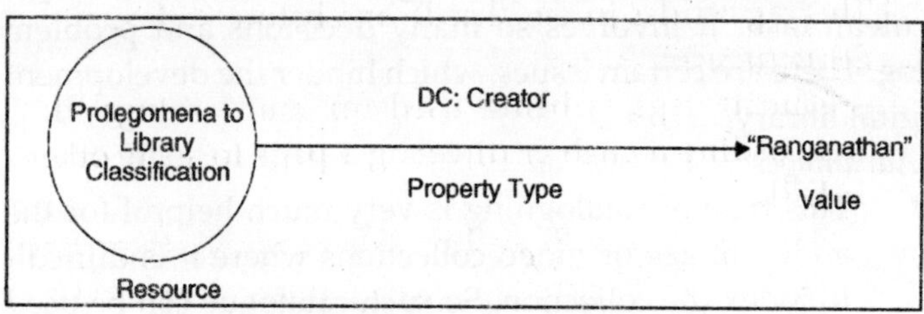


**Fig 3.2.** RDF Model Representation

Basically RDF uses XML, where one can define its own tags unlike to HTML.

### Databases

The current approach is to store information in databases. These databases are made accessible through web-browsers or any other interface depending on the library. Any user can search these information using search techniques and a search engine. In such databases search can be done on a specific field and it removes the need of catalogue.

*Disadvantage:*

* The major disadvantage of this system is that the reader has to browse the whole document to find its relevancy.
* It makes mandatory to use bibliographic database system, because commercially available popular database systems do not give sub-field level description of document.

## AN EXPERIMENT

A catalogue-based approach has been adopted for developing Digital Library model. The library gives access to all sorts of documents including text, audio, video and image in different formats. Browser is used as front end for search and delivery of documents. For searching the document, search engine, provided within MS-Frontpage, is used. The formulated query uses catalogue for search and displays the hit records in a list format. Each item in list is hyper- linked to the catalogue entry page. Each catalogue page in-turn is hyper- linked to the original document. Establishing a digital library is definitely a Herculean task. It involves so many decisions and problem solving. There are certain issues, which hinder the development of digital library.

*Advantages:*

* This type of cataloguing is very much helpful for the audio, image or video collections where it is difficult to index the collection. So such catalogue can be used as document surrogate and can be searched easily using any search engine.

* An abstract gives a clear view to reader about the usefulness of document for his/her study.
* It is a simple approach and can be built using common softwares like, Frontpage.
* It does not use any database.

*Disadvantages:*

* This approach is only feasible in the small libraries and specialized libraries, which have collection that can't be indexed.
* For large size library, powerful search engine is required, because search engine indexes the content of whole catalogue pages and searches through them, which takes time.
* The results are only based on pattern matching so there are no semantics associated to search.

## CHALLENGES FOR DIGITAL LIBRARY

### Intellectual Property Rights (IPR)

No doubt the primary aim of life is to earn. Due to this approach of life the concept of IPR came in picture, which suggests the benefit of creator if his/her work is used for the monetary gain or so. This monetary gain became the chief concept in publishing industry. This particular concept really hurts the library philosophy, because it stops copying of documents or its any part for use, without the prior permission of copyright holder. In digital library, actually the media of document is changed which is even more serious problem than the earlier.

At this particular juncture many of the digital library projects die. In such an environment, even if library somehow gets the permission to change the document form or accepts the publication in digital form, it is difficult to save the document from unauthorized distribution and copying. Watermarking is a sort of a solution of it. There is wide variety of softwares, which can be used for watermarking like Digimarc, SysCoP etc. But side-by-side there are softwares, which can change watermarks, for example, StirMark. IPR and security are the two major issues, which dampen digital library projects.

## Economic Issues

Development of digital library involves lot of resources and in terms of money it is not a small amount, which has to be dealt with.

### *Operating Cost*

It is true that to set up a digital library, big money is required. Once it is set up the operating cost for maintenance has to be considered. No doubt duplication and printing cost is negligible, but it really doesn't cut some of the costs, which are there in traditional library. Readers are still very comfortable in reading through printed form and on demand it is library's duty to give in print. So paper stationeries and printing may still be required. Side by side money is required to have backups, buying electronic stationeries, system maintenance, electric charges etc. Besides, library has to consider payment to ISP and telephone line and any other communication mode.

### *Revenue*

Copying can be done in digital environment with 100% fidelity without cost. But to distribute a non-digital product in a digital form, library must have to pay to copyright holder, and if all agree that library should generate its own funds, the question of HOW comes. Charging to user is big problem, because as it is known that publishing industry works on nonlinear pricing, which influences libraries to have nonlinear prices. For example, for two different products if library is paying different amount then it is required to charge differently to users. Thus publishing industry plays havoc for digital libraries.

### *Monitoring*

If digital library, working on Internet, gives links to other Internet resources, due to volatile nature of web documents, it is a must to keep track of presence of web documents. There are few softwares, which do this work like MoMSpider and Web:

lookout, which can trace any changes on the linked webpages. But the real issue is that if the link is entirely changed how to trace that which is quite common on Internet.

### *Communication*

If library delivers its service through the Internet or Intranet it has to have a user interface. Now it should be taken care that how fast the interface get loaded to reader's machine and how fast the results of searches are displayed. For that, librarians should have sound knowledge of technology and changing web environment.

### WRAPPING UP

In library development movement, digital library is a milestone. Though developing a digital library seems to be easy from the point of view of technology but the real challenge lies in the culture of society. To propagate the knowledge it is required to have a sharing of knowledge and in which the publication industry poses biggest challenge. That is why, many of the digital library projects went up to putting the home publication on digitized form not the collection of library. It seems that such problems can be solved if learned bodies or libraries start publishing themselves. But this revolutionary concept may rouse many moral and ethical issues in the librarian's lobby. It is a matter of debate or deep discussion which librarians have to go through and finally again we have a Yaksha Prashana- Are we really ready for this change?

## TOTAL QUALITY MANAGEMENT (TQM) IN LIBRARIES: A PERSPECTIVE APPROACH

TQM is a " system of continuous improvement employing participative Management and centered on the needs of customers". Key components of TQM are employee involvement and training. Problem solving teams, statistical methods, long term goals, thinking and recognition that the system, not people produces inefficiencies. Libraries can benefit from TQM in three ways: breaking down interdepartmental barriers; redefining the beneficiaries and library services as internal customers and external customers; and reaching a state of continuous improvement. A library should always focus on providing the best services possible, and be willing to charge to service its customers.

## TOTAL QUALITY MANAGEMENT

Total quality management is an approach that an organization takes for improving its performance on systematic and continuous basis. This is achieved by involving all employees throughout the organization in satisfying all requirements of every customer, whoever the customer may be either external or internal. Quality Management is the basis for library management in general.

Such principles of TQM as meeting the Customer needs, exact assessment, continuous improvement, team work and enthusiasm of the leaders are typically for library services:

* *Total:* Everyone in the organization is involved in creating and maintaining the quality of the services and the products offered.
* *Quality:* The organization through individual and collections focuses on meeting customer needs, recognizing that customer perception identities quality.
* *Management:* In managing the system, the emphasis les on continuously improving his system in order to achieve the best results.

Above all TQM is a management philosophy embracing all activities through which the needs of the customer and the community, and the objectives of the organization, are satisfied in the most efficient and the cost-effective way by maximizing he potential of all employees in a continuing drive for improvement.

## 14 STEPS TO TOTAL QUALITY MANAGEMENT

Based on the work of Japanese managers, Demirs outlined 14 steps that managers in any types of organization can take to implement a total quality management programme:

* Create constancy of purpose for improvement of product and service. Constancy of purpose requires

innovation, investment in research and education. Continuous improvement of product and service, maintenance of equipment, furniture and fixtures and new aids to production.

* Adopt the new philosophy management must undergo a transformation and begin to believe in quality products and services.
* Cease dependence on mass inspection. Inspect product and services only enough to be able to identify ways to improve the process.
* End the practice off awarding business o price tag alone. The lowest priced goods are not always the highest quality.
* Improve constancy and forever the system of product and service. Improvement is not a one time effort; management is responsible for leading the organization into the practice of continual improvement in quality and productivity.
* Institute training and retraining. Workers need to know how to do their jobs correctly even they need to learn new skills.
* Institute leadership: Leadership is the job of management. Managers have the responsibility to discover the barriers that prevent staff from taking pride in what they do. The staff will know what those barriers are.
* Drive out fear people often bear reprisal if they "make waves" at work. Managers need to create an environment where works can express concerns with confidence.
* Brake down barriers between staff areas. Managers should promote teamwork by helping staff in different areas/departments work together. Fostering interrelationship among departments encourages higher quality decision-making.
* Eliminate slogans, exhortations and targets for the workforce. Using slogans alone, without an investigation into the process of the workplace can be

offensive to workers because they imply that a better job could be done. Managers need to learn real ways of motivating people in their organization.

* Eliminate numerical quotas. Quotas impede quality more than another working condition they leave noncoms for improvement. Workers need the flexibility to give customers in level of service they need.
* Remove barriers to pride of workmanship, give workers respect and feed back about how they are doing their jobs..
* Institute a vigourous programme of education and retaining. With continuous improvement, job descriptions will change. As a result employees need to be educated and retained so they will successful at new job responsibilities.
* Take action to accomplish the transformation. Management must work as a team to carry out these above 13 steps.

## BENEFITS OF LIBRARY ORGANIZATION BY THE SERVICES WITH TQM

"Sirkin" suggests some ways a library might use the principles of TQM to enhance library services:

* Create service broachers and information kits.
* Conduct a user survey about library services.
* Improve signage.
* Change hours of operation.
* Provide a more convenient material return.
* Simplify checkout of material.
* Use flexibility in staff assignment.
* Co-operate with local government.
* Ask vendors to give products demonstration.
* Give new staff a through orientation.
* Create inter departmental library advisory groups.
* Improve the physical layout of the library.
* Track complaints.
* Develop an active outreach programme.

* Open satellite offices.
* Publicize new or changes services.
* Develop user and staff training materials
* Target services o specific groups.
* Offer electronic document delivery.
* Follow the mission statement.

While TQM clearly has positive aspects implementing it can have potential challenges "Jurow" ad "barnnard" identify four barriers to the adoption of TQM in libraries:

* *Vocabulary:* Objections to terms such as "total" "quality and "management" which imply that high standards are not already being met.
* *Commitment:* TQM takes several years to implement and requires a long term commitment by library managers
* *Process:* Our culture tends to be impatient and we try to solve problems quickly, contrary to TQM ' careful process analysis; and
* *Professionalization:* Professional can be resist to turning over their practices and services to what they perceive as the "uniformed whims of the customer."

"Sitckin"also notes that it is not possible to satisfy everyone's demands; choices will need to be made.

## WHY LIBRARIES SHOULD ADOPT TQM

Libraries are among the most ancient social and cultural institutions in existence. Ancient libraries as well as modern ones have one thing in common: all of them have a body of information recorded on of them have a body of information could be retrieved when needed. The accessibility of information requires good organizational ability from those who are structure of the organization where desired information is retrieved and made accessible efficiently and in a timely manner to the users. Creation and maintenance of such a structure requires an effective management process that facilitates work towards the goal.

Today technology has changed our social and economic life. In the workplace methodologies change people work at home or on the web with flexible time table, and more and more virtual communities are emerging in different fields. The most important stakeholders in the library are customers, providers of subsidies, staff and other libraries. These stakeholders are interested for various reasons, in the introduction of TQM. The introduction of TQM makes great demands on the staff.

The following factors in particular need to be taken into account:

* TQM involves a process of change and therefore requires of staff that they be ready to play a constructive role in that process.
* TQM requires a basic re-orientation from the media stock towards customer and markets. For TQM a result oriented approach, not the input of resources, is of vital importance.
* A strongly hierarchical organization with fragmented responsibilities is not well suited to the introduction of TQM since all staff needs to feel a responsibility for influencing quality.
* The effort necessary for implementing TQM is at the same time rewarding for both staff and the institution: Improvement of the institution in which they work, a strengthening of that institutions position, and more opportunity of staff to influence their own work.

The management of quality in libraries, as a management method that allows the improvement of performance, has been the object of interest for the managers of these services. In this context, that permits the reality of the information service is essential to better adequate and quality proposals.

## FINAL COMMENTS

Quality can be described right time as well as doing it right the first time and doing it right each time.

It requires continuous improvement. In this context of the library, it can be described as:-

* Q – Quest for excellence of knowledge
* U – Understanding the user's demand.
* L – Leadership quality for librarian.

* I – Involving all staffs.
* T – Team spirit for achieving common goal.
* Y – Yardstick to measure progress.

There are various aspects of dimensions of quality that are utilized by a user to evaluate library service:

* *Performance*: Performance of library services according to the user's need.
* *Features*: Special features of library, that appeals to users.
* *Access*: Approachability to library and easy access to document.
* *Competence*: Possession of special skills and knowledge required performing the library services in the changing content.
* *Responsiveness*: Whole-heartedly endeavour to provide services as soon as possible.
* *Courtesy*: Respects, politeness as tidy appearance of library staff.
* *Communication*: Listening carefully to the users educating and informing them in the language in which they can understand easily.
* *Reliability*: Providing reliable information thus making users free from doubt and confusion.
* *Credibility*: Trust worthiness, belief having the user's best interest at heart.
* *Tangibles*: The physical evidence of various services, tools, equipments, and latest information technologies.
* *Availability*: Unlimited access to the library.
* *Maintainability*: Restoration of service immediately if it has failed at any juncture.

## DYNAMIC DIGITAL LIBRARY CONSTRUCTION AND CONFIGURATION

### BACKGROUND

Over the years the Greenstone digital library software has been employed by many users internationally to develop a wide variety of digital libraries. In addition to operation over the Web, an early application, and still a major one, is collections of humanitarian information in the form of CD-ROMs that run on any Windows computer. There are now over two dozen of these collections, and they have been distributed widely by the United Nations and other non government agencies. Many other styles of collection have been developed under Greenstone.

They range from numerous personal collections based around common document formats such as E-mail, photographs, Word, and PDF documents through to largescale bibliographic catalogs such as the BBC radio and TV archives. There are mixed media collections involving text, images and audio drawn from data such as historic newspapers and oral history. Several demonstration music collections support direct content-based retrieval through "query by humming."

Many customised and branded user interfaces exist, such as the New York Botanical Gardens, and many international collections in local languages created by institutions in China, India, Croatia, Russia and Israel. The software is distributed in source form, and for convenience binaries are available for Windows, Linux and MacOS X. The user interface is available in 30 languages. A recent addition is a graphical interface for collection design and construction which is also multilingual.

## WEAKNESSES

Many experimental interfaces have been built for Greenstone, some of which make use of a CORBA-based protocol to support distributed client-server interaction. These include a Venn diagram tool for formulating Boolean queries graphically, and a bibliographic visualization tool that plots matching citations on an x-y grid based on publication year and ranked relevance score to the query terms. However, while perfectly functional, some of these variants are implemented inelegantly, exposing limitations caused by certain aspects of the design. For instance, the immutable nature of the index files generated during the building process makes incremental adjustments to a collection expensive.

Another hindrance is the low level of functional customization supported by the runtime system. Although minor presentation tweaks are easy, more extensive changes involve modifying and recompiling the source code. The strongly typed nature of the CORBA protocol was also found to be overly restrictive in many practical situations.

## REQUIREMENTS

From these and other considerations arose the following requirements for an improved design:

* *Backwards Compatibility*: Naturally we wish to retain the existing system's strengths. This is accomplished by ensuring that the new design is backward compatible, which has the added benefit of providing existing developers and users with an easy migration path.
* *Levels of Customization*: To match the different categories of people involved in constructing digital libraries, different levels of customization are required. For instance, a content developer may wish to include source documents in a new format; a collection editor may seek influence over diverse issues of presentation.
* *Software Modularity*: To facilitate development and long-term management of the software, code modularization—a mantra of any software engineering approach—is essential. This is promoted by adopting off-the-shelf technology such as a database system, indexing tools, and page rendering software; and by the use of standards.
* *Service Based*: Basing a digital library around a set of services is another way to accomplish modularity—in this case, modularity of function.
* *Distributed Architecture:* A rich digital library infrastructure can only be supported by a distributed architecture, and the addition of an open protocol helps to foster interoperability.
* *Future Compatibility*: Libraries are long-term institutions with a mandate for preservation, and it is essential that old collections can be presented by future versions of the system. This is a more ambitious

requirement than mere extensibility which, although an admirable quality in any design, does not necessarily ensure that future versions can safely interact with current ones.

* *Dynamic*: Many aspects of the library should be dynamic, for example content, whereby documents and metadata can be added, revised and removed while a repository remains on-line, and configuration, where presentational issues can be adjusted and services added at runtime.
* *Integrated Documentation*: Large-scale software systems such as digital libraries benefit immensely from the use of an integrated documentation system.
* *Self-describing Modules*: This goes a stage further than the previous item: modules describe themselves in a machine-readable format so that other modules can interact with them without the need for explicit control.
* *Computer Environment Integration*: A digital library should mesh well into a user's existing computer environment. Full integration makes a digital library become a seamless component of each user's work environment.

## SOFTWARE DESIGN

The new software design has evolved from the requirements articulated above, our own experience of developing digital library systems, and studies of other open source software and research projects. This section provides an overview of modularity and inter-module communication, and then works through a simple, stand-alone example. The next section describes four very different examples built using the new design, to illustrate the general applicability of the approach.

### Modularity

We decided that the best way to meet the challenges posed by the list of requirements was to reimplement Greenstone using a modular topology. In the design, a digital library manifests itself as a network of modules, and communication between them is expressed through an instantiation of XML. A mandatory requirement for a module—enforced through its base class definition—is that it handles "describe yourself" messages. What kinds of messages follow typically depend on the outcome of an initial "describe yourself". Modules have the ability to transform messages by applying an XSL Transform. This is a particularly useful mechanism for dynamically controlling levels of configurability—one of our requirements. Within the network of modules comprising a digital library, a set of services are defined that prescribe the functionality supported by that particular digital library configuration.

### Communication

Modules communicate using synchronous request-response pairs. Figure 3.3 shows an example XML exchange, where the Text Query module in a collection called "demo" is asked to describe itself. It does this, providing information about the structure of the service as well as fragments of text to be used for display. These are returned in the language specified in the request. While the language used is structured and typed, it has been crafted in such a way that the information it contains can be open-ended. For example, in figire, the param List structure allows other items to be included, such as whether stemming is on or off. In addition to supporting optional parameters, extensions can be introduced without having to update the protocol's API, thereby avoiding the need to propagate code changes to the entire distributed network.

*A Sample XML Exchange as a Request/Response Pair:*

```
<request to='demo/TextQuery' lang='en'
type='describe' uid='21'/>
<response from='demo/TextQuery' lang='en'
type='describe'>
<service name='TextQuery' type='query'>
<displayItem name='name'>Search</displayItem>
<displayItem name='description'>Full text search</
displayItem>
<displayItem name='submit'>Search</displayItem>
<paramList>
```

```
<param name='index' type='enum_single' default='stx'>
<displayItem name="name">Index to search in</
displayItem>
<option name="dtx">
<displayItem name="name">entire documents</
displayItem>
</option>
<option name="stx">
<displayItem name="name">chapters</displayItem>
</option>
</param>
<param name='maxDocs' type='integer' default='10'>
<displayItem name="name">Maximum hits to return</
displayItem>
</param>
<param name="query" type="string">
<displayItem name="name">Query string</displayItem>
</param>
</paramList>
</service>
</response>
```

Fig. 3.3

## A SIMPLE STAND-ALONE EXAMPLE

The simple stand-alone example shown in figure encapsulates many of the design's key features. It comprises a "back end" server, termed a digital library site in our design, coupled to a "front end" that provides the user interface. The modules' names were chosen to emphasize the roles they play. The Receptionist's point of contact with the server is the *Message Router* (MR) module—all communication with the site occurs through this module. The configuration is designed to generalize to a distributed environment.

The digital library back end in figure contains two collections, demo and fao, and a cluster of collection-formation services. Add Document is a service that adds a document to a collection. Import Collection imports into the system all documents associated with a collection, converting them where necessary from their original form. Build Collection builds all indexes and browsing structures that are associated with a collection. Activate Collection makes a newly-built collection active, so that it can be seen by digital library users. These services are all concerned with creating a digital library collection. Being related, they are grouped together into a "service cluster." In figure, the services just listed are accessed through the Collection Formation service cluster module. As far as the digital library user is concerned, a "collection" is a focused group of documents with a uniform means of access. For the system, it is a service cluster that groups a set of services that are related by the data they work on. For example, the demo collection towards the lower left of figure contains three modules providing four services to the user. The modules are called "Search," which provides a Text Query service, "Retrieve," which provides a document retrieval service Resource Retrieve and a metadata retrieval service Metadata Retrieve, and "Browse," which provides a metadata browsing service Classifier Browse.

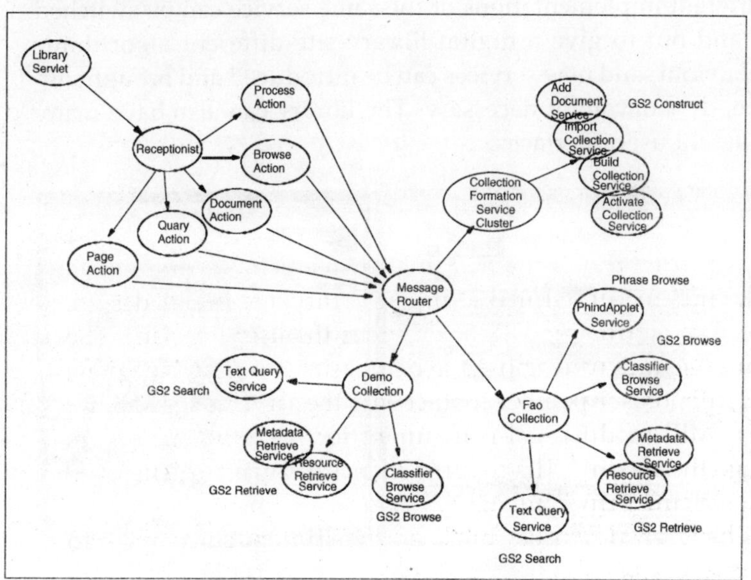


**Fig 3.4.** A Simple Stand-Alone Site

The Web-based front end at the upper left of figure centers

around the Receptionist, which is the point of contact for the interface generator. A servlet takes HTTP commands in the form of URLs and arguments and translates them into XML for the Receptionist. The Receptionist is capable of executing various different actions, each of which involves many calls to the digital library's Message Router. The built in ability for Receptionist modules to transform XML messages using XSLT is used—in conjunction with a style sheet-to generate the HTML that is finally presented to the user.

## EXAMPLES

For pedagogical purposes, the example configuration in figure is rudimentary. The front and back ends are compiled together into a single executable process with a single Message Router handling all communication between them. However, the design supports a far richer infrastructure than this. Message Routers have the capability to communicate across a distributed network with other Message Routers and with Receptionists. Different implementations of the same service can be switched in and out to give a digital library site different algorithmic behaviour; and new services can be introduced and brought on-line, dynamically if necessary. The library can also have many different user interfaces.

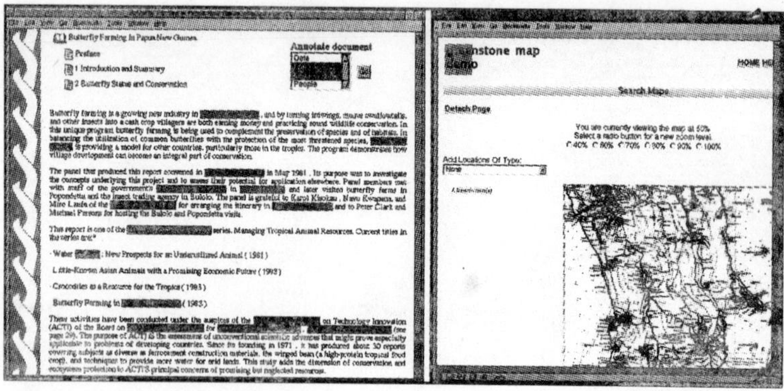


**Fig 3.5.** Additional Services to Agument Run-Time Functionally (a) Text Agumentation of Place Names; (b) Novel Map-Based Interface

We now describe four more interesting scenarios. The first

emulates "classic" Greenstone to demonstrate backwards compatibility, with a distributed configuration a straightforward addition. The second augments text at display time, to show how functionality can be enriched through the introduction of a new service. The third and fourth utilize novel interfaces to enrich the interaction: the former is specialized for geographic maps, and the latter for text based collections.

### Classic Greenstone, with Collections on Remote Sites

To provide backwards compatibility, a set of Greenstone3 services have been implemented that access index and database files generated by a Greenstone2 system. Indeed we have already seen these in figure. Moreover, using *Cascading Style Sheets* (CSS), the look and feel of the traditional interface has been matched one-for-one, so that the user's experience of the digital library remains the same. Of course with the more versatile design, more sophisticated internal structures can be built within the digital libary.

For instance, because of the design decision that all communication be XML based, it is straightforward to arrange for the XML messages sent between modules to be seamlessly streamed across remote machines. For this we employ the *Simple Object Access Protocol* (SOAP), but any protocol that can process text can be used. To the user there is no disernable difference accessing collections this way. Backwards compatability is not the sole aim, however, and the structure allows increasingly interesting digital library designs—ones that do provide a distinctly different expierence for the user. We discuss three such examples next.

### Dynamic Text Mining

The next example shows how a new Greenstone3 service can be provided that enhances documents for the reader based upon the open source GATE system for text mining. The motivation is that highlighting selected items in documents can make it easier for users to scan them for particular pieces of information. In this implementation, digital library documents, once located, are mined on the fly marking up entities such as keywords and place names before presenting them to the user. Figure shows a section of a book on Butterfly Farming in Papua New Guinea that the user is reading. The Annotate document menu at the top right calls the display time text mining feature. When items on this menu are selected, text of the selected type is highlighted in the document displayed. In this case the user has selected Places and Organizations, and these are highlighted wherever they occur, in different colours.

The selectable items in figure were identified and extracted by ANNIE, GATE's information extraction system. Whenever an annotation type is selected from the menu, Greenstone3 calls the information extraction module dynamically to identify items of that type. This incurs a delay that depends on the document's size but is usually short: the system processes text at the average rate of 15 Kb/sec on a typical workstation. In order to achieve this the software is loaded when the Greenstone3 server is executed and remains resident in memory thereafter, to avoid a start-up delay in which all the text processors are initialized and prepared for use. In Greenstone3, GATE is encapsulated in a module as just another service.

It takes messages with two parameters, the type of annotation and a document, and returns the document with relevant items marked up with XML tags. A style sheet in the server module chooses the colours in which the items are displayed. In order to generate the menu in the figure, a "describe you" message is sent to the GATE module, which returns a list of the annotations that are available. Apart from this one module, the rest of the digital library system knows nothing of GATE. However, it does know about a general class of services, Enrich, that take a document and return the same document with some elements marked up. To add this text-mining ability to an existing Greenstone3 site dynamically the Java class files for the new service need to added to the correct folder on the DL site's file system, the site's configuration file updated to name the new service, and a "reconfigure" signal sent to the DL site server.

**Geographical Map Based Interface**

Figure 3.6 is taken from a site configured to support map

searching based on a small collection of New Zealand maps drawn between 1770 and 1953, part of our university library's special collections. It shows the result of searching for "Rangiriri"—a township in the North Island of New Zealand and, on a hill nearby of the same name, the scene of a battle in 1863 between Maori and British soldiers. Two crosses have been overlaid on the map showing the position of the township and hill, and can be seen slightly above the center of the map.

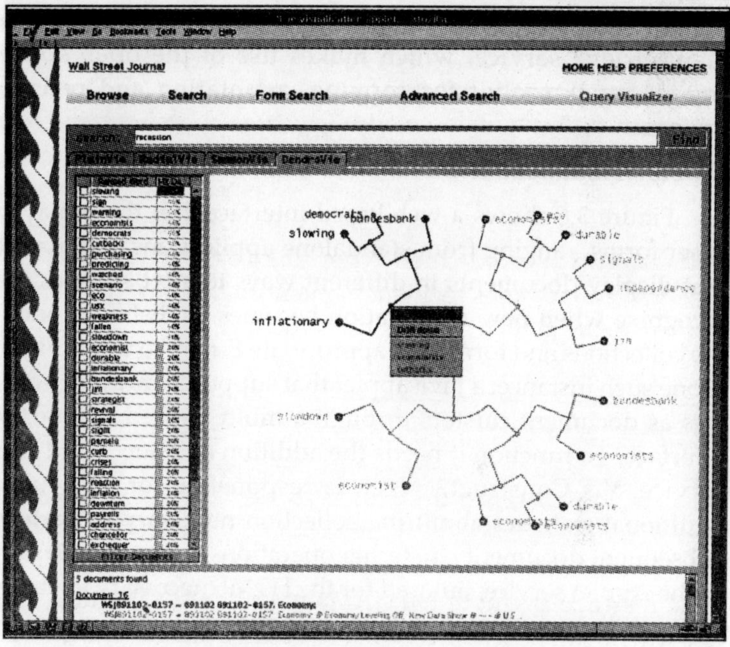


**Fig 3.6.** Applet based Dendro Visualization of Clustered Documents Matching Query

The query interface and presentation of the results is similar to the traditional interface, except that against each matching item a thumbnail of the map containing the place name is given. Figure is the result of honing in on one such map appearing in the result set. Through the interface the user can change the level of magnification of the map and request that additional features such as cemeteries, bridges, and estuaries be marked.

This new functionality is provided by adding two new

services, including geographic metadata with the collection's source documents and a gazetteer of over 40,000 entries from *Land Information New Zealand* (LINZ). Searching is handled by the Map Query service. For each place name query term that is located in the gazetteer, its longitude and latitude are checked against each map to see if it falls within its boundaries. Once all cross-referencing is complete, the list of maps with matching entries is sorted by the number of query terms on each map. Image manipulation and the results display are handled by the MapRetrieve service, which makes use of the open source ImageMagick toolkit for copying, annotating and resizing images.

### Cluster Visualizations

Figure 3.6 shows a web-based interface, but there may be other forms, ranging from standalone applications and applets that display documents in different ways to alert services that recognize when new information becomes available in one of the collections and formulate appropriate E-mail to users. Figure is one such instance: a Java applet that supports browsing result sets as document clusters through a multi viewed, interactive interface. To function it needs the addition of a new build-time service, Vis Construct, which is responsible for computing additional statistics about the collection necessary to perform subsequent document clustering operations, and a sub-classing of the Applet service, tailored for the HTML necessary to embed the visualization applet within a web page.

Besides this, the visualization can interact with any text-based Greenstone collection that defines keyword metadata. The distinctly different interface behaviour is achieved through fine-grained interaction with the existing Text Query and Metadata Retrieve services using SOAP. Derived from the query term entered, there are four views in the visualization. The first is the standard result list format; the other three are based around a shared model of hierarchically clustered documents.

In figure, the user has entered the query term "recession" to a collection based on the Wall Street Journal and is viewing the result as a Dendro map—the circular arranged tree displayed in the main panel—which contains words like slowing, slowdown and inflationary around the circumference. The size of nodes in the tree represents the number of documents clustered at that point in the hierarchy, and for reasons of space only five levels of the tree are shown at a time. Clicking on a node shows a popup menu with the precise number of documents in the cluster and the option of "drilling down" as shown in the figure. The consequence of choosing this option is for the tree to be redrawn with the selected node at the center of the map, thereby exposing more of the detail in that part of the hierarchy. While all this is going on, the left-panel displays the keywords relevant to the selected cluster, and the bottom panel lists the documents involved. Within the left panel, keywords can be activated or deactivated and the bottom panel dynamically filtered to reflect the changes.

## INTEROPERABILITY FRAMEWORKS

This modular, service-based and dynamically configurable approach to digital library architecture can be found in other designs and systems. Two key examples are the Extended Open Archives Initiative protocol proposed by Suleman and Fox and the Open DLib system of Castelli and Pagano. The XOAI protocol, based upon XML and related technologies, builds upon the basic OAI Protocol for Metadata Harvesting. It is a modular protocol which represents each service as a different type of OAI request.

This service-based approach is readily seen in Greenstone3's protocol, where each service has its own request and response format. Like OAI and XOAI, Greenstone3 uses XML for representing requests and responses; providing a gateway between Greenstone3 and XOAI servers and clients should be readily achievable. The OpenDLib system also takes a modular approach to service communication and library construction. Many of its features are similar to those of XOAI and Greenstone3, and the handling of requests to the library map as readily as for XOAI.

However, Open DLib is centered upon a "manager" service that coordinates services, responding to the introduction of new services and alterations to existing ones. Coordination is achieved through a communication protocol between the manager and each service. Individual services, including each library in a federation, acquire data from the manager. The manager does not itself control or direct requests for searches, documents, and so on but instead coordinates between services to ensure consistency. Greenstone3 provides many of these features—for instance, service description requests—without requiring a centralized manager.

The similarity of protocols between Greenstone3, XOAI and Open DLib echoes experience with the previous generation of DL protocols and augers well for interoperability. Greenstone's widespread adoption and free availability allows others to adopt it as a platform for experimenting with the service-centered design approach. It facilitates the addition of new digital library features which would have been hampered by the less open structures of Greenstone2 and its contemporaries. Greenstone3 retains and extends the lightweight configurability of its predecessor without requiring centralized management processes.

## ROLE OF TECHNOLOGICAL INNOVATIONS IN IMPROVING LIBRARY SERVICES

Once librarians were considered only the custodians of the library collection, but the change in information media from print to electronic has shown the new sunrise in the life of librarians. The basic aim of a library is to meet the teaching, learning, scholarly-research and other information needs of its faculty, students and research scholars and that too effectively and with efficiency. Medical library and information professionals ensures that health care providers have access to reliable, relevant, accurate, up to date and timely information that enhances the quality of health care.

The migration of information from paper to electronic media has changed the whole nature of research. With the easy availability of office computers and the transformation of media, the popularity and usage of digital and virtual libraries has been increased. World Wide Web has totally changed the meaning of a library. Physical presence has been decreased rapidly with the invention of virtual library. There is a universal assumption that man was born innocent or ignorant and should actively seek knowledge. "Information seeking is thus a natural and necessary mechanism of human existence". Information seeking behaviour is the purposive seeking for information as a consequence of a need to satisfy some goal. In the course of seeking, the individual may interact with manual information systems or with computer-based systems.

Information seeking behaviour involves personal reasons for seeking information, the kinds of information which are being sought and the ways and sources with which needed information is being sought. Information seeking behaviour is expressed in various forms, from reading printed material to research and experimentation. Scholars, students and faculties actively seek current information from the various media available in libraries, *e.g.* encyclopedias, journals and more currently, electronic media. In this era of 'E', a sea change can be seen in the information-seeking behaviour of the users of library. In the phase of print media, users had no choice except going to the library and search for the material in books, journals and archives for hours. Search was very time consuming in print phase. Changing needs of users have changed the role of a librarian, which has transformed a librarian into information professional. Librarians have always acted as a link between knowledge source and its users.

In this era of 'E', librarians are playing the role of an electronic middleman. They are now helping the readers in the best possible way by using the latest technology and searching techniques. Users are being connected to the information resources via Internet for hyper-links and for many more options and choices for advance search. The change in the information-seeking behaviour is the result of the invention of E-resources. Readers felt relaxed with this invention and inclination towards these resources was natural.

There are many types of E-resources like Ebooks, E-journals, various open sources, gateways and databases. Chronologically we can divide these resources specifically journals as, in-print journals, on-line journals free with print, only on-line journals, on-line databases. In the era of 'E', readers demand has become significant as they ask for an article or topic in place of a book or journal and at the same time they prefer to search online databases to fulfill their needs. With the invention E-resources quantity and quality of research both have been affected. Different search techniques are undertaken by library users to search and locate relevant information. To understand how users of libraries search and locate relevant documents, we librarians, need to understand the search techniques and what resources and sources of information they generally use and require. Information professionals and users both suffer from the problem of exhaustive information, from a wide range of sources and shortage of time to find, manage and evaluate.

Sometimes users search internet indiscriminately without knowing the facts. Here librarian plays an important role by making the users aware of the importance of the evaluation of the retrieved information by guiding them, how to retrieve, what to retrieve and how to further use that retrieved information, which is called evaluation of information. The challenge posed by the information explosion is being successfully met by electronic information sources. Further this information explosion, diversity of user need, financial crunch and impossibility of self-sufficiency has led to the formation of consortia at local, regional, national and international level.

## OBJECTIVE

The main objective of this study is to know the changing needs and information-seeking behaviour of the users and further various methods and resources being adopted by the librarians to fulfil these needs, which is the result of various technological innovations. Information seeking is a fluid and situation dependent activity where a seeker's actions are influenced by access to information, perceived quality and trust in the information source. This reminds the necessity of regular study and development of information system and management information services in North Indian Medical Institutes.

This work intends to study followings in libraries as a prototype of North Indian Medical Institutes:

* To examine information seeking behaviour of library

users of North Indian Medical Institutes.

* To study the problems faced by the library users of North Indian Medical Institutes while seeking and using information.
* To explore the role of the library consortia's for providing service to the library users.
* To review the use of E-databases in this era of information explosion.

## HYPOTHESIS

In this study it is hypothesized that:

* Physical visit to the libraries has been declined.
* Preference of users has been shifted to online documents from print one.
* Lack of knowledge about IT is the main problem the user face in the information searching process.

## METHODOLOGY AND SCOPE

There are many ways to get information. The most common research methods are: literature searches, talking with people, focus groups, personal interviews, telephone surveys, mail surveys, e-mail surveys and internet surveys. A survey has been conducted on North Indian Medical Libraries through a questionnaire to know the changes in the information-seeking behaviour and needs of the users in this era of 'E'. So the medical professionals who were enrolled as member in the various medical libraries of Chandigarh and adjoining areas were considered for the study in hand. Further it can be stated that there were about 720 active library users of these libraries, so these users were taken as the subject for the study.

Through the stratified random sampling technique 72. Questionnaire method was used as it can be completed in one of the two basic ways. Firstly, respondents were asked to complete the questionnaire with the researcher not present and thus data was collected from 72 medical professionals, out of which 33 were students and 39 were senior residents, Assistant professor and professors. Secondly, respondents were asked to complete the questionnaire by verbally responding to questions in the presence of the researcher. This variation is called a structured interview and this method was applied on 28 librarians to know their observations.

## FINDINGS (USERS)

### Visits to the Library

Twenty-nine respondents (40%) reported frequently visiting a medical library, 18 (25%) rarely visited and 24 (33%) never visited; one respondent did not answer this question. Respondents in their first year reported frequent visits to the library more often than those did in their second year. In the overall group, those who never or rarely visited a library indicated that E-resources are not sufficient; documents that they needed were not available or libraries were not needed because of the Internet.

So the main observation regarding visit to the library is that students visit library more frequently in their initial years of college/ institute. Overall group of users prefer to search Internet as they are not satisfied with the available E-resources in their library. They only visit the library after making sure that this required information is available in the library. This service is being provided through WEB OPAC in most of the libraries today. So hypothesis 1 stands proved.

### Preference of Information Sources

Most respondents reported performing database searches independently. Among those who did their own searches, MEDLINE and PUBMED was the bestknown and most frequently used database: only 1 of 72 respondents did not know of MEDLINE. HINARI is being used by some users but the main problem with this database is that site is very slow. When asked about criteria for selecting references, the most important feature was free full-text availability with the demand of online database and formation of consortia. Regarding access to the full text, few respondents said they visited a library to check document availability and ordered articles through a library. More than half of respondents preferred electronic tools for literature searching. Yet most indicated they preferred to print documents rather than read them online. Respondents were further asked about their preferences about the form of the document. An online database is the most preferred format (39%) in contrast to the print only format that is the least preferred one (10%). This observation directly shows the shift of the preferences of the users from print to the online formats. It is strongly supported by the findings in which online journals and databases have become the most preferred form of document as 75% users need only online resources in form or the other. Further users prefer taking print of the required information as they feel discomfort in reading directly from the screen. So hypothesis 2 stands proved.

## Problems in Information Seeking

Several problems were identified in the information searching process. Many respondents found difficulties in choosing among the large number of documents retrieved in searches and lack of time was also noted as a problem. Common obstacles in the information-seeking process identified by respondents include lack of time, doubt about the existence of relevant information, retrieval of too much information and difficulties with navigation and searching. Since latest innovations have made the search easier with the latest options like E-mail alerts, send articles etc., but problem in information searching still persists due to the lack of knowledge of I.T. So the hypothesis no. 3 also stands proved.

## OBSERVATIONS (LIBRARIANS)

According to the librarians, Internet search engines, E-print services, author Websites, full-text databases, electronic journals and print resources are all used to some extent by most of the users. Convenience remains the single most important factor for information retrieval. Speed of access, ability to download, print and send articles are top advantages of electronic journals for all groups. All these services and facilities are possible with the application of IT.

These observations reaffirm that important opportunities remain for librarians and libraries in providing both access to information resources and educating clinicians in how to effectively utilize such tools. Determining the relevance of a document or source is solely an individual's perspective, so the library or librarian is not a determining factor in differentiating sources. It would, however, be advantageous for a library to know and have the relevant material available for use. Library users expect their libraries to obtain new electronic resources while simultaneously maintaining or growing traditional print collections until the electronic resources are fully stable. Libraries are expecting to do this with no additional funding. Research has also concluded that information sources like electronic databases are of fundamental importance in a clinical environment giving their direct contribution to decision making in health issues, often making the difference in patient survival. Increasing demand of E-databases can be met with the formation of consortia only, as E-databases are the main feature of consortia these days. Important observation is that these databases have become addiction for the users.

## Library Consortia

Information explosion, diversity of user need, financial crunch and impossibility of self-sufficiency has led to the formation of consortia at local, regional, national and international level. A library consortium is an association of a group of libraries to achieve mutually the common objective. Working in an atmosphere, which is fully affected by *Information Communication Technology* (ICT), librarians are mastering the use of electronic resources to better understand and meet the information needs of the users and further train them in using new searching tools for better search.

Consortia provide the following common benefits to the libraries involved:

* Access to otherwise un-subscribed reading materials.
* Scope for electronic archives.
* Getting deep discounts through joint pricing negotiations.

* Developing common resources databases.
* Effective document delivery system.
* Enhanced search facilities
* Better scope for developing a union catalogue among participating libraries.
* By forming consortia, librarians are contributing to the economy of their country by saving Government revenue to a great extent. Following are some of the big and successful consortia's of India.

## E-DATABASE

Understanding the user needs play an important role in growing the libraries and librarians; otherwise the library profession may grey in future. To meet the increasing and advanced demands of the user, consortia are playing an important role. Secondly to avail full fruit of consortia a very sincere suggestion to library professionals is to be in touch with whole of the new technology, bridging the libraries through I.T and ICT. One should know the inside out of all the E-databases and involved I.T application.

An E-database is an organized collection of information, of a particular subject or multidisciplinary subject areas; Information within an Edatabase can be searched and retrieved electronically. Edatabase can be full-text or bibliographic. Full-text databases contain the whole content of an article such as citation information, text, illustrations, diagrams and tables. Bibliographic databases contain only citation information of an article, such as author name, journal title and publication date and page numbers. There are many Edatabases and all these databases have various features of searching techniques and tools, which are being used by the librarians to help the users in finding best information in less time.

Some of the popular medical E-databases are mentioned below:

* Academic Search Premier:
  - BMJ
  - MEDLINE
  - OVID

- PROQUEST
- PUBMED
- SCOPUS
- WEB OF SCIENCE
- HINARI

Almost all the reputed publishers have come up with the Edatabases like Oxford University Press, American academy of Pediatrics, Cambridge University press and many more. All these e-databases can be considered as the latest technological innovation in the field of information.

# 4

# Library Resources and Technical Services

## THE CONCEPTUAL FRAMEWORK

The conceptual framework rests on a synthesis of cognitive learning theories about scientific reasoning and concepts. Many theories discuss learning and define the characteristic steps of learning: component display, information- processing theory, modes of learning, and mental models. From the perspective of cognitive processes that make up a scientific reasoning skill set, these theories show general agreement that scientific reasoning is closely related to problem solving and that it involves both inductive and deductive reasoning.

A spatial representation theory of reasoning suggests that people do better when visualizing things, and therefore successful scientific reasoning includes observation and visualization skills. Ziman in his discussion of scientific research and knowledge provides a summary of many important aspects of science, such as patterns of fact, differentiating facts into categories, skills of observation, accuracy, relevancy, explanation, description, generality, and extensive reliance on and use of instrumentation, measurement, and models. From these theories and research studies, it is possible to derive an operational definition of the selective skills and critical steps in learning that are an integral part of the scientific reasoning process. We define scientific reasoning as inductive and deductive thinking. Inductive thinking includes concept development, which is composed of concept acquisition, concept formation, and concept mapping. Deductive thinking includes hypothesis development, which comprises discovery, observation, model building, and evaluation/proof formulation based on empirical evidence. This definition can be correlated with educational objectives when teaching, and with learning outcomes while or after being exposed to learning activities such as lectures and laboratories. For example, training in concept mapping has been shown to facilitate acquisition of text information.

Therefore, in measurable terms of cognitive processes, scientific reasoning comprises:

* Concept acquisition
* Concept formation and analysis
* Concept mapping
* Instantiation
* Generalization and categorization
* Problem formulation
* Hypothesis generation
* Explanation
* Prediction
* Evaluation

This is neither a comprehensive, definitive, nor sequential list of scientific reasoning skills. It provides the theoretical framework for our design and prototype development of learning spaces. In this framework, concepts emerge as the foundational units for facilitating science learning. For a similar approach based on concepts. There are a number of definitions of the word "concept" in the learning sciences.

These definitions have been contributed by psychologists, educators, philosophers, linguists, and cognitive scientists and include the following:

* A concept is an idea or thought, more precisely the abstraction that represents or signifies the unifying principle of various distinct particulars.
* Concepts represent the fundamental elements of all concept areas. In formal content situations, concepts are classes of objects, symbols, and events that are grouped together in some fashion by shared characteristics.

* Most concepts are structured mental representations that encode a set of necessary and sufficient conditions for their application, if possible, in sensory or perceptual terms.

These definitions show that concepts are not studied in an isolated manner; rather, they are studied in their associations or relationships with other concepts. An important component of instructional design is the analysis of the concepts to be learned.

Two basic types of analysis are:

* Content task analysis, which focuses on defining the critical characteristics of the concepts and the relationship of those characteristics according to superordinate and subordinate organizations, and
* Contextual analysis, which focuses on the memory and organization of the concepts.

Both types of concept analysis imply the specification of relationships among concepts. These relationships can be restated in the terminology of librarians: analysing characteristics and superordinate and subordinate organizations of concepts, students define generic-specific and object-property types of relationships. During contextual analysis, students determine other types of relationships between concepts, which librarians know as associative relationships. Associations can also be defined between objects and processes, objects and events, tools and methods, etc. Related to concepts, but not quite the same from the standpoint of educators, are the words "subject," "topic," and "class."

The subject is a field of knowledge or established area of instruction, for example, the subject of mathematics. Subjects are often associated with disciplines. Teachers, scholars, and other workers tend to specialize in the study or use of a particular body of knowledge—or we could say subject/discipline. Subjects involve not merely their particular subject matter, but a particular kind of activity related to it. Topics, on the other hand, are subjects that invite treatment by a number of disciplines. The topic may involve a number of concepts from different subjects, or it may be led or dominated by a single subject. The topic web is a schematic, annotated way of planning the topic, showing how a variety of ideas, activities, subject areas, or skills are related to the core idea. Class is a group, set, or kind of things sharing common attributes. It is frequently associated with the set: a number of things of the same kind that belong or are used together. Theoretically, a discipline determines its subject, identifies topics, breaks them down into classes and concepts, determines relationships, and teaches them via a number of activities. Physical geography is the domain used here to investigate how concepts are organized in classroom teaching and learning.

## THE DISCIPLINE OF PHYSICAL GEOGRAPHY

Document analysis was used to examine the organization of content in one textbook as well as traditional classroom lectures supplemented by Microsoft PowerPoint presentations. We chose materials from introductory freshman and sophomore courses in physical geography. Informal interviews with two teaching faculty supplemented the formal document analyses. Curriculum materials used include Christopherson. Document analysis is a method of research that is used to study historical documents, usually primary source materials.

This method can be used to investigate details like document type, date, creator, as well as answer questions like why was the document written and what can be inferred about the document creator and other pertinent subject matters. Education staff at the National Archives and Historical Administration have created and made publicly available via their Web site a number of document analysis worksheets for different types of documents, such as maps, text, etc. Lectures and textbooks have been the primary tools of Western education for some time now. Lecture materials are unusual in that they can be considered as both primary and secondary source materials.

Textbooks are clearly secondary source materials. Good lectures summarize, synthesize, and present a vast amount of material in a bite-sized chunk. Textbooks provide explanation, corroboration, and pointers to more materials on the subject. Both types of materials were examined in order to identify key aspects of their organizational structure. A limitation of these analyses is the lack of observation of real learning activities, evaluation, and user studies of physical geography learning in students. However, we feel that such studies, while useful, should be preceded by a clear understanding of the nature of the discipline as perceived and presented by its expert teachers. We found that organization by concepts is the preferred method for presenting learning material. Concepts are the building blocks in the educational process. Instructors teaching concepts also defined the terminology and explained the relationships among concepts.

Thus, in geography teaching, a variety of resources for particular natural processes or phenomena are presented as terms selected and defined by the instructor; and relationships within and external to other processes, phenomena, tools, methods, classifications, theories, and states are explained, explored, and studied. One of the key aspects of geography learning at the undergraduate level is vocabulary–terminological lists, lists of standard terms, and their definitions. Additionally, many geographic terms and concepts represent details of natural phenomena and require pictorial explanation. For example, alluvial fans and geologic folds are explained with text, verbal analogies, images, diagrams, maps, and photographs. Educators create personalized collections of images of natural phenomena, processes, and objects.

These are accompanied by definitions, which sometimes are cross-linked with others, offered as a glossary, and used for presenting new material to students. Scientific classifications are of great importance. The textbook contained about 70 classifications, ranging from objects to phenomena to spatial and temporal divisions such as geologic time periods. Additionally, instructional materials pointed to a number of other classifications of objects and phenomena. For example, there are more than 2,000 coordinate systems alone.

A final aspect of organizing for learning in geography is the attention given to the expression of geographical concepts and their relationships using mathematics–measurements from instruments for specific concepts, equations that specify relationships. Through computation, most of these are ultimately transformed and represented as visualizations such as climographs, hydrographs, hypsographic curves, etc. These visual and mathematical representations are used extensively to promote basic scientific interpretation of complex phenomena and processes, often not possible by mere observation. Real-world phenomena taught in physical geography are presented under disciplinary aspects of geography, geology, physics, biology, chemistry, astronomy, and other science and engineering disciplines. Synthesis of diverse perspectives is considered to be an outcome and strength of geographical knowledge and is consistently highlighted in presentations. This contrasts directly with the widely held view of science as essentially reductionist in nature. But it fits with the study of geography as an applied science, dealing with measurements, forecasting and modeling, and interpretation of natural phenomena.

## SIMILARITIES AND DIFFERENCES BETWEEN ORGANIZATION FOR LEARNING AND KNOWLEDGE ORGANIZATION IN LIBRARIES

Summarizing, the two activities of organization for learning and organization for information retrieval in libraries appear to have many similarities. Concepts, relationships, and classifications are also key tools that are used to organize knowledge in libraries. Librarians, like educators, use the same concept-related terminology, specify the same relationships, and are involved in similar processes related to concept analyses. How are library concepts different from concepts used by educators? Are terms, classes, facets, and subjects the same as concepts? How are concepts arranged in library classification schemes? How do librarians analyse concepts? For librarians, a concept is a knowledge unit with similar characteristics.

Often, the term "concept" is used interchangeably with words such as "term," "subject," "subject heading," "topic," and "facet." "Terms" are the main components of thesauruses, while "subjects" or "subject headings" comprise the subject heading lists, like:

* Library of Congress Subject Headings or
* Dewey Decimal Classification.

Unlike terms, which mainly include concepts from a specific domain related to phenomena, subject headings—human constructs—may include different types of concepts, specifically names, time periods, form, and topics.

The main differences between terms and subjects can be described as follows:

* In general, a term denotes a single concept, while a subject heading may consist of composites of terms, although it also may consist of a single concept.
* The guidelines for thesauruses give rules for establishing hierarchical relationships and for assigning associative and hierarchical terms. LCSH also has rules that are used when establishing new headings; however, composite headings are more difficult to relate than terms, and there remain many headings and relationships that were established before the rules were made.

The term "topic" is frequently used interchangeably with the terms "subject" and "subject heading," or "topical subject." Topic represents an aspect of the main subject other than form, place, or period—for example, headings: Libraries, Agriculture. "Subject" is defined as any one of the topics or themes of a work, stated explicitly in the title or text or implicitly in its message. In library cataloguing, books and other items are assigned one or more subject headings that represent their content to assist users in locating information by subject.

In indexes and bibliographic databases, the subject headings assigned to documents are called descriptors. Topics and subjects in library classifications are associated with document aboutness. In library cataloguing, subject analysis has traditionally been carried out on the summarization level that is finding the one overall subject concept that encompasses or can represent what the whole item is about.

Alternatively, the 20% rule is invoked where 20% of the document is about the subject. In library and information science, class is "the first order of structure in a hierarchical classification, at which level major disciplines are represented. A class may incorporate one or more divisions, which in turn may incorporate one or more subdivisions". Examples of classes are the fundamental disciplines or what educators refer to as subjects that are the foundation of the main classification systems: mathematics, physical science, human science, history, art, and so on. Classes are usually divided and arranged according to principles of categorization, such as shared properties and exclusivity. Relationships among concepts are specified to varying degrees by different types of classificatory structures. For example, thesauruses generally specify only three types of semantic relationships. Library classifications are limited in how relationships can be constructed or how many can be specified by many factors, such as the type of scheme and the hospitality of the inherent notation.

In faceted thesauruses or faceted classifications, the relationships are structured with a central idea in mind—for example, object, process, or event. However, most library classifications attempt to preserve the principle of containing relationships.

Containing relationships include:

* Main class or basic subject in relation to all its subdivisions
* Genus in relation to species
* Whole in relation to part
* Class in relation to its members.

The principle of containing relationships does not mean that each item must be more special than the one preceding it. Many items are neither more general nor more special than those adjacent. For example, a book on Mozart in general would precede one on Mozart's operas, etc. Such knowledge organization structures correlate well to topics in education, where concepts from different knowledge domains are related to one topic.

These relationships are often based on contextual analysis, and the relatedness is based on proximity of concepts in the text. For instance, the concept "drainage basin" is highlighted as a heading in a textbook; other concepts like sheetflow, interfluves, gullies. The inclusion relationships principle, drainage basin is a broad term, and sheet flow, interfluves, gullies, and continental divides are narrow terms. Concept, subject, and facet analyses are the processes by which public knowledge structures are used and created. They are familiar activities to librarians, and distinctions between them are often not made. Concept analysis, usually done by indexers, uses an indexing language or thesaurus. Subject analysis as done in library cataloguing is the process of assigning subjects from a controlled vocabulary list to a document. Discourse communities interpret facet analysis in different ways. Classificationists, designers of classification schemes, perform facet analysis when they try to identify the fundamental classes needed or inherent in a subject.

The definition of facet analysis we use in this study is based on the original work of Ranganthan. It is also currently used by the Facet Analysis Theory project to create subject-based portals for the Web. Facet analysis is the "rigorous process of terminological analysis where the vocabulary of a given subject is organized into facets and arrays, resulting in a complex knowledge structure with both semantic and syntactic relationships clearly delineated". These analysis techniques are used to solve the disambiguation problems of semantics, which are well-known problems in information retrieval. When a user searches using a word or phrase, do the records that are retrieved with the same words or phrase really correspond to what the user meant? Classificatory structures take care of semantic problems such as synonyms and homographs in many different ways—for example, thesauruses use qualifiers and parenthetical statements.

They also specify relationships between terms. Semantics therefore refers to the meaning of the term, both its dictionary definition as well as all the associations to it. Definitions are called the "reference" or "denotation," and associations are called "connotation." Definitions are limited and often standardized by community consent and use, but connotations may be infinite since they are determined by personal experience. Thesauruses select associations and include them in three kinds of semantic relationships; indexing languages try to describe many more associations. However, we find that in geography teaching many more associations need to be specified and described for the novice learner. This is one important difference. Another difference is that definitions must also be provided. Given these surface similarities, we decided to find out how, if, and what knowledge organization system could be used to facilitate physical geography science learning.

Our specific questions: How can library classification schemes and thesaurus-type knowledge structures be used for educational purposes? How can differences between organization for learning and for information retrieval be reconciled? There are a number of earth sciences thesauruses that include physical geography. To answer the question of whether a thesaurus can be used for educational purposes, a comparison of concepts in two types of information resources was carried out. Concepts from physical geography texts and the major thesaurus in the geosciences, *GeoRef*, were compared. We also examined the information system *GEOBASE*, a database that indexes materials in physical geography. Physical geography is one of the subjects in geosciences; it may be considered a marginalized knowledge domain because it does not have a major classification scheme or a thesaurus devoted only to it.

We found that documents on physical geography have just a linear list of terms rather than a thesaurus for collection indexing and retrieval. The *GeoRef* thesaurus does contain some terms used in physical geography, but many of them are not included. Our preliminary estimates, 65% of concepts explained in the textbook cannot be found in *GeoRef*. Examples of concepts not found in *GeoRef* are angle of incidence, angle of repose, atomic number, atomic weight, autumnal equinox, available water, average global temperature, azimuth.

To answer the question of how a library classification scheme can be used to support science learning, we examined two widely used classification schemes: Library of Congress Classification and the Dewey Decimal Classification. We found that many physical geography concepts are excluded from these major, albeit general, classification schemes. We speculate that this is so because concepts are neither subjects nor topics. Examples of geography concepts not found in these tools are open and closed systems, law of basin areas, leeward. However, these terms are needed if geographic information resources such as maps and datasets are to be more adequately described for information retrieval in a library catalog that supports science learning. Some universal classification schemes are employed primarily outside the United States, but many of these are based on subjects and disciplines similar to LCSH and DDC, so geology concepts would be separated from geography, resulting in educational limitations.

Another disadvantage of current universal classification schemes is their use of the principle of containing relationships, not the principle of building relationships around the main idea—object, process, or event—as the guideline for knowledge organization. Thus, they do not represent the concept relationships that reflect the order of things in science. Scientific classifications differ from library classifications and subject thesauruses in many ways. One significant difference is that library classifications are based on the literary warrant and link topics to subtopics. Many scientific classifications belong to disciplines that have widely accepted classifications and categorizations.

Most of the concepts in these disciplines might naturally fit into thesaurus hierarchies based on the is- A relationship, often referred to as broad term - narrow term relationship. The proliferation of special library classifications and thesauruses in many science disciplines shows that many more relationships and deeper subject intension is often needed than provided by general-purpose schemes. Physical geography, however, is a discipline that is somewhat unique. Geographers and geomorphologists do not have unanimous approaches to classifying real-world phenomena or processes; rather they have multiple classifications based on various criteria. All are considered equally important for teaching the science of geography.

## LIMITATIONS OF EXISTING KNOWLEDGE STRUCTURES

As early as 1944, Swank pleaded for a critical discussion that recognized the interrelationships between classification, library catalogs, indexes, and bibliographies. While in the digital world these tools are certainly merging and can be merged, our analysis shows that other critical interrelationships that need to be considered for the development of digital learning spaces are the ones that integrate knowledge structures and reference sources. This means that we should explore the merging of knowledge structures such as classification schemes and thesauruses with reference works such as encyclopedias and dictionaries. Included in this list are glossaries, gazetteers, and terminology lists.

Reference tools like:

* Xrefer and Atomica
* Thesaurus
* Definition
* Encyclopedia linkages.

We focus only on the limitations of classificatory concepts such as hierarchy, semantic relationships, and order as they are currently implemented or used in knowledge structures. The enhancements needed are also discussed. The thesaurus' hierarchical relationships–generic, instance, and partitive–are not enough to describe the full granularity of how phenomena or processes or objects are analysed in physical geography. To illustrate this point, let us consider types of "atmosphere," specifically, its NTG relationships. Figure shows them listed in alphabetical order (fig. 4.1).

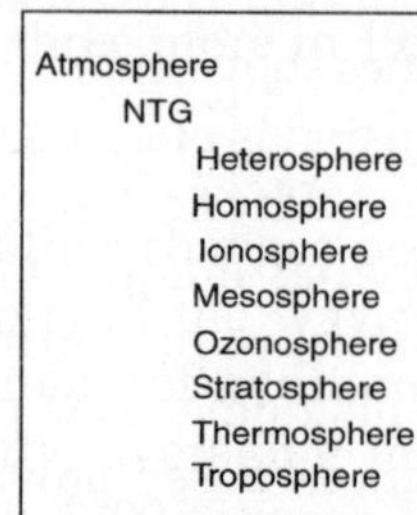


**Fig 4.1.** NTG Relationships for "Atmosphere"

All these concepts represent types of atmosphere. They are all linked to atmosphere with one type of relationship, NTG. However, for a specialist in the field, these concepts differ in their relationship to the concept atmosphere; namely, they are based on different classifications that consider different criteria. Following the faceted thesauruses' practices, such as those in the Art and Architecture Thesaurus, these different classifications can be maintained in different "nodes", which simply mean different sets of subtypes. Nodes themselves are treated as nonindexing terms and are shown in angular brackets in figure.

Atmosphere
NTG
<Composition Criterion>
Homosphere
Heterosphere
<Temperature Criterion>
Mesosphere
Stratosphere
Thermosphere
Troposphere
<Function Criterion>
Ionosphere
Ozonosphere

**Fig 4.2.** Nodes for "Atmosphere"

By default, the conventional thesauruses and thesaurus construction software, such as Multi-Tes, arrange narrower concepts in alphabetical order. Such an arrangement is not a satisfactory foundation for building learning spaces in physical geography. In real geography learning, concepts are arranged in a certain order, which is by no means alphabetical, and differs depending on the concept. It may be chronological or based on disciplinary logic. For example, geological time periods are arranged in a chronological order that is based on macro time scales. Other times, arrangements are based on micro time scales. The need for ordering concepts exists in library classification schemes too.

However, general thesauruses usually do not specify a citation or preference order. The exception is faceted thesauruses, such as the A&AT. Our findings suggest that ordering of concepts in sets is desirable for enabling learning. It would also be useful to add multiple ordering of concepts–for example, as the concepts are organized in the textbook.

In the literature, concepts can be repeated as subtypes of one concept under different classifications.

For instance:

* N. Lancaster differentiates the following dune types:
  - Crescentic dunes
  - Linear dunes
  - Star dunes
  - Parabolic dunes
  - Nebkhas
  - Lunettes
* E. D. McKee differentiates:
  - Crescentic dunes
  - Linear dunes
  - Star dunes
  - Other dunes
* L. Aufrere classifies dune in the following way:
  - Longitudinal
  - Oblique
  - Transverse

In these classifications, linear, crescentic, and star dunes appear in two classifications. To incorporate all these classifications into a thesaurus, we would have to list some of the terms as subtypes of sand dunes twice or more. The classifications are taken from Nicholas. Some universal classification schemes are employed primarily outside the United States, but many of these are based on subjects and disciplines, so geology concepts would be separated from geography, resulting in educational limitations. Another peculiarity of concept arrangements in textbooks is that they are not in the alphabetical order usually found in thesauruses. Very often orderings carry additional semantic information-for instance, they show chronological sequence or evolution.

Thesauruses should reflect such scientific orders. These orderings do not necessarily have to be displayed for the users; they can be used only by librarians or in the background. The users will just see the sequence of concepts in a way the phenomena or their types are arranged in nature, or in chronological order or the order in which scientists usually arrange them.

Ranganathan suggested the following possibilities for order in array within a facet in addition to alphabetical order:

* Increasing quantity. Types of polygons could be arranged in this order: triangle, quadrilateral, pentagon, hexagon, heptagon, octagon, nonagon, decagon, hendecagon, dodecagon, etc.
* Later in time. Writers in literature could be arranged according to their date of birth.
* Later in evolution. Living things could be arranged in this way.
* Spatial contiguity
* Increasing complexity. Methods, instruments, machinery could be arranged in this way.
* Canonical order. This means a traditional order, such as arithmetic, algebra, geometry.
* Favoured category or literary warrant. This order could give precedence to the subjects in the array about which most had been published.

Subject intension is depth of the subject, the microtopics. If relationships that support scientific theories, classifications and categorizations, and concepts on a level of even micro-topics are available, they can be used for the construction of concept maps. Concept maps are gaining quick popularity as a favoured instructional material in many disciplines. There are a number of software packages that allow students and instructors to construct concept maps. However, our experience at ADEPT indicates that many instructors do not have the time to build concept maps and organize their materials using them. Another reason why concepts maps are not widely constructed in science is because it is very difficult to build a concept map from scratch and show the complexity of relationships on one plane, as opposed to multidimensional space. However, instructors are often willing to use concept maps in instruction if they are constructed, maintained, and organized by other responsible entities, such as libraries.

## CONVERGENCE

We conclude that a faceted thesaurus based on scientific classifications of disciplinary-specific facets such as objects, processes, phenomena, and methods can provide the foundation for developing digital learning spaces in physical geography. It must be constructed with great care given to the contents, categorization, and quality of the hierarchies. For example, polyhierarchies must specify roles and have more detailed associative relationships. An ALCTS committee has been investigating the area of subject relationships. Hierarchies must also link types and parts of objects to objects, processes to processes, etc.

## FACETS

Facets are "clearly defined, mutually exclusive, and collectively exhaustive aspects, properties or characteristics of a class or specific subject".

Our analysis derived similar facets in physical geography that were originally assembled as universals in the context of all disciplines:

* Objects
* Properties, attributes
* Processes and activities
* Instruments
* Theories, principles, classifications
* Applications
* Disciplines

### Names for Relationships

Another desirable enhancement that should not be overlooked is more detailed specification of the associative relationships among concepts. Relational structures—indicated usually by an abbreviation RT for related term or by AS, often used for associative relationships—are neither sufficient nor explicit.

While the task of decoding what is hidden behind the abbreviation would not seem to be complex for the more experienced users of a specific domain, for the novice domain users, in our case, students, it will be difficult to understand the nature of RT relationships without specification. Therefore, for students a short explanation of the associative relationships is necessary.

## Labels for Nodes

Node labels are organizational devices that are often used to arrange hierarchical displays. Node labels are enclosed within angled brackets.

## Support for Orders in Arrays of Related Concepts

As discussed previously, concepts in the relationships can be ordered not only alphabetically, but also in chronological, evolutional, canonical, and other sequences. Agreement is needed for how objects should be ordered in geosciences. For instance, in our example with atmospheres, the flexibility of defining sequential orders lets us arrange concepts of atmospheric types in the natural order as is shown in fig. 4.3.

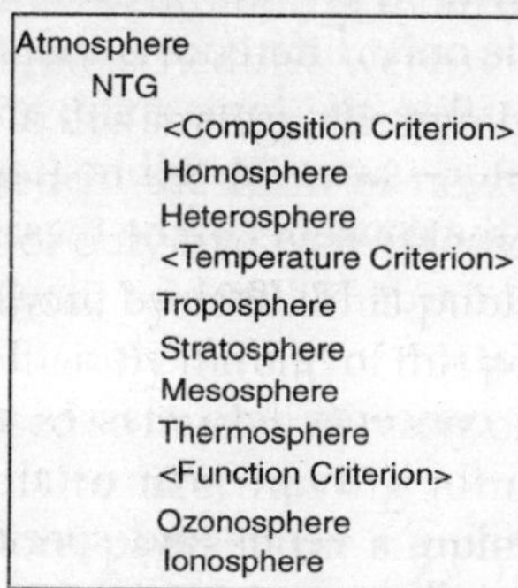


**Fig 4.3.** Natural Order for "Atmosphere"

# USING TOPIC MAPS FOR DIGITAL LEARNING SPACES

Many technical and theoretical approaches offer solutions to interlink concepts; semantic nets, ontologies, topic maps, and concept maps are some of them. The use of the ISO Topic Map standard, XTM. Topic maps provide "a standardized notation for interchangeably representing information about the structure of information resources used to define topics, and the relationships between topics". The topic definition in the standard is similar to the librarian's definitions of topics or subjects. However, it is possible to use topic maps for linking concepts and specifying relationships between them. In other words, it is possible to construct information resources such as concept maps based on classificatory knowledge structures, like the faceted thesaurus using the XTM standard. In doing so, no significant distinction between concepts and topics is made.

As examples of topic maps, XTM and faceted thesauruses have many features in common:

* Both link concepts.
* Both treat concepts and relationships separately.
* Both use controlled vocabularies.
* Most relationships in both standards have symmetrical counterparts.
* Both serve as backbones in information systems that allow linking the information resources to the concepts; the only difference is that topic maps do this internally within the topic map, and thesauruses do this externally—surrogate bibliographic records carry linkages to the concepts in the thesaurus.
* In both standards hierarchies play an important role in information organization. The first step of organizing concepts into classes and subclasses of concepts in topic map construction is similar to the task of defining a genus and species, a primary task in building a thesaurus.
* Classes in topic maps and hierarchies in thesauruses facilitate a systematic approach to cross-referencing concepts from different facets; from these an ontologist will have a clear picture in terms of the categories for characterizing the concepts.

Standard thesaurus relationships can be mapped to topic map terminology as shown in fig. 4.4.

| Thesaurus | Topic Map |
|---|---|
| BTG-NTG-General Term | <Instance> |
| USE-Use this Term | <BaseNameString> |
| UF - Use this Term Instead | <VariantName> |
| SN - Scope Note | <Scope> |
| NTG-BTG - Narrower Term | <InstanceOf> |

**Fig 4.4.** Thesaurus—Topic Map Relationships Mapping

The advantages of topic maps are that they are in XML format and have a number of software packages–for authoring, navigating, and displaying. These software packages help users and creators visualize the contents of the concept space and display explicitly concepts and relationships among concepts. The visualizations can be shown to users as concept maps. Concepts immediately related to a particular concept can be viewed as a concept map for the particular concept. The relationships in topic maps also have a much richer structure than the relationships in thesauruses.

While thesauruses have only a predefined set of relationships, the XTM standard gives full semantic freedom in the specification of relationships. This is both an advantage and a disadvantage. Since concepts and relationships are important for librarians and educators and may vary based on discipline, different learning spaces can be designed for different domains. Relationships in topic maps have two components: roledefining topic and role. Role-defining topic can be expressed as a verb; for example, written by, has, originates. The idea of including verbs in a concept space is interesting, since most library knowledge organization schemes have always tried to avoid verbs.

In science education, verbs are important information elements and are used quite extensively: modify, move/transport, measure, capture, produce, protect, damage, form, originate, re/distribute, dissipate, accumulate, gravitate, occupy, cover, resist, protect, dissolve, decrease, increase, exist, generate. For the role-defining topics we initially recommend implementing isAssociatedWith, Has-Constitute/Comprise, IsStudiedIn-Studies, Uses- IsUsedBy, IsCausedBy-Causes using XTM. However, a more complex typology of relationships can also be specified. Roles refer to the related concept and explain its category.

For roles, names of basic categories–or facets–such as, processes, methods, tools, properties, objects; or their more detailed subcategories: landforms, landscapes, hydrologic bodies, vegetation, fluvial processes, and other can be applied. Roles are the elements that can make the topic map model especially attractive to educators and novice learners. Figure shows the list of relationships and roles needed for teaching and learning about atmosphere.

Typology of Associative (Related) Relationships for Atmosphere:

* IsStateOf
* IsMethodFor
* IsClassificationFor
* HasClassification
* HasAssociatedMethods
* HasStates
* CanBeMeasuredWith
* IsForMeasuring
* HasProcesses
* IsProcessOf
* HasProperties
* IsPropertyFor
* IsAssociatedWithGeosystem
* IsUsedFor.

Due to the complexity of the relationship structure in the XTM standard, the relationships have to be specified in both directions: from concept a to concept b and from concept b to concept a. From this perspective, the thesaurus appears to be a more efficient model; the symmetrical relationships are derived from the relationship between a and b. The weakness of both standards though is that they lack the predefined behaviour of relationships. While in thesaurus the behaviours are described in the NISO standard, no action is taken upon it by the existing software packages.

For instance, knowing classes of concepts and the directionality of relationships, one could impose the constraints that would disallow such entries as *Hamlet* wrote Shakespeare, or erosion is made of sand. The constraints that would disallow such entries are necessary if we are going to use the help of the scientific community in building the relationships. Additional research of relationship behaviour in concept spaces is highly desirable. The basic idea of topic maps is that all concepts are grouped around one central concept—topic via the inclusive relationship—*instanceOf*—instance. Each relationship can have a reference to a specific role-defining topic. The examples used in the XTM standard indicate that the topics for the relationships can be expressed as verbs. For instance, in creating a topic map about streams we could say: topic streams includes instance—*has*. Further, all related-to-stream concepts that can be linked with the verb has can perform specific roles in the relationship—in this specific case, all the components will have a role—*Part*.

Different types of stream parts can be disambiguated by the more specification of roles:

* Longitudinal Part,
* Cross Sectional Part, and
* Component.

While the topic map standard offers a nice data model, it does not describe the theoretical details of construction for concept spaces: what relationships can be used, or how the relationships should be specified. Such principles must be developed. We believe that the underlying principles that are well suited for topic map construction are the principles of faceted thesauruses. These include strictly defined rules about specification of hierarchical relationships, use of controlled vocabularies, and construction of associative relationships. As a general organizational principle, we also propose using the "natural order of things" approach, described earlier. This means that as suggested, structure relationships according to the order of things as perceived in science/nature. Streams will be related to streams, parts of streams, stream properties, and other objects related to the streams: *e.g.*, terraces, fluvial processes, and physical, chemical, and biological properties.

When this approach is followed, a subject ontogeny is maintained as well and becomes a part of public knowledge structures. Topic maps can provide the conceptual framework for developing the content domain and scientific reasoning processes of student learning that can be associated with information resources. Because the standard builds a structured semantic network over heterogeneous and topically diverse resources, it allows easy and selective navigation to the requested information as well as easy maintenance. The interface for topic maps can be either conventional with hyperlinks, or graphical, the so-called hyperbolic browser interface that represents concepts as the nodes in hierarchies. Hyperbolic navigation where the user can rearrange nodes and bring areas into focus with the mouse has been shown to be a better interface for understanding of complex, heterogeneous data sets. Hyperbolic visualizations with Empolis or Ontopia allow users to enter a search term/concept phrase.

The system responds with a concept map for the term/ phrase. Each node of this map has other concepts associated with it with specific roles such as *has-parts, isCausedBy-Process,* and so on. Each node can be activated as a live hyperlink to provide entry into other thesaurus maps that extend or narrow the relationships and concepts as appropriate. Each node also has occurrence roles, the information resources associated with each concept.

The use of topic maps for educational purposes may need certain improvements to visualizations, such as:

* Support for multiple ordering
* Display of hierarchical relationships
* More interactive features that allow a user to select and save existing learning spaces. A click on a concept node should display the information about a concept—its scope and variant notes.
* Aggregation of resources by form/type and number of resources
* Visualization limited to one concept with immediate relationships, not the whole body of concepts.

Summarizing, we find that classificatory notions, such as hierarchy, concepts, classes, facets, and vocabulary can be used to provide the digital learning spaces needed to support science education in physical geography. To do so, the critical places where the enhancements need to take place in a faceted thesaurus are described: terms to be more rigorously defined and maintained as concepts and facets, scope notes to include nodes that make the relationships explicit, semantic relationships to be extended with other disciplinary classifications and associations, and display of concepts and relationships in multiple orders. Other enhancements needed, such as combining definitions and illustrations with thesaurus terms and better understanding of the behaviour of relationships in concept spaces, have been identified and further investigation is recommended. Development alternatives include concept maps using concept mapping software or ISO topic map authoring. These approaches, specifically XTM, have been compared with existing principles and protocols for thesaurus construction and maintenance, and the advantages and disadvantages have been highlighted.

## USE AND PERCEPTION OF THE DESCRIPTIVE CATALOGUING OF RARE BOOKS (DCRB) CORE STANDARD

Bibliographic control of rare book collections has always been a time-consuming and specialized process. The materials in special collections are there for particular and compelling reasons. Catalogers of such collections have traditionally identified those special attributes in catalog records with full-level bibliographic description, extensive notes, and as many access points as are deemed appropriate by both catalogers and curators. The bibliographic standards for cataloguing rare books, with the principles of *Anglo-American Cataloguing Rules,* (AACR2) underlying them, have evolved over a number of years, first in 1981 in *Bibliographic Description of Rare Books* (BDRB)and most recently in *Descriptive Cataloguing of Rare Books* (DCRB), published in 1991. A new edition, with the title *Descriptive Cataloguing of Rare Materials (DCRM),* is now in preparation by the Association of College and Research Libraries, Rare Books and Manuscripts Section (RBMS), Bibliographic Standards Committee.

The new edition will include rules for the various formats of materials. The documentation for books will be known as DCRM(B). While the current standard of DCRB is written primarily for books printed before 1801, it can be used for post-1800 imprints as well. The Programme for Cooperative Cataloguing (PCC) has defined and approved core standards for many of the bibliographic formats, beginning with the standard for books in the mid-1990s. All the core standards, written for use by the participants in the Bibliographic Records Cooperative (BIBCO) programme, are intended to encourage "faster, better, cheaper" cataloguing. They ensure the same reliability in description, authorized headings, and call numbers as full-level records, but they do not require as many notes or subject headings.

In January 1999, the PCC approved the Core Standard for Rare Books (CSRB). Called DCRB Core because it is based on the full standard of DCRB, the standard is intended for use in cataloguing books with imprint dates between 1500 and 1800. The text of the standard was written and proposed by the Task Group for Developing a Standard for Core Treatment of Rare Books, a group that was charged with the creation of the core standard by the PCC Standards Committee and that included several members of the RBMS Bibliographic Standards Committee. The expected use of the DCRB Core standard is for cataloguing books that have been chosen more for their need of accessibility than for their full bibliographic details.

## DEFINITION OF THE DCRB CORE STANDARD

Two documents define the core record for rare books: Core Standard for Books and the DCRB Core. The Books Core requires authorized headings, a call number from a standard classification system, full fixed-field data, descriptive fields 245-4XX but fewer notes only one or two subject headings, and as many added entries as the cataloger judges to be appropriate. Significantly, notes for justification of added entries are not required. The frequently occurring bibliographical references note is also not required.

With the requirements of the Books Core as a base, the DCRB Core standard specifies additional or differing elements.

Figure presents the DCRB Core elements arranged in MARC tag order, with an indication of how or why the elements should be used. The code "DCRB" in field 040 $e is mandatory because the bibliographic description is based on the full standard of DCRB.

Differing from the Books Core, the DCRB Core does not require a standard call number. Many libraries do classify their rare books, but other libraries use local call numbers. The DCRB Core standard does not require that catalogers who use local call numbers go an extra step and assign a standard call number as well.

| | |
|---|---|
| 040 $e Dcrb | Cataloguing Source: Description Convention<br>Mandatory (Since the Full Standard is DCRB) |
| 050, 082, 086, 090, etc. | Call Number Fields<br>Not Required (Because many Rare Book Collections use Special Call Numbers) |
| 245-4XX | Title, Edition, Imprint, Physical Description, and Series Fields<br>(Following the more Inclusive Descriptive Method and Extent for Recording Biblio-Graphic Details and the Options Prescribed by DCRB) |
| 500 | Note Field<br>Mandatory (If Elements on the Title Page have been Transposed in the 245 Field) |
| 510 | Citation/References Note Field<br>Mandatory (If One of the Five Citations Specifically Required by DCRB) |
| 655 | Index Term – Genre/form Term<br>Not Required but Encouraged |

**Fig 4.5.** Elements of the DCRB Core Standard Required in Addition to the Requirements of the Books Core

The title, edition, imprint, physical description, and series areas are all required if appropriate to the item being cataloged, just as they are in the Books Core, but their inclusion follows the descriptive method prescribed by DCRB and may apply the options for shortening the bibliographic record. The DCRB Core standard specifies two note fields in addition to those required by the Books Core. If the cataloger transposes the elements on the title page in the transcription in the title field of the bibliographic record, the transposition must be acknowledged in a 500 field.

The citation/references note field provides, in standard form, reference to bibliographic sources. In a fulllevel DCRB record, the 510 field may provide justification for information included in the catalog record. In a DCRB Core record the same reference may lead the user to information that has been omitted from the record, but DCRB Core requires only the five sources listed in DCRB rule 7C14 for post-1500 imprints. The final element of the DCRB Core standard, the index term field that employs genre, form, or physical characteristic terms from standard thesauri, is encouraged but not required. DCRB Core defines the minimum requirements for the bibliographic record. At the discretion of the cataloger, more note fields and more access points may be added to a given record. This flexibility means that a core record may contain more than the minimally required fields without attaining the level of a full record.

Examples of a full-level DCRB bibliographic record and its corresponding DCRB Core record illustrate significant differences between the two standards. A DCRB Core record can be recognized by the encoding level code "4" and "dcrb" in the cataloguing source field 040 $e. The examples used here have the appearance of OCLC records, and the full-level record has been adapted from an existing OCLC record. Other examples illustrating the differences between the two standards can be found on the Web pages of the RBMS Bibliographic Standards Committee.

The difference in the length of the two records is immediately noticeable. The core record has been created by using the options in the full DCRB standard for shortening the bibliographic description in several areas and by omitting fields not required by the core standard. In the publication area, the cataloger has followed the option in rule 4C6 in the full standard to shorten the field. Instead of transcribing all six names of the printers of the book, the cataloger has given the name of the first printer and a bracketed statement that there are five other printers.

The DCRB Core standard does not require any of the thirteen notes used in the full-level record, including the notes that justify the main and added entries. The thirteen note fields in the full-level record have been reduced to one note in the core-level record, the 510 field. While the 510 is not one of the five citations required by the full standard, the cataloger has chosen to include the 510 that gives the reference to the bibliography of Daniel Defoe because the bibliography contains substantially all of the information in the other notes in the full-level record.

Even though this work is a multipart title, the contents note as taken from the title page does not reflect distinct titles of the individual volumes. The contents note, therefore, has been left out of the core record. The DCRB Core record contains only one of the subject headings and one of the added entries used in the full-level record. While the examples are coded as BIBCO records, any library that is not a participating BIBCO member may also create core records. The 042 will be absent from a non-BIBCO record. Creating a core bibliographic record would obviously take much less of the cataloger's time. The time savings and therefore the cost savings may be significant factors for some libraries.

To implement the standard, however, may alter the past practice of describing a book to the fullest to help users find the edition or issue of a title that they are looking for. The DCRB Core standard was written to give catalogers the option and discretion of using a less-than-full standard when collections have been identified as more important for access than for fuller bibliographic details. The flexibility of adding more to the core record and the dependence on the cataloger's judgment in choosing to add more are two key principles of all the core standards. These two characteristics may make use of the DCRB Core, in particular, an attractive alternative to the time-consuming full-level record.

## TEXT APPRAISAL

Although a number of articles have been written about the Books Core and other core standards, little has been published about the DCRB Core standard. When the standard was being written, discussion and reports at the RBMS Bibliographic Standards Committee meetings were recorded in the minutes of the committee. The work of the DCRB Task Group was documented in its final report. During the time of the task group's work on the standard, discussion and comments were solicited on the Exlibris list.

All of those exchanges are available in the archives of the list. After the standard was written and approved, discussion concerning issues of its actual implementation and use was not initiated on Exlibris or Autocat, two lists to which many rare book catalogers subscribe. Much of the literature treating the core record describes its development within the context of the history of the PCC, its purpose in encouraging "faster, better, cheaper" cataloguing that can be relied on for quality of description and authorized headings, and its potential contribution to the success of the national programme. There are, however, some studies and reports that investigate particular issues that are relevant to the DCRB Core. Several studies have been done to evaluate the time savings and cost-effectiveness of the core record. Thomas notes that an unpublished study done at Cornell University by Boissonnas found that core records could be created 25% faster than full-level records.

The UCLA/OCLC Core Record Project, conducted from December 1994 to April 1995 with the same group of catalogers creating core- and full-level records, confirmed the assumption that core-level cataloguing is faster than full-level cataloguing and further confirmed that fewer subject headings and added entries are used in the core records. Other libraries' subsequent use of those core records in the OCLC database with little additional editing attested to the reliability of the records. Hyslop discusses an unpublished study of experimental core cataloguing done at the Library of Congress in 1996.

The experiment underscored the efficiency and productivity of cataloguing using the core standard. Cataloguing statistics at Colorado State University over several years indicated that the use of the Books Core to catalog government publications primarily in the backlog was successful in making a greater number of books accessible more quickly than before the core standard was used. Two recent studies explore the sufficiency of the core record. The first study analyses the access points and notes in the core- and full-level records and finds statistically significant differences in the two levels of records. While the authors indicate the fields that catalogers may want to augment, they acknowledge that catalogers may want to accept basic corelevel requirements unless the need for additional fields outweighs the time savings in the creation of core records.

The second study is a pilot study of library users' opinions about the usefulness of the various elements in the core and full records. Although the study finds the need for further research to confirm the preliminary indications about users' preferences concerning the usefulness of the various access points in the bibliographic records, it does indicate that even though users prefer fulllevel records, they still feel the core record is sufficient for finding the materials they need. In a study conducted by interview of cataloger and cataloguing manager attitudes towards the BIBCO core record, Banush found that both groups of participants, while generally satisfied with the core record, expressed varying opinions about its problems and benefits.

The cataloguing managers expressed more satisfaction with the core record than did the catalogers. Banush notes that this attitude of satisfaction with the core record is in contrast to the reduced percentage of core records actually created by the BIBCO participants during 2000 and early 2001. He also reports that there is a distinction between those accepting core records created by other libraries as copy cataloguing and those creating original core bibliographic records. Even though libraries readily use other libraries' core contributions to the shared cataloguing databases, often without revision, they are more reluctant to create them, preferring instead to create fulllevel records. Cromwell reports that even before the Books Core standard was implemented as part of the BIBCO programme, Stanford University used a similar standard with varying success.

She suggests that the use of the core record cannot achieve the level of cost-effectiveness that is expected without the acceptance and understanding of the catalogers themselves about its purpose and its concomitant emphasis on catalogers' judgment and flexibility. The published and reported studies of the efficiency and cost-effectiveness of creating core records point to an encouraging potential for the application of all the PCC core standards. The research about access points, users' perceptions, and practitioners' opinions tempers the findings of the efficiency of the core record while producing some statistical and qualitative data that encourages further study.

While the DCRB Core standard bears the approval of the PCC to be used by the libraries participating in the BIBCO programme, it may be applied by any library, whether a BIBCO participant or not. In the three years since the approval of the DCRB Core standard by the PCC, however, there has been little evidence that the standard is being widely used. This study investigates the trends in the use of the DCRB Core by means of a survey designed to investigate catalogers' use and perceptions of the standard.

## METHOD

To reach catalogers and special collections librarians who would be able to provide information about their experience with the DCRB Core standard, a query was posted to three lists: Autocat, Pcclist, and Exlibris. Although many people subscribe to all three lists, the profile of subscribers is different for each. Autocat is a list of several thousand people worldwide who are interested in cataloguing issues; Pcclist is a list whose subscribers are from participating PCC libraries; and the subscribers to Exlibris are those who have an interest in the field of rare books and special collections.

In November 2001, the query was posted to the three lists, asking three questions:

* If anyone has cataloged using the DCRB Core standard;
* If not, has a decision been made not to use the standard; and
* If either is the case, would the recipient be willing to participate in a longer survey about the use and perceptions of the DCRB Core.

The questions were posed in this way to find catalogers who have given some thought to the use of the core standard, whether or not they actually use it. The intent was not to seek responses from catalogers who do not use the core and have never considered doing so. Within a reasonable amount of time, only 15 libraries had sent responses, and of those, only 4 indicated that they use the DCRB Core standard. Thirteen, however, said they were willing to participate in a survey.

A few respondents to the query to the three lists indicated that they were responding because someone else had forwarded the query to them. Several more focused groups of potential respondents, therefore, were polled by e-mail: the liaisons at the BIBCO libraries, the members of the RBMS Bibliographic Standards Committee for the past several years, and the heads of cataloguing, heads of special collections or special collections catalogers at member libraries of the Association of Research Libraries (ARL). Using this second method, 135 queries were sent to the three groups. Sixty-five libraries responded and, of those, 30 indicated that they would participate in a survey. By using these two methods, posting to the lists and soliciting individual libraries, 43 libraries were identified that were willing to participate in the survey.

In March 2002, the 43 surveys were distributed to the participants as Word and rich-text-format attachments to e-mail messages. All participants were assured that their names and the names of their institutions would be kept confidential. Thirty-seven surveys were returned. Since most of the solicited libraries are large research institutions, the majority of the returned surveys are from that category of library. The responses to the list postings, however, came from a broader range of libraries. The overall group of respondents therefore has more diverse representation and includes public, private, university, government/national, and special libraries.

The geographic distribution of the respondents includes libraries from the United States, Canada, and the United Kingdom. Fifteen libraries participate in the BIBCO programme of the PCC. Twenty participants are OCLC member libraries, two are exclusively RLIN libraries, and 14 contribute catalog records to both utilities. One library catalogues solely in its own system. Although the initial query was designed to identify willingness to participate in a survey and some responses indicated only yes or no to the three questions, 54 respondents supplied additional comments about the DCRB Core standard or characterized their cataloguing practices or their collections. Of the 54 initial respondents, 24 did not wish to participate further.

In addition, the six libraries that received the survey but did not return it provided some information about their reasons for using or not using the core standard. Their comments will also be included in the following discussion as indicators of perceptions about the DCRB Core standard.

## THE SURVEY AND RESULTS

The survey document contained 12 questions, most of which included multiple parts. The first two questions sought information about the type of library, the rare book collection, and the catalogers of the collection. Succeeding questions asked about the original cataloguing policies of the library, whether the DCRB Core standard has been considered, what decision has been made about its use, and whether any DCRB Core cataloguing records have been created. Questions in the next part of the survey suggested reasons for either using or not using the core standard.

Further questions asked how DCRB Core records created by other institutions are handled and whether any studies of users' perceptions have been done. Space for other comments was provided in question 12. While it was expected that the institutional data would vary from the responding libraries, questions 1 and 2 were asked to determine ranges of information to characterize the participants. No clear conclusions can be drawn about the relevance of the type of library, the size of the collection, the number of volumes cataloged or in the backlog, the number of rare book catalogers, or the reporting hierarchy within the institution. Both large and small collections are represented among the responses, ranging between a few hundred rare volumes in a collection to close to or more than one million rare volumes, with dozens to more than 175,000 volumes in the backlog.

The number of original rare book cataloguers ranges from 25 full-time equivalents (FTE) to nine FTE. Only eight of the 37 libraries have more than 1 FTE rare book cataloger, 11 have less than one FTE, and two did not specify a number; the remaining 16 have only a single full-time cataloger. The questions about the size of the collection and the degree to which it is cataloged fully, minimally, or not at all seemed to pose more problems for the respondents than any other questions. Several respondents indicated they would be delayed in returning the questionnaire until they were able to determine the statistical information about their collections. Rare book cataloguers report to cataloguing or technical services departments in 19 of the responding libraries, to special collections departments in 12 libraries, and to both departments in six libraries. The survey asked about the cataloguing policies of the libraries to determine how many libraries use full-level DCRB or full-level AACR2 for cataloguing pre-1801 books.

The answers were not as straightforward as expected. In responding to how much original cataloguing follows the full DCRB standard, 11 libraries responded that they do all their pre-1801 cataloguing using that standard, and 13 libraries responded that they catalog none of their books using the standard. When answering the reverse question of how much original cataloguing of pre-1801 books follows the AACR2 full standard, 14 libraries indicated all and 15 libraries indicated none. One library catalogs none of its books according to either standard, but instead creates bibliographic records that are fuller than either DCRB or AACR2. Among libraries that do not adhere strictly to one standard, 12 libraries answered that they catalog some of their sixteenth- to eighteenth-century books using the full DCRB standard, and seven indicated that they use full-level AACR2 for some of their books.

The differences can only be attributed to the complexity with which catalogers of rare material view their work and to exceptions in cataloguing practices. To begin the enquiry about the use of DCRB Core by the responding libraries, four questions were asked: have you considered using the DCRB Core standard, have you decided to use it, have you decided not to use it, and have you actually used it? Eighteen of the 37 libraries have considered using the DCRB Core, 14 have decided not to use it, and six have decided they will use it. Six libraries have, in fact, created records using the standard.

Six libraries that have decided to use DCRB Core are not the same 6 that actually have used the standard. One library said that the decision has been made to use the standard, but implementation has been hindered by staffing difficulties. Another library has applied the core standard without having made the policy decision that it expects to make in the near future.

Two other libraries expressed their intention to use the standard in the future, one as soon as appropriate collections have been identified. Depending on the answer to the question of use of the DCRB Core, respondents were asked to indicate why and how they use the standard or why they do not. In each case, a list of reasons was given for potential responses with additional space for other comments. In the discussion that follows, the responses of those libraries that use the DCRB Core standard will precede the responses of those libraries that do not use the standard.

Each of the six libraries that use the DCRB Core did not answer all the questions; and since the number is small, only the positive responses will be noted. One library uses the DCRB Core standard to catalog all of its sixteenth- to eighteenth-century books. Four use DCRB Core for some of their cataloguing; 1 among them uses the standard as the default, but enhances the record if there is a compelling reason. The sixth library uses the DCRB Core to catalog its rare books even though none are pre-1801 imprints. Three of the 6 libraries use the DCRB Core for particular reasons: for a specific collection or when lack of expertise or want of a significant reference work would make it impossible to catalog at the full level.

All the six have applied the standard at cataloguer discretion. and two of the six also have applied it at curator discretion. In response to why and how they use the DCRB Core standard, four libraries answered that they use it to save time, three to increase production, four to gain faster control over their backlog, and three because it is more costeffective. In addition, one librarian whose institution does not hold any pre-1801 imprints replied that they use the DCRB Core because it is "better to capture the uniqueness of what we own in the archival and special collections department", and another respondent noted that they upgrade to the level of the DCRB Core standard some of the brief records for early imprints that can be found in the OCLC database.

Only one library uses the standard as it is written, "since it is written to be flexible"; two other libraries sometimes use it as written. Four libraries add more fields than the standard requires. The additional fields include: notes for contents, immediate source of acquisition, and ownership and custodial history; genre, form, or physical characteristic terms; added titles; and local information required by the library's online system or cataloguing policies. Five of the libraries encourage cataloger's discretion to determine whether to include additional fields and what the fields should be.

The six libraries indicated the percentage of bibliographic records created using the DCRB Core standard to be less than 1%, 1%, less than 5%, less than 10%, and 100%, with one library reporting that no statistical records had been kept for DCRB Core records. In actual numbers 4 libraries reported they have created the following numbers of records: 10, 10–15, 18, and ca. 4400. The fifth and sixth libraries were unable to give figures. The library that catalogs all its sixteenth- to eighteenthcentury books using the DCRB Core standard does not add bibliographic records immediately to OCLC, and there may be a period of time before they appear in the utility's database.

The library that said it starts with the DCRB Core record as the default and enhances as necessary, creates its original catalog records locally without an 040 field because the generic 040 with the library's holding symbol is added automatically when the records are sent to OCLC. This library has not kept records of the number of DCRB Core records created. Given that these two libraries may create a considerable number of DCRB Core records without a way to track them in OCLC and that other libraries, that they have created a minimal number of DCRB Core records, it would be surprising if the national databases have a significant number of DCRB Core records.

The initial responses of the 2 libraries that said they have used the DCRB Core but did not return the survey indicate that they probably have created few catalog records using the standard. When 1 of the 2 libraries applies the DCRB Core, it does so only for seventeenth and eighteenth century books, not for fifteenth- and sixteenth-century books, and it never omits notes justifying added entries.

The other library applies the standard in limited instances because it feels that rare books should be given full-level cataloguing. Since the DCRB Core does not require a standard call number, this second library can contribute BIBCO records for broadsides and pamphlets that it does not classify. Adding these two libraries that did not participate in the survey to the six that did participate brings the total of known users of the DCRB Core standard to eight.

Thirty one libraries that do not use the DCRB Core standard indicated their reasons in response to a ten-part question that suggested 9 possible reasons and asked for others in the tenth part. Each of the reasons was affirmed by some of the libraries.

**Table 4.1. Thirty-one Survey Respondents'Ranked Choices for Not Using the DCRB Core Standard (from Question 9)**

| Reasons | Yes | % Yes | No | Unanswered |
|---|---|---|---|---|
| Core is inferior | 19 | 61.3 | 11 | 1 |
| Description not accurate enough | 15 | 48.4 | 14 | 2 |
| Too few access points | 15 | 48.4 | 16 | – |
| Requires learning new standard | 11 | 35.5 | 18 | 2 |
| Unfamiliarity with standard | 8 | 25.8 | 22 | 1 |
| Shortages or changes in staff | 6 | 19.4 | 24 | 1 |
| Use would disrupt workflow | 5 | 16.1 | 24 | 2 |
| Training is unavailable | 5 | 16.1 | 25 | 1 |
| Material not appropriate | 4 | 12.9 | 27 | – |
| Additional reasons | 18 | 58.1 | – | 13 |

That the DCRB Core standard is inferior was the reason cited by most of the libraries, 19, that have not used it in their original cataloguing records for rare books. Fifteen respondents said that the description is not accurate enough and that there are not enough access points with the use of the standard. Eleven stated that they have not used the DCRB Core because it would require learning a new standard, and eight said they do not use the standard because they are unfamiliar with it. Six respondents reported shortages or changes in staff that have kept them from using the standard.

Five libraries said that training is unavailable, and five also indicated that the use of the DCRB Core standard would disrupt the established workflow. Only four said they do not have material appropriate to catalog using the standard. The opinion and perception of nearly two-thirds of the libraries responding that they do not use the DCRB Core standard is that the DCRB Core record is inferior to the full record. Almost half think that the standard does not provide enough access points and that the description is not accurate enough. Clearly these three most prevalent perceptions indicate that the survey respondents have not been willing to give up fuller bibliographic treatment for their rare books.

This opinion of the lesser quality of the DCRB Core record as a reason for nonadoption by most of the respondents is reminiscent of a similar kind of negative perception and resistance to acceptance that were noted for the Books Core by Cromwell in her observation that cataloger's attitude and acceptance are needed for the success of the Books Core. The six other reasons that the respondents affirmed for not using the DCRB Core standard are all operational obstacles within their libraries more than opinions or perceptions. Changes in libraries' current personnel, procedures, or materials issues might create more acceptable conditions for the adoption of the DCRB Core standard. Catalogers could learn the new standard or become familiar with it, changes or shortages in staff could be overcome with time or more money, a new workflow could be established, training could be sought, and appropriate materials might be acquired.

The participants gave a number of other reasons, however,

for not undertaking use of the DCRB Core. In response to the possibility that a library may not have appropriate materials for using the core standard, some libraries qualified that reason noting the small quantity of rare books they catalog. Seven libraries said that they do not catalog many rare books, that they do so little original cataloguing, especially of rare books, or that they have so few pre-1801 imprints that it is easier to apply the full standard and not worth applying a different standard when they encounter a title that may be eligible for core-level cataloguing.

One librarian replied that the categories of materials that would be candidates for DCRB Core-level cataloguing are generally cataloged to their own minimal-level standard. Administrative or departmental policy to catalog all books at full-level DCRB was cited by 6 libraries as the reason for not applying the DCRB Core standard. Although 13 libraries answered that they do not use full-level DCRB for cataloguing any of their sixteenth- to eighteenth- century books, 4 specifically reiterated that they use only AACR2 full for cataloguing rare books.

Two libraries emphasized their production goals and decisions to apply certain standards as reasons for not taking time to learn a new standard. One librarian thinks "the introduction of a DCRB Core standard runs contrary to the whole intent of DCRB to provide fuller description than AACR2."

Another librarian said that not justifying access points is confusing to users and that if the cataloger starts to add more fields, it would be easier to create full-level records. Two respondents said their reference collections are not comprehensive enough to provide references in a 510 field to allow the abbreviated description of the DCRB Core standard.

Two other libraries indicated that their backlogs are not large enough to need to implement DCRB Core cataloguing. Four librarians each offered one of the following reasons: use of the Core does not increase production, it would create more inconsistencies in the catalog than are already there from so many changes in standards over the years, there is little time for the catalogers to assimilate the new standard, and catalogers prefer one standard not choices

These additional reasons and comments express strong opposition to the use of the DCRB Core standard. For the most part, they are internal or operational issues that pose obstacles to the adoption of the standard. Remarks from the 24 libraries that did not wish to participate in the survey provide further insight into why some libraries do not use the DCRB Core. Their reasons are categorized in Table 4.2.

**Table 4.2. Categorized Reasons for Not Using DCRB Core from Twenty-four Nonparticipants in Survey**

| Reasons | No. |
|---|---|
| Not enough of a collection to make it worthwhile | 11 |
| Not informed enough or aware of DCRB Core | 6 |
| Cataloger is retiring or have a change of staff | 5 |
| Do not use DCRB full | 4 |
| Have a shortage of staff | 4 |
| Do not use any core standard | 3 |
| Policy is to catalog at full level (including BIBCO records) | 3 |
| Other libraries would not be able to enhance records to full level | 2 |
| Feels the need to justify added entries | 1 |
| Feels limitation in training | 1 |
| Feels limitation in knowledge | 1 |
| Does not do BIBCO for books | 1 |
| Has not cataloged rare books in a while | 1 |
| Does not create BIBCO records for rare books | 1 |
| Only a few catalogers are trained in DCRB | 1 |
| Too little time to discuss issues related to DCRB Core | 1 |
| Has a large backlog | 1 |
| Uses Books Core | 1 |
| Catalogs few original records for rare books | 1 |
| Differences between core and full are minor | 1 |
| Using core does not save much time | 1 |
| Doubts can convince Special Collections of value of core records | 1 |
| E-resources are becoming priorities | 1 |

Some of the reasons are identical to those of the survey participants:

* The rare book collection is not sufficiently large to warrant learning to catalog by any standard other than full-level DCRB (11 libraries);
* The library is not familiar with or even aware of DCRB Core (6 libraries);
* There are changes (5 libraries) or shortages (4 libraries) in staff;
* The DCRB full standard is not used (4 libraries);
* The policy is to catalog at the full level (3 libraries); and
* Training poses a problem (1 library).

In addition to these commonly held reasons for not applying the DCRB Core, three libraries indicated that they do not use any of the core standards, and two libraries hesitate to use the DCRB Core because it might prohibit a non-BIBCO library from enhancing the core record to a full-level record in OCLC. Each of the following reasons was cited by a single library for not employing the DCRB Core standard: added entries should be justified in a note; knowledge is too limited to apply the standard; BIBCO books records are not created; BIBCO rare books records are not created; rare books have not been cataloged recently; only a few catalogers are trained to use DCRB; too little time is available to discuss DCRB Core and issues related to it; the backlog is large; the Books Core is used instead; too few original records for rare books are created; the differences between core and full level are minor; the core standard does not save much time; the value of DCRB Core records cannot be sold to Special Collections; and, finally, e-resources are becoming more of a cataloguing priority than printed special collections materials.

Common emphases and implications that run through many of these reasons are the little availability of time and the desire for adherence to fuller standards, two characteristics that have long been in competition in technical services processes in libraries. One library, however, intends to use the DCRB Core standard, and two others are considering using it. How well cataloguing copy is viewed and used by other libraries is one way of evaluating the efficacy of a cataloguing standard. Responding to question 10, nine participants in the survey said their copy catalogers accept DCRB Core records without changing them, although one library said there was room for cataloger's judgment and two libraries indicated that they might add subject headings or local notes. Nineteen respondents said their copy catalogers edit DCRB Core records locally.

In response to the question of whether original catalogers enhance DCRB Core records to full level locally, 29 libraries answered in the affirmative; five do not enhance core records to full level locally. At 16 libraries, original catalogers enhance DCRB Core records to full level nationally; at 16 libraries they do not enhance nationally, although two libraries said they may do so in the future. Four of the respondents noted that their catalogers have never seen a DCRB Core record; 1 of them would edit if a core record were encountered. Since there is so little evidence for the creation of DCRB Core records, it is surprising that not more libraries commented that they have not seen them in the bibliographic utilities.

Further research in the databases of the bibliographic utilities is needed to confirm that the DCRB Core standard has as yet found little acceptance and use among rare book catalogers and curators. The final question on the survey asked if any use studies of DCRB Core records have been conducted. Not surprisingly, none of the respondents has done such a survey. In their additional comments, however, three librarians said they think the purported time savings of core cataloguing records are not worth the cost to the users in locating materials they need. These opinions are greatly supported by many special collections departments' preferences for using the DCRB full standard.

## WRAPPING UP

Clearly, the preponderance of the evidence indicates that most libraries surveyed have not used the DCRB Core standard and prefer to catalog their rare books using a full standard, whether DCRB or AACR2. The DCRB Core standard was not written as a replacement for full-level cataloguing for all rare books. The standard states that the expectation is that materials cataloged using the DCRB Core will be chosen more for their accessibility than for full bibliographic treatment. Eight libraries have identified appropriate collections to catalog using the DCRB Core standard.

Among the responses received both in the initial query and in the survey itself, six additional libraries indicated that although they do not now use the DCRB Core standard in their cataloguing, they are expecting to do so in the future or seriously want to consider using it. The total of fourteen libraries that either do use the DCRB Core or almost assuredly will use it in the future indicates the beginning of acknowledgement of the value of the standard and a more positive attitude among some catalogers towards the standard. A recent survey of the special collections departments of the ARL libraries finds that large portions of the collections are uncataloged.

Although formats other than books form the bulk of the uncataloged collections, an average of 15% of the book collections have no access through any form of bibliographic description, and 49% have access only through a card catalog. Many non-ARL libraries may also have large proportions of their special collections in uncataloged backlogs. According to the minutes of recent meetings of the ARL Task Force on Special Collections, one primary issue under discussion is the question of providing increased access to those backlogged materials through bibliographic control.

Many of the books in backlogs may have existing bibliographic records in OCLC and RLIN that can be used by copy catalogers. For those books that do not already have catalog records in the bibliographic utilities, however, the application of the DCRB Core standard in creating original bibliographic records has potential. To begin a project to catalog backlogged material using the DCRB Core standard, a primary task for special collections librarians is to identify specific collections that will be appropriate for DCRB Corelevel cataloguing. One library among the survey respondents is considering cataloguing its early French pamphlets using the DCRB Core. Other pamphlet collections or subject collections, such as political or religious tracts, may be candidates for DCRB Core cataloguing.

One librarian said that using a cataloguing template for materials issued by the same publisher would make DCRB Core cataloguing even more efficient. Several libraries indicated that they are looking for appropriate collections. One respondent noted that sometimes the DCRB Core standard is applied to enhance a brief cataloguing record to bring it up to a higher level without the necessity of enhancing to the full level. In addition to identifying collections that are candidates for DCRB Core cataloguing, libraries will need to encourage cataloguer's judgment to help overcome the resistance to using core standards. Because the flexibility of the core standard permits a wide range of additional elements in the core record, the cataloger is not limited to the bare minimum requirements. Not every book in a backlog will be a candidate for core-level cataloguing, but identifying the proper collections and undertaking DCRB Core-level cataloguing projects can help increase accessibility to those materials that users do not know exist in rare book collections.

## MANAGING ADMINISTRATIVE METADATA

A growing need exists for metadata management of administrative issues related to electronic resources. Some of these issues include license restrictions, authentication means, technical contacts, and statistics availability. *Integrated library systems* (ILS) do not easily accommodate such metadata, and paper files maintained by serials librarians have proven inadequate both in accessibility and organization. Making e-resource metadata quickly available to interlibrary loan and reference staffs is facilitated by an online gateway of the ERTS model.

### IN THE BEGINNING

Discussions about the state of Tri-College e-resources were held in 2001. The focus of these discussions, which were sponsored by a Mellon Foundation grant, was ensuring consistent access to e-journals throughout the consortium. This original charge was broadened later that year and resulted in development of the ERTS system. The authors comprise the founding members of the ERTS Team. We held a number of brainstorming sessions to identify the results each library hoped to achieve with ERTS.

Particularly due to our consortium status, numerous discussions were necessary so as not to overlook any one library's specific needs. Some of the goals for ERTS included:

* Immediate access to license information for all e-resources purchased by the Tri-College Consortium libraries
* Various statistical reports not easily available, if at all, through our integrated library system
* Notification services that alert staff when e-resources are about to expire

We began identifying data elements based on these needs.

The suggested fields, and the information we expected to place within them, fit into four categories:

* *Licensors:* Entities from whom we license e-resources
* *Items:* Individual e-resource titles
* *Purchases:* Acquisitions data concerning e-resources
* *Vendors:* Entities from whom we purchase e-resources

After consulting established element sets, particularly those maintained by the University of Washington and Johns Hopkins University, it was comforting to see that our direction was quite similar.

## SCOPE

ERTS exists in large part because of limitations inherent within integrated library systems. That said, the ERTS Team was wary of duplicating information already held in our local catalog. Thus we sought to restrict ERTS's scope to those data either unavailable, or not easily retrievable, through our ILS. Since the predominant mission of ERTS is to track license information, few freely available electronic resources are entered. Only in cases where a certain aspect of a freely available e-resource requires tracking, such as how the consortium has decided to catalog it, is it entered in ERTS. In cases of volatile aggregators, only a collectionlevel record is maintained.

Resources we have decided to exclude from ERTS generally fall into these categories:

* Extending less than a year's guarantee of access
* Delivering incomplete holdings
* Not providing ready title-level access

## LICENCE INFORMATION

As in many institutions, electronic resources are heavily used in our libraries. As a result, serials and acquisitions personnel field numerous questions from public services staff regarding license restrictions. The paper files we maintained before ERTS were not an adequate medium for promulgating license-related information. Ellen Finnie Duranceau's efforts with license tracking at MIT were influential at pointing the way towards a networked file for staff use. Apart from the license terms related to legal responsibilities, ERTS stores elements that directly address what library services we can provide and what our patrons can do with a given resource.

Some of these data include:

* *ILL Allowability:* We have buttons for yes, no, n/a, and unknown. There is also a free text box to allow for further details. Our ILL staffs need to know this information, and occasionally reference librarians are asked about such restrictions.
* *Number of Simultaneous Users:* Because certain resources carry this restriction, this element helps public services staff troubleshoot the cause of a user not being allowed access. Documenting simultaneous user limits in ERTS provides a check that may help public services staff before assuming a more involved access problem is the culprit.
* *Print Restrictions:* Some resources limit the number of pages printed per session, and others even prohibit printing. This element prevents the expenditure of valuable time trying to diagnose an apparent printing problem.
* *Reserve Restrictions:* Staff responsible for electronic reserves need to know if such mounting is restricted

in any way. An example of such a restriction is having a strict time frame for the duration of the e-reserve link. As with print restrictions, the licensor may obligate us to inform users of such restrictions or other license terms.

* *SDI Availability:* This element indicates the availability of a service allowing patrons to register for e-mail notification when new content becomes available. Often, such content is in the form of journal issues or tables of contents.
* *Archival Guarantee:* As we exchange print subscriptions for electronic equivalents, access to this information has become a great concern, especially since it is often hard to tease out of veiled licensing language.
* *Negotiation Contact:* This element stores the name of the licensor's negotiation representative. This information is useful when we wish to alter the language in our license.
* *General Comments:* This catch-all field is used to capture license data not covered in the fields, such as a note concerning licence revision dates.

## CATALOGUING INFORMATION

Cataloguing electronic resources in the Tri-College setting poses complications beyond the natural challenges inherent with this ever-changing media. When the Tri-Colleges first purchased electronic resources, a commitment was made to provide individual bibliographic records in our local catalog for each title. During this time, many journal publishers provided online access to their content, often free with the print subscriptions. As aggregators and large publisher collections became available, the challenge to provide title and subject access grew into an even more formidable task.

In order to continue providing individual title access in this environment, the Tri-Colleges employed several methods of cataloguing, including a locally derived batch method, along with the more standard copy cataloguing via cooperative resources like OCLC.

Further adding to this quandary, the consortium libraries share a catalog. Although the libraries purchase many online resources collectively, there are numerous eresources unique to a single library. Maintaining consistent cataloguing standards across three separate technical services units is a challenge. ERTS supports sharing of these standards by centralizing cataloguing information for the Tri-Colleges. Initially, the cataloguing elements in ERTS were linked to the licensor database.

This architecture posed three problems, however:

* The licensor name is generally not used by cataloguing and reference staff to identify an electronic resource.
* Catalogue librarians describe information about individual and collection titles that is not always consistent across multiple resources offered by the same licensor. For instance, a licensor may place title lists and holdings information for one of its collections on the Web, but not for another. This may affect the way the resources are cataloged. Appending these cataloguing data to title records, rather than licensor records, gives us the flexibility necessary to record differences among collections.
* Several freely available collections for which the Tri-Colleges maintain cataloguing procedures do not warrant a licensor record.

The cataloguing database consists of approximately sixteen fields that are divided into four sections on the cataloguing information page:

* Title;
* Tripod Searching Information;
* Technical Cataloguing Information; and
* Publisher-Related Information.

## Title

Cataloguing uses this section, consisting of one element "Title", to identify the individual journal, collection-level, or aggregator title. The Tri-Colleges use the MARC 130 tag for local collocation and retrieval purposes within Tripod. The title field in ERTS replicates the locally derived 130 field. The intention is to facilitate ease of searching for public services staff. If they require more information about an electronic resource, they can then search the title in ERTS.

## Tripod Title Searching Information (for Public Services)

This section, designed for use by public services staff, consists of two elements that identify the search keys necessary for retrieval of all titles in a collection or aggregation. The first field contains a URL that invokes an OPAC search in Tripod. The second element contains the Tripod search key and search term. Such a field might look like this: author=Project Muse.

## Technical Cataloguing Information

This section centralizes local decisions for Tri-College cataloguing staff. It consists of three elements. The first field notes, whether individual titles within a collection, aggregation, or database, are analysed. The second field indicates what method is used to catalog analysed titles and where the file used for the locally batch-created records resides. The third field records any MARC fields that are unique to each collection, aggregate, or database. For instance, a cataloger might decide to use a series entry to help collocate related electronic resources. When this is the case, the 4XX field would be recorded in this field. Also, if a 7XX field is recorded for a person or corporate body, it would be accordingly noted in this area.

## Publisher-related Information

This section incorporates URL and note fields. The URL field directs catalogers to a title list, usually located on the licensor's Web site, that is used in our batch load procedures. A brief note about the update pattern and frequency of these titles lists is also located here. The final element in this section is a note about whom to contact at the vendor for service updates. Overall, the cataloguing database is a modest component of ERTS. Yet it provides the Tri-College's cataloguing community an invaluable tool. ERTS circumvents the need to record cataloguing decisions on paper files or "in our heads," making for a stronger, more fluid approach to cataloguing electronic materials throughout the consortium.

## PURCHASE INFORMATION

Although much purchase information is available in our local catalog, we felt it would be useful to be able to view a title's cost over a five-year period, as well as to easily distinguish any one-time fees. Additionally, we wanted to have the ability to gene0rate reports that would tell us how much we were spending on different categories of electronic titles.

Each purchase event is captured in ERTS by entering the following data:

* *Library:* This is the purchasing library or in some cases may be the consortium as a whole.
* *Licensor:* Selected from a drop-down list of licensors; this is usually the publisher/creator of the title.
* *Vendor:* Also selected from a drop-down list; this is from whom we purchase the title. For cases in which one of the libraries acts as purchasing agent for the other two, that library would be recorded as the vendor.
* *Purchase Type:* We have a need to distinguish among titles that are paid as electronic only, titles that carry an added cost over the cost of the print subscription, and titles that offer free online access as a consequence of a print subscription.
* *One-time Charges:* We wanted to record this information separately so that it could be distinguished from annual costs. Price, paid date, expiration date, and ILS order number are also entered.

Generally, much discussion surrounds the initial decision to purchase a particular resource. The decision to renew a resource, however, is often made with less thought and in a very short time frame. It is most often the case that the need to make the renewal decision is prompted by a renewal form or invoice from a vendor and is sometimes received after the previous subscription has expired.

We often do not take the time to ask ourselves important questions such as: How often was this resource used? Has the licensor provided good service in the case of technical problems? Can we justify the cost? Instead, we often rely on the gut feeling of our bibliographers. While their sense of the usefulness of the resource may be valid, we want to be able to provide more data and more time for them to make the renewal decision. Therefore, we have added an e-mail-alerting component to ERTS which uses the expiration date in the purchase record and notifies selected staff sixty days prior to the expiration of a title. This is a strategy we learned from the HERMES system implemented at Johns Hopkins University. We believe this gives us sufficient time to analyse usage statistics, cost, and service issues so that we can make informed renewal decisions.

A 'renew' button in the purchase record moves the previous year's purchase data to a new column, retaining the ILS order number and purchase type. ERTS uses the price entered for the new year to calculate the price change from the previous to the current year. A variety of reports can be generated from the purchase data in ERTS. For example, we can create reports totaling electronic acquisitions by purchase type for the fiscal year or for any selected time period, giving us the title, the most recent paid date, and amount of each electronic resource, sorted by type of resource, then by title. A report on the number of records by purchase type and an annual expenditure comparison report can also be generated. Other report types can be created as needed.

## TECHNICAL SPECIFICATIONS

ERTS runs on FileMaker Pro, currently version 5.5 desktop software at Haverford's Magill Library. ERTS was developed on a Mac, but currently runs on Windows. Staff use Macintosh and Windows computers to access the database, which performs well on both platforms. Readonly access to ERTS is restricted to the three college campuses by IP address; editing privileges are restricted by passwords.

The staff functions of inputting, editing, and reporting are available in all three campus libraries through FileMaker's sharing system. Search functions for public services staff are available through a Web interface using the FileMaker CDML tags. Through the Web, users on the three campuses can search by licensor name or title and view the license restrictions that apply. Staff can also enter comments about an e-resource's system performance or access difficulties, which can then be made available to them at renewal time.

*ERTS consists of six interrelated files or "tables"*:

* Licensors—One record is entered for each licensor and used by all three libraries.
* Items—One record is entered for each title and used by all three libraries.
* Purchases— Each library maintains a separate purchase record.
* Vendors—One record is entered for each vendor and used by all three libraries.
* Service comments
* Administration

# 5

# Technology-enhanced Library

## INTRODUCTION

Libraries across India, as in other parts of the world, are facing sweeping changes on account of the media in which information is generated, transmitted, disseminated and archived due to the increasing presence of electronic formats. There is no doubt that information in electronic form is a potential asset, and that it can be vigourously applied in any environment. The advent and spread of electronic formats has made a major difference in the information processing and service environments in libraries, especially after the emergence of the Internet and Web as the dominant pathway and repository of electronic information resources.

In an increasingly networked world, it is possible that universities may be able to take back control of scholarly information, and libraries may risk being cut out of the author-publisher-dissemination loop. Libraries act as facilitators to provide the right information to the right user at the right time. Users visit libraries to borrow identified documents, or to take photocopies/printouts of those documents from reference collections or journals not issued out normally.

The advent of Web-enabled information resources, such as e-journals, e-books and e-reference sources, and their access through networks has taken the library to the users and a significant amount of information access is now taking place beyond the four walls of the library. In many cases users want a 'pinpointed precision' in the information search process whereas the library attempts for an 'exhaustive recall' to comply with the various ways in which an information source is approached and to satisfy each user's diverse interests. This information overload may cause doubts in the users regarding the relevance of information services as perceived from a professional angle. Along with quantifying use, it is equally important to assess the qualitative attributes of implicit and explicit use and examine the difficulties of users in properly framing their requests for information.

The limitation on the part of library professionals to perceive and represent what is demanded by users in information systems, and the dilemmas of information organization and retrieval to handle these demands must be effectively addressed. Libraries and professionals are equally concerned about the emergence of Internet as an information repository beyond the library's walls, as amply demonstrated by enhanced citations of Web resources. As library acquisitions are falling, information sources are increasing, and a single site library satisfying the user's needs is a doubtful proposition; users are forced to look beyond the library for their information needs. Thus the only option for the libraries is to enter into collaborations, networking and consortia and to reorient their roles as information services and access centres from their previous roles as information warehouses.

At the same time, the technical advances resulting from enhanced research in science and technology have made it possible to reduce drastically the time involved in information collection and identification. Also the extra time required in adapting printed information to client service through cumbersome manual routines of classification and cataloguing is considerably reduced by the availability of electronic information, leaving the professionals to concentrate more on tasks to support the extensive teaching and intensive research environment.

## ACADEMIC AND RESEARCH LIBRARIES

The application of computing to library work in India has a history of at least three decades because since the time the computer entered premier academic institutions and selected R & D facilities, it has been explored for improving information processing and management routines. *Information technology* (IT) enriched library services arrived initially for *science and technology* (S&T) information handling and for the special libraries attached to *research and development* (R&D) centres and academic libraries in higher education institutions.

In comparison to other libraries, academic and research libraries have better infrastructure and skilled manpower in greater numbers, making them able to offer information services comparable to advanced countries. Like qualified teaching and research personnel and well-equipped laboratories, the right information service is another vital element in the trinity which completes a fruitful academic or research environment.

## MARKET-DRIVEN COLLABORATION

Academic and research libraries, especially in developing countries, are passing through a very challenging phase in their existence due to unfriendly trends in the emerging information market. On the one hand, these libraries are still left with many of the old problems such as poor budgetary support and weak infrastructure, as well as staff in fewer numbers and often with less expertise. But the new information marketing techniques, like the possibilities of delivering and accessing electronic information in diverse channels, force these libraries to be very vigilant and cautious in their approach towards information acquisition and services. Libraries and professionals in India were quick to understand the emerging information environment was forcing their users to depend largely on those resources, which are becoming more expensive day by day due to the rise in production costs, fall in subscriptions and inflationary trends of Indian currency.

When individual libraries found that alone they are not in a position to satisfy the information requirements of their clients, they formulated various collaborative arrangements with other libraries such as,

* *Interlibrary loan* (ILL) services,
* *Document delivery services* (DDS),

* Resource-sharing, and
* Consortia-based subscriptions.

## PRESENT PRACTICES AND EMERGING GOALS

The special libraries attached to research and higher education were lucky enough to garner resources to automate their in-house routine operations and for hosting online public access catalogues (OPACs); some of them also set up facilities to search electronic databases. A few of them evolved the desired infrastructure for Internet surfing, for hosting of full-text database access, and for setting up digital libraries. The major advantage of the progress in computerization is a considerable increase in the amount of information available online. We have experienced that at the start of computer applications only the surrogates (metadata) existed online, but some full-text content has been made accessible online in recent years.

These libraries are experiencing the virtues of electronic information in different forms such as e-journals, e-books, bibliographic/full-text electronic databases on CD-ROMs and through Web access. Due to publishers' 'electronic plus' policies, libraries are able to access electronic versions of printed sources such as journals either for free or by paying an additional fee. However the goal these libraries in specialized research and academic centres should have set for themselves is to enhance their information facilities to fully functional digital libraries, comparable with similar facilities in the developed countries.

## CULTURES AND CONFLICTS FACED BY LIBRARIES

The fixed roles suggested by Levy for researchers, publishers and libraries are either overlapping or changing in the electronic scene. There are cases where an author or a library is acting as electronic publisher, and there are publishers providing a wide variety of information packages beyond the contents of printed journals.

The real question is: has the library really lost ground in the emerging information scene? Even the critics will not say so. The concerns expressed are only to revitalize the professional skills of librarians, rejuvenate the style of working and reorient the library towards its rightful place in effective dissemination of information. Maybe the common feeling that the library is a central place in the institution visited everyday by large numbers of users, like any public utility, has lost some ground in the electronic scene. Nonetheless, apart the continuing provision of information services for print sources, the electronic revolution has reaffirmed the library more as an information service and access centre than as an information storehouse.

## TECHNOLOGY-ENHANCED LIBRARY SERVICES

### TECHNOLOGY ADVANCES

The major technology breakthroughs in the context of libraries include:

* Advent of printing press and mass production of printed documents enabled democratization of information. Libraries had a major role in the print era, as no one can own a large number of books on a particular subject whereas libraries by their very purpose concentrated on doing so.
* Microforms helped to preserve less used information in a compact space and as a smoother delivery option for voluminous sources. Libraries had their unchallenged role even in the microform era as the special purpose readers for microfilms and microfiche were costly and exclusively housed in the library.
* The economical and affordable copying technology revolutionized the concept of information use as it spearheaded the trend of owning copies of relevant portions of library resources. The copying technology freed the user from sitting in the library for long duration for reading, since one can simply get a copy quickly and leave.
* Computing is the biggest technology revolution so far, as it is a major enabler in the information dissemination chain; also it is not a stand-alone technology unlike earlier technologies and can be networked and integrated with a whole lot of other

devices and technologies. It not only revolutionized the production of books and microforms but also brought the arrival of online and CD-ROM databases, electronic information resources, Internet and the digital revolution.

## PRODUCTS AND SERVICES

Adapting IT for library applications is an ongoing process, right from procuring or developing IT enabled information products through computer aided processing and management to delivering IT-enriched services. Library professionals in India are already exposed to the different offshoots of IT for library organization and information services.

### LIBRARY AUTOMATION PACKAGES

The availability of a wide variety of library automation software to suit the varied needs of libraries themselves is a reflection of the progress libraries have made in automating the operations of procuring, processing and providing information sources. Procurement is the end of the story for many other software/databases used in a library, whereas library automation systems will open a floodgate of issues. What the vendor provides is a structure to build information concerning the collection and users, to conduct various aspects of organizing the collection and offering information services.

Thus software needs to be evaluated for its suitability for the target library before purchase. This may include case studies from other libraries using the software, evaluation of hardware and operating system required, computer awareness among staff and users, network as well as computer infrastructure in the institution, and above all estimation of cost and charges for after-sales support. Using suitable software for library automation will significantly reduce manual operations and enable professionals to dedicate more time for professional jobs.

### CD-ROM AND ELECTRONIC DATABASES

Due to the poor communication infrastructure prevalent in India and to the immense costs involved, online database services were used only by few institutions. The distribution of the same content of online data repositories subsequently in CD-ROMs made it affordable to a larger number of institutions. While the library automation package gave search-and access facility to information sources present in the local collection, CD-ROM databases attempted consolidated access irrespective of holdings to the bibliographic data of publications in a discipline. CD-ROM databases have also freed library professionals from conducting searches and allowed the end user to conduct the searches. CD-ROM is so common nowadays that a library holds a good number of them not only for bibliographic, numeric and full-text databases, but also those received along with printed books and other reference sources. Managing and serving these high capacity discs was a problem earlier due to the stand-alone software required, whereas the onset of networking and hard-disk cached solutions provides an effective and functional way to enable access to them through the intranet.

## WEB

Since the 1990s, the Internet has changed the dissemination of information, such as electronic copies of traditional paper-based journals and conference proceedings, free electronic-only refereed journals, haphazard copies of all kinds of material on home pages and a handful of electronic preprints archives. Most libraries in India now have a website and they use the site to present the basic strengths of the library and to host services such as the OPAC and Web access to electronic information.

The 'size of the catalogue card' and the field lengths of primitive database technology are surpassed in the Web era. Types of information resources on the Web also vary from authentic primary information about the latest research results to ephemeral product catalogues. Issues worth consideration are often the content of the sites that are deleted, modified or changed to new machines without proper redirection and the extraction mechanism through search engines, when a flood of sources is retrieved against a query, of which few are relevant. The Internet and Web demonstrate that a large amount of electronic information can be hosted in a decentralized fashion in a cost-effective manner. The Web has also freed the user's dependence on library resources for finding information related to address and contact details of a person/institution, contents pages of books, journals, etc.

As far as possible, especially for reference and information services, looking at the Web has become an innovative trend in the reference service to complement dated print sources. Many publishers visibly feel the benefits and reach of the Web, and have considered it as an alternate medium for delivering information sources; some publishers even permit unrestricted access of tables of contents and abstracts of their primary journals. As a result of these initiatives, the 'print and distribute' paradigm is challenged by 'distribute and print' paradigm.

## CONSORTIAL LICENCES

The term 'consortial licences' designates library groupings to negotiate access rights to electronic information with publishers and vendors aiming at enhanced access to more resources at better pricing. "Consortia can be a means to introduce products to a previously untapped market" for vendors and "consortia provide shared expertise, access to new electronic and print resources, professional development, new sources of funds, and safety in numbers" for libraries. In contrast to earlier library collaborative arrangements such as ILL and resource sharing, the publisher and trade community are parties in the consortial agreements.

In resource-sharing, libraries concentrate on collaborative subscriptions by avoiding duplication, where as in consortial licenses, the emphasis is to strike the 'best deals' even if the library suffers some duplication. The publisher community experience is that increased subscription costs lead to a reduction in the total number of subscriptions, further raising the subscription cost every year. Publishers also found it difficult to enforce ownership rights with electronic sources, even after adopting the latest technology tools and forcing libraries to sign the toughest of the legal clauses.

The good marketing wisdom of the publisher and trade community prevailed to open up information access rights through consortial licenses for a large part of the product spectrum to at least those libraries or groups of libraries which procure products beyond a certain threshold value. The *Indian National Digital Library in Engineering Science and Technology* (INDEST) is the first and the major consortium in India. It is under the aegis of the *Ministry of Human Resource Development* (MHRD). Before the creation of the consortium, access to electronic journals in these institutions remained at 60% of subscribed titles, but the number of online journals has increased 10 times after the establishment of the consortium.

The rates for access offered to the consortium are lower by 50% to 90% depending upon the category of institution and the consortium paid only 11% of the list price to access these resources. Info net, another consortium, floated by the *University Grants Commission* (UGC) for Universities, is also gaining strength. Similar consortia are also operational for research institutions under the Council of Scientific and Industrial Research (CSIR) and the Department of Atomic Energy (DAE).

## DIGITAL LIBRARIES

Libraries in India are engaged in the development of prototypes of digital information resources, as influenced by developments in other countries. There are certain types of content which lie inaccessible or less used in their present physical forms that can be put to more visible and enhanced use through digitization. Also heavily used content presently available in limited numbers of copies can be identified for conversion to electronic format. The linear text in many of the print sources presents difficulties for providing a hypertext approach or a multimedia feeling, for simulating learning by doing; sustaining attention and interest for long duration calls for using electronic technologies to enable content to be more functional.

The static content in printed sources fails to attract users who are increasingly exposed to the widely appealing features of broadcasting and IT-intensive presentation tools. Multimedia-enabled digital information will be useful to a large percentage of illiterate and older population also. There are cases such as papers in journals and conferences in print form that never get their deserved visibility and often end up with out reaching the target population. The digital dissemination of this content may lead to very effective teaching and more focused research in most areas.

To demonstrate the efficacy of digital libraries and collections, libraries must be able to identify materials in the public domain, sources generated in-house, and similar materials to overcome the constraints of copyright. Digital library (DL) development needs a two pronged strategy to digitize local content as well as to devise options for providing access to external resources obtained as free or as part of existing subscriptions or access licenses.

The typical academic or research library in-house digital library on an Intranet must include the following components:

* Consortial access to electronic journals and electronic databases;
* Free/paid Web access to journals subscribed in print format;
* Subject gateways and virtual libraries;
* Free/paid e-books from publishers and portals;
* Intranet access to bibliographic and full-text databases, and CD-ROM publications;
* Local archiving of free and paid e-books;
* LAN serving of e-supplements of purchased books;
* In-house digitization of copyright-owned and copyright- free printed books in the collection;
* Born-digital in-house publications such as research reports, annual reports, convocation reports, teaching materials, theses and dissertations, in-house journals, proceedings of conferences, seminars, workshops, etc., conducted by the institution;
* Preprints and post-prints of research papers sent for publication to journals, conferences, and books, especially with respect to the Open Archives Initiative gaining ground to provide further access to research published in toll journals and to make the results of publicly funded research available to those who need them;

* Publications in the public domain, such as government publications, publications from non-profit institutions, etc.

But many libraries are unable to provide these components due to lack of awareness or due to the hurdles invariably faced by libraries in India. The lack of interest on the part of parent institutions and the absence of action plans or priorities is the major hindrance. Though computer and communication infrastructure is improving, their availability for information work is not appreciated in many organizations. Paschoud commented how several of the speakers and many of the delegates at the International Conference on Digital Libraries (ICDL) 2004 conference in New Delhi focussed on addressing what most European libraries would consider very basic issues such as network/Internet connectivity and management.

Even in places where infrastructure is available, there is an acute shortage of competent labour to take up the task of digitizing local content and evolving digital information repositories. The students, faculty, curriculum and training methodology at the disposal of library schools have to be improved visibly to meet this challenge. Coupled with this is the need for continuing education for retraining the working professionals. Institutions, individuals, or private publishers have rights over content, and motivating them to ease these rights when they are not inclined towards digitization is not a simple task. Levying charges for access is a distant proposition; instead sponsorships from institutions, government bodies and library suppliers can be explored.

Even when hosted as a free facility, enough security mechanisms must be evolved to prevent any trespassing by hackers. Selecting useful content requires careful review and evaluation by subject experts, as digitization will only help to preserve the record, and not its enhanced and continued access. Internet bandwidth in India has to be sufficiently augmented to allow faster access to Web content as more content is being hosted on the Web. The different funding agencies, research councils and institutions are not currently offering monetary support to the desired extent for digital library development.

## CULTURE AND CONFLICTS FACED BY USERS

### MANUAL AND ELECTRONIC SEARCH

Searching for manual sources required scanning catalogue cards or indexing and abstracting sources. As cross-references often increase the number of cards or pages, there was a difficulty in being very exhaustive. Conducting selective dissemination of information (SDI) services had been extremely difficult as the document profiles must be matched with user profiles with the aid of semi mechanical systems. Most of these limitations are easily eliminated in the electronic environment due to the very nature of information processing and organization in electronic form.

The inherent advantages of indexing electronic information help the user to search for any or all the fields in a timesaving manner. Since document profiles are already stored in the database and search software supports creation of user profiles, current awareness services (CAS) and SDI services are achieved more easily. The concern for end-user searching was dominant right from the beginning of early CD-ROM database systems since the time spent for searching does not involve communication costs as is the case with online searching. Also with the universe of knowledge getting increasingly complex as a result of continuing advances in research in intra and inter-disciplinary areas, vitiating the search conducted by a generalist like a librarian may not be effective in amassing the user's information requirements completely or not achieving the desired results expected by the user.

The convoluted information requirements of present day researchers require sufficient knowledge of their disciplines and since the users are increasingly exposed to the computerized work environment, they feel very confident to conduct information searching on electronic systems. The professional ethos and egos also plays a part as users find more satisfactory results from electronic systems than manual systems, and in a relatively easy and convenient way. The librarians should recognize the confidence and maturity of users to conduct searches on their own as they have better knowledge of their disciplines, more exposure to the different keywords and their relationships and because of the inherent advantages of locating related sources serendipitously while scanning the retrieved results.

There should be closer interaction and effective communication between library professionals and users to understand each other's views about information needs and use. Library user meetings, orientation sessions for new users, special help for research scholars, training programmes about usage of print and electronic resources, a help desk at reference counter, holdings locator services, interacting with users through phone and e-mail, encouraging users to approach the librarian, ask a librarian, and user friendly websites are some options practiced in libraries in India.

## INFORMATION USE

Information services provided by a library are primarily based on subjective input from users and hence justify users commenting about misses or noise in electronic information service outputs. An information need is what an individual *ought* to have; an information want is what an individual *would* like to have; an information demand is what an individual *asks* for; an information use is what an individual actually *uses*; and an information requirement denotes what is *needed*, what is *wanted* or what is *demanded*. Information needs are affected by a variety of factors such as the range of sources available, the uses to which information will be put, individual characteristics of the user, social, political and economic systems surrounding the user, and the consequences of information use.

Accessibility of information resources is usually assumed to depend on a range of cognitive, social, and physical factors, such as whether a person is aware of a resource, has the knowledge and skills needed to access it, and has the resource close at hand. Scientists spend 50–60% of their time communicating. The computerised environment has increased the quantum of information available nearby, but it has not enhanced a person's information consumption skills. There is a burden of effort in information storage and retrieval that may be shifted from author to indexer to index language designer to searcher to user. Though the user is exposed to more microfilms, Xerox copies, and electronic information on desktop/ Intranet/ Web, ready to display at the touch of a button, the more time one spends in searching and collecting information, the less time s/he gets to use the information. Scholarly articles are identified for reading in five basic ways: browsing, automated searches, citations found in the literature, mentions by other people, and current-awareness tools.

How much information one requires to work on a particular problem is also subjective as human beings observe the 'principle of least effort'. Perhaps one may easily deal with an information crisis by identifying a part of the total references and by using few of what is identified.

## USER BYPASSING

Though libraries in India are progressing well on the automation and information access front, there is a definite case of fewer users present in the library due to different reasons. The real question is whether electronic services of libraries have in any way affected the user interests or have the users found more confidence in an information superhighway beyond the library. The same proportions of scientists still browse to identify scholarly articles to read, but more are using online searches and the proportion of readings identified through online searches appears to be increasing. Library acquisitions suffered a serious setback in recent years unable to withstand the price rise and these budgetary constraints forced users to look beyond the library for their varied information requirements.

Hence research publications in some disciplines now cite more Web resources. Librarians are not yet acting as true consumers and hence cannot blame predatory publishers for taking advantage of the situation. Another issue involves the very large and rapidly increasing number of articles obtained through photocopying, interlibrary loan, document delivery, preprints, and reprints. The right step in assessing whether there is a depleted user interest in libraries is to study use patterns over the years and, in a populous country like India, just going by the numbers will not address the qualitative aspects. There has not been much reduction in book issues in an academic library, but are the new acquisitions being used to the same extent? But what is seen is the fall in library attendance, as observed and reported by many library managers.

It is evident that fewer users actually visit the library, and very few still spend more time, a lot of others use the library through lending, photocopies, electronic access through networks, etc. It becomes difficult to quantify use as the library has statistics only about explicit use, but there are also implicit uses through browsing or reading inside the library, which are difficult to quantify. There are also vital questions about whether mere issuing a book or taking a photocopy of a journal article attribute to use and hence comes the need for a qualitative assessment of use. Perhaps professionals are afraid to look at these issues as the results of such assessment may force the authorities to examine critically the investments in a service institution like the library. Like Reenen's comment about false consumers, it seems that librarians fear self-assessment of library usage or to undergo a performance audit.

## THE LIBRARIAN'S IDENTITY CRISIS

### Education and Training

As stated previously, the students, faculty, curriculum and training methodology at the library schools have to be visibly improved to meet the challenges posed by electronic information and impatient, highly demanding users. There are also problems of infrastructure and a directionless attitude in the teaching and research sector often forgetting the interdisciplinary aspect of the subject. Working librarians have good exposure to new databases, their acquisition and use, pragmatic implementation of various routines etc., which are not accessible to library schools.

Thus apart from teaching faculty, expert practitioners in the discipline would also be involved in education programmes to bridge the gap between preaching and practice. The existing courses must always look at the sweeping changes in the library workplace and adapt well to enable the students to face the challenges with confidence, giving ample opportunities for improving reasoning, communication skills, general awareness, and other characteristics identified for a multi-tasking service organization. The age-old teacher-centric teaching has to be circumvented by student oriented and professional (job)-centric teaching.

## Job Opportunities

Though the major employer, the government is not recruiting many, more and more universities/institutions are offering library courses in the regular and distance modes. And this upheaval in quantity does not contribute in any way to the quality of these courses. For a prospective student/parent, the job advertisements provide an impression of plenty of jobs in the field, as library jobs at different levels in different institutions do not follow standard designations. But only when one finishes the course and looks for job openings, does the actual state of affairs come to light. Actually the increase in library-related jobs is merely additive, and not multiplicative, like computers, management or engineering, and should not show an exponential rise at any point of time.

## Continuing Education

Since the mode and rate at which information is generated, organized and used is witnessing sweeping changes in the perfectly wired information age, a continuously evolving discipline like LIS is meant to tackle the intricacies of information for societal development; thus it shall not be learned effectively and practiced perfectly by exposing students to a framed curriculum in formal education only.

The discipline has changed drastically from being based totally on print sources; aware of the increasing richness of information in electronic forms and available over networks thus is leading to embracing vigourously other disciplines like computers, management, and information and communication technology. It is imperative for the information practitioners to continuously monitor and augment their professional skills through continuing education (CE) to discharge their duties to users, employer and profession. The present initiatives on CE are generally being made by national institutions and suffer limitations such as: they are of short duration, generally infrequent, claiming comparatively high fees, working professionals finding it difficult to get sponsorship from their institutions, involve travelling to far off destinations hampering their regular work, etc.

## Cultures and Conflicts Faced by Librarians

Gone are the days of close-minded librarians and the quality of candidates entering the profession is continuously improving. As technology-intensive librarianship is gaining ground in the country, working librarians are getting much exposure to new technology tools for providing better information products and improved information services. Working librarians in at least the major academic and research institutions have better computer infrastructure and possess better expertise on the latest information products and services.

It is quite natural in the emerging print plus electronic hybrid library scenario that a library professional right from first job is expected to be conversant with the electronic apart from the manual means of information collection, processing, management and servicing. But there are also apprehensions about the level of technology appropriate to conducting well in the challenging and demanding academic and research setup. A library professional must be distinct from a computer professional due to the very nature of their profession and the expected deliverables. But the acute emphasis on technology has created a situation that a professional can hide many of his/her professional ignorance by a little computer knowledge which is not going to be good either for the profession or for the libraries. Google cannot and will not be replacing libraries because both can co-exist with their diverse functionalities catching the attention of users at different occasions.

The professional nature of the librarian's job always motivates him or her to help the users unlike administrative staff in the institution who are always rule-based; sometimes this may lead to not so proper upkeep of administrative procedures and records, and in some cases cause unnecessary rivalry with the administrative staff. There are also personnel problems as the librarians fail to command a leadership role in many institutions thereby eclipsing their role in strategic planning. Institutions attach prime importance to libraries but are they doing the same towards the personnel in their libraries? It is a strange case of all the virtues are of the system and the problems are due to the staff. Largely a service wing in many institutions, not enjoying the power, visibility, service conditions, and career prospects of the research and teaching staff, the status of library professionals in many of these institutions is not a morale booster, leaving many of them underperforming.

It is not uncommon to see non-professionals heading many libraries, maybe just because they are senior teachers or good administrators or researchers and not because they are good as librarians. There are also problems of the lack of a peer group in the profession resisting such attacks on the profession as many senior professionals have become self-centred, and professional associations compete for minor issues. The professional staff members working in many libraries in developing countries are totally engrossed in administrative and routine jobs related to library operation and administration. Many institutions do not demand their library professionals to pursue an offensive role. The users always need quick services and they never respond to any of the reasonable operational or managerial delays.

The real situation is that the libraries have very little control over their suppliers whereas their consumers have too much control over them. Users are not patient enough to interact constantly with the library staff to tune their profiles to improve the relevance of information services, maybe due to time constraints on their parts. Again by a rough assessment, it seems that less than 10% of the users usually respond to SDI results and the remaining are either using it as it is or rejecting it straightaway. Out of those responding, only a few show their willingness to give feedback to modify their keywords to improve the utility of such services. Users may sometimes get so arrogant with the helpful nature of library staff and doubt it as their weakness.

## CONCLUSIONS

Like building collection and providing services, improving access to information should be the guiding criteria for libraries in the electronic era. Apart from hosting external information, they should also evolve local digitization ventures to give more visibility to internal information. We have to design a new set of parameters to judge operational efficiency and performance effectiveness of libraries. Traditional libraries boasted that they attracted a lot of users to stay inside their premises for comparatively longer duration whereas a modern librarian will be more concerned about carrying information to users' desktops. No library, no matter how rich its budget allocation and collection may be, is in a position to satisfy all the information needs of its users.

As a person well versed in the intricacies of the emerging information market, the librarian should be frank enough to admit that the information needs of all users are not met by the library alone. Collaboration with other libraries through consortia or networks increases the amount of resources available to users. Most academic and research libraries spend a lot of public money for information needs of a small percentage of the population and optimizing that spending for the benefit of more number of users is the need of the hour. Library professionals have a major role in the emerging print plus digital hybrid information environment that is looming large in many academic and research libraries.

This role can be properly identified and refined only through constructive interaction of administrative heads of institutions, library professionals and professional associations. There is no doubt that we are passing through a severe phase and this is the right time to have a close introspective and critical look at collections developed, services offered and professional skills required in the light of complex user needs, hazy use patterns and the ever-increasing spread of Internet, electronic databases and digital libraries.

# 6

# Implications of Monumental Construction

## INTRODUCTION

In 2001, when the new public library in Alexandria opened, the designers and developers of the project declared that they planned to establish one of the largest libraries in the world and thereby revitalize the idea of the antique library of Alexandria. Similarly, the builders of the library in Shanghai, who call it the "palace of knowledge," include its large dimensions among its unique characteristics.

The size of the building housing Library 21, in Stuttgart, Germany, described by its manager as the city's "meteor," is said to reflect the library's tremendous significance. Indeed, since the 1990s we have witnessed a wave of construction of large, even monumental, libraries around the world, construction of the type that characterized the ancient world.

This phenomenon occurs in an age of advanced information technologies; an age which is characterized by developments in computerization, in general, and the development of telecommunications and the Internet, in particular, which enable easy access to information.

It is characterized as well by the development of user friendly search engines which provide access to sources from any place at any time; and in addition by the rapid development of advanced technologies for non-paper storage and preservation of information which saves space. The purpose of the present study is to examine the implications of the current wave of large, even monumental, library buildings for the functioning and status of public libraries.

## LITERATURE REVIEW

### FUNCTIONS OF PUBLIC LIBRARIES OVER TIME

In the library in Nineveh, all collections were gathered: documents, certificates, correspondence, religious writings and historical descriptions, as well as works in various scientific fields. Hessel claims that these collections effectively declare the purpose of establishment of the library, to serve the state, to glorify the eternal memory of its founder and also for science. Since those distant days, libraries have assumed a variety of forms but their primary, "classical" function as guardians of the collective memory of human culture has remained unchanged from their earliest development until today. Over the years, another central function has been added: not only do libraries collect and preserve information, but also they now routinely process and disseminate new information.

This change occurred gradually, beginning with the introduction of paper and the invention of the printing press and climaxed in the 20th century. This development occurred simultaneously with the continued strengthening of libraries' position as public institutions with a social-education function of the utmost importance. Throughout the 150 years of its existence, the modern public library has undergone changes in its goals and functions, and as a result in the services it offers the public.

During each period, it attempted to meet the demands of the times. Since the latter half of the 19th century, libraries have become a part of the public sector and are funded by public monies. Therefore, they not only protect and preserve the knowledge that belongs to the community, but also have added services intended for the general public, in order to make education available not only to elites and academics. Initially, the library was an auxiliary institution in the field of education, a continuation of, and supplement to, the public schools that were established during the same period. As an adaptive institution, its functions have changed with the times. Therefore, in the late 19th century, the public library moved into the field of leisure and began offering popular books for pleasure reading or folklore evenings, following the waves of immigration at the time.

Furthermore, in the 1950s and 1960s, the library began to serve as an information centre for the general public and fulfilling a supplementary role by providing information services to public and economic institutions, both governmental and voluntary. In the 1960s and 1970s, libraries began to participate in social projects and reach out to various groups of non-users. IFLA clearly states that other functions have been added to the library's traditional role as a supplier of books, because the library has become a cultural and social centre in the community. As such, the library offers the community lectures, clubs, exhibitions, concerts, films, a venue for performances, the possibility of integrating a museum into the library and even a meeting place for different groups, including the elderly.

It is almost superfluous to note that in recent years, libraries have been required to go beyond their traditional services and adapt themselves to the information revolution by supplying their clients with new services using advanced technologies.

However, the IFLA Core Programme repeatedly emphasizes and reaffirms the value of library collections and archives as vital for both the survival and development of culture and scholarship. It seems that among those working on the portrait of the current and future library, the voices that tend towards greater emphasis on social-cultural aspects are increasing.

### Vision of the Virtual Library versus the Reality of the Monumental Library

Many people would claim that the future has already arrived. Not only have the needs of information consumers changed significantly, but most importantly, the variety of means and possibilities for obtaining information have changed. It is hard to imagine the library's clients continuing waiting for a busy librarian to supply traditional service when they have not only telephone, facsimile and e-mail at their disposal, but also a home computer or laptop which can be used to connect directly to the Internet. Young people tend to position the library as a marginal institution in future society and expect that it will become sort of a museum for "antique" materials. Awareness of the possibility that libraries might disappear is evident in almost every treatment of the issue.

For example, in their book *The Incredible Vanishing Library*, Gross and Borgman describe the importance of the library both as a social institution and as an organization that supplies information from various sources. However, they claim that decision makers do not sufficiently understand and acknowledge the great importance of the library in fulfilling these roles and, therefore, they are gradually becoming an invisible institution. Hage believes that the basic tools used by libraries will remain unchanged despite the advanced technology. A similar line of argument is taken by Schement, who believes that even in the digital age, the role of librarians as skilled mediators between information and the public should be maintained since most people lack the skills to navigate between the many sources of information.

Despite this, Schement does consider the possibility of the vanishing library realistic and believes that librarians should also provide "remote" information services outside of the library building. As early as 1972, almost 20 years before the trend towards building new, large libraries began, Rohlf claimed that public libraries would not only continue to exist and expand the variety of services they offer, but also grow in size. Architects, Rohlf claimed, are currently required to plan libraries with a long-term vision and create buildings that are capable of adapting to developments and changes, house large quantities of electronic gadgetry, while at the same time being filled with light, space and having a layout that gives people a feeling of belonging and humanity.

In the face of all of the predictions of a world without books and without libraries, Naisbitt and Aburdene claim, "In every place where the information economy has spread... the need for arts, new museums, cultural and literary renewal has experienced unprecedented growth." The authors even present data showing that more new titles and new editions of books are published in the United States every year. A similar spirit of wonder, it appears, rests on most representatives of the large libraries that were constructed or expanded in the late 20th Century. Beyond the superlatives used to describe the buildings themselves, most of the library directors refer to the close connection between the rejuvenation of the library's visual aspect and its content and popularity level.

For example, the directors of the new public library in Rotterdam, the new library in Stuttgart, Germany, the new Queens Borough Public Library, New York and the new library of San Antonio, Texas all describe the impressive building as one of the city's outstanding landmarks and note an increase in the number of visitors and users of library services. Do these changes in the character and image of the public library help strengthen and preserve its original goals and will they, in the future, position it as an institution with a central role in society? The purpose of this study is to attempt to clarify these issues.

## METHODOLOGY

### RESEARCH QUESTIONS

* Does the change in a library building have implications for its popularity? In other words, is there a significant increase in the number of visitors and users to monumental library buildings?
* Is the change in the form of library buildings indeed being accompanied by a change in content? In other words, in the new public library, is it possible to identify a change in direction, transforming it from an institution that focuses on "traditional" services into a significant cultural centre in the community and society?

## RESEARCH POPULATION

The research population included:

* Directors of 24 libraries in Israel and other Western countries, whose libraries meet two criteria:
  - The library was built and opened to the public after 1990.
  - The library could be included in the category of monumental structures. To meet these criteria, the study included libraries in Israel with a constructed area of more than 2,000 square meters and libraries in other countries that are five or more stories tall or cover an area of 10,000 meters square or more.
  - Most of the large libraries in the study were opened to the public between 1995 and 2001. Out of the 24 libraries included in the study, 79.2% are in new buildings and 28.8% are libraries that continue to function in an old building that has been expanded.
* In addition, we interviewed 42 people from five relevant professions: nine futurists, seven sociologists, ten architects, seven urban planners and nine experts from the fields of information and library science.

## RESEARCH TOOLS

* A questionnaire was completed by the directors of the 24 selected libraries. The purpose of the 15-question questionnaire was to examine the characteristics of the people who use the library services and to see whether there had been a quantitative increase, in addition to examining the functioning of the public library through the lens of the services that it offers in the new building and the different ways it is used, as compared to how it functioned in its previous building.
* Structured interviews with 42 experts and a questionnaire each interviewee was asked to complete at the end of the interview. Analysis of the interviews was done according to a qualitative research approach, while the accompanying questionnaire was analysed quantitatively.

The interviews lasted between 30 and 90 minutes. All of the interviews were recorded, with the consent of the interviewees, transcribed and processed with a long process of summarization and adaptation of the statements to categories relevant to the research questions.

## FINDINGS

### Large Buildings– more Users

#### *Can a Public Library in a Magnificent Building Serve as a Centre of Attraction*

One of the questions asked of the experts in various professions was whether, in their opinion, a magnificent, respectable public library building would encourage more people to visit the library. Table presents the division of answers given by the interviewees who answered the question positively, according to professional groups. The data in table indicate that most of the interviewees, including all of the architects and most of the information and library scientists and futurists and more than half of the others, indeed believe that a large, respectable public library building will encourage more people to visit the library.

**Table 6.1. Does a Magnificent New Public Library Building Encourage More People to Visit the Library? Comparison between Groups of Interviewees (by Percentage)**

| Profession | Architects | Information and Library Scientists | Futurists | Urban Planners | Sociologists | Total |
|---|---|---|---|---|---|---|
| Percentage of positive answers | 100.0 | 88.9 | 77.8 | 57.1 | 50.0 | 77.5 |

### Did the Number of Visitors to the Library Increase

From the research data we received, it emerges that after the construction of a new library building, there is a dramatic increase (in percentage) in the number of library visitors. Of the library directors, 96% answered that there had been an increase in the number of visitors. Most responded there was a 100% increase in the number of people visiting the library, meaning that the number doubled. Two directors reported an even higher increase.

### *Was there an Increase in the Number of Regular Clients*

Most of the libraries that participated in the study (68.4%) reported that one-fifth of the city's residents are registered subscribers. Four libraries reported that over half of the residents are registered as regular users. These numbers represented the number of subscribers *registered* as regular library clients. To these numbers, we must add the other, unregistered residents, who the library, as a public institution, serves with a variety of services that do not require registration. All of the libraries, except one, reported a significant increase in the number of registered clients.

From the data that we received, it emerges that the average increase in the number of registered subscribers at the new large libraries was 95.8%. This means that the number of regular clients increased by the same amount as the number of visitors to the library. From these findings, it clearly appears that the construction of a large library building increases the number of people who use the library whether they come to visit, surf the Internet or even just to be with people. Furthermore, it increases the percentage of regular customers who take advantage of the services offered by the public library.

## Functions of the Public Library in the Virtual Age

### *The Library as a Centre of Social-cultural Life in the City*

Experts in various professions were asked to express their position regarding the library as a social- cultural centre. Figure presents the percentage of respondents who believe the library is a centre for social-cultural activity in city. It shows that 90%

of the architects would locate the library in the centre of a city's social and cultural life.

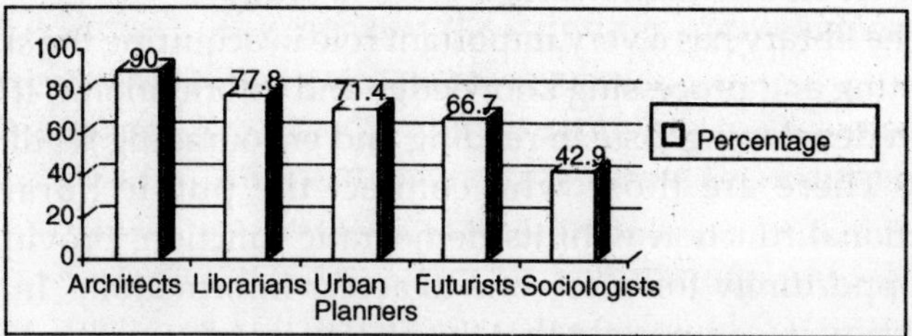


**Fig 6.1.** Division, by Professional Group, of Answers Regarding the Library Placement in the City's Social_Cultural Center

They are followed by the information and library scientists and urban planners. Only 42.9% of the sociologists believe that a library needs to be in the centre of social or cultural life in the city. Most of the interviewees (71.4%) believed that libraries should be in the social-cultural centre of the city.

## Roles of the Public Library in the 21st Century – Analysis of the Interviews

After we learned about the interviewees' opinions regarding the public library and its location in the centre of the city's social and cultural activity, we continued by asking what, in the interviewees opinions, should be the library's role in future society.

### *Information and Library Scientists*

After analysing the statements by the interviewees from the field of information and library science regarding this question, it emerges that all members of this group agreed on one function: the library is a place for holding cultural activities and a meeting place for spending leisure time. "We are a society that is built on personal meetings some of the readers have a limited need for the collection ... they come in order to meet therefore the place is lively. "The library of the 21st century is a social meeting place beyond this, the library needs to allow for clubs and generally be a cultural centre". Regarding other library functions, approximately one-half of the interviewees from this group said that the library should be a place to learn and acquire skills, in addition to locating the necessary information. "The library is a place to sit and do homework, a place to study".

"The library has a very important role in acquiring the skills for locating and processing knowledge and information... it has a role in developing taste in reading and encouraging reading" (M.R.). There are those who connect the public library's instructional function with its democratic function: providing equal opportunity for every one to access information. "In the 21st century it is important that the library instruction teach the use of computer and Internet – to reduce the digital gap". Only two of the information and library scientists interviewed mentioned the traditional functions of the public library – preserving knowledge and lending books. Perhaps these things seem to be self-evident.

### *Architects*

The function of the public library all of the architects agreed upon and mentioned was social meeting. "Library is like a house of prayer – these are buildings where large numbers of people gather". The library has a role in preserving books and also in bringing together resources in all existing media. Most of the architects agreed on this point. "Practically speaking, a library is 'a museum of knowledge,' a warehouse of information for coming generations ... on paper and on electronics".

### *Urban Planners*

This group had many doubts and there was not even a single function mentioned by all members of this group. Despite this, most of the urban planners interviewed noted that in the future the library would be a place for preservation or storage, but with the possibility of accessing this preserved material. "First of all, preservation for future generations is necessary but also presentation, to make all of the literature accessible and visual".

### *Sociologists*

In this group, too, there was no agreement regarding the main purpose of the library. However, most of the sociologists interviewed think that the library must make information broadly available on a full range of media. "First of all, a centre of knowledge, a centre that facilitates access to knowledge ...".

There were those who made a connection between libraries' offerings and equality in society. "This is in the context of people who do not have the means to purchase all of the books ... to provide information at no cost". Of the sociologists, three noted that libraries should continue their traditional functions of "lending, reading, guidance and reference".

### Futurists

Most of the futurists interviewed do not consider the public library an essential institution, because of the technological changes that have already occurred and which are continuing to occur. However, when we asked what, despite this, roles of a library would have in the future society, several of the interviewees mention the role of the library as a meeting place and also the necessity of a place that will gather and organize information and be responsible for preserving the culture.

Several of the people interviewed referred to the role of the library in providing professional instruction and assisting the educational system:

> The public library will not remain a source of information – that's over, but it will have other functions such as meetings with books, meeting to exchange information... people need the social interaction and everyone looks for an appropriate place. People are looking for a reason to meet. Some meet in a restaurant, others in a movie theatre, others in their living room and yet others in a library.

### Functions of the Public Library in the Opinion of All Groups (Analysis of Questionnaires)

#### *Functions of the Public Library in the Opinion of All Respondents*

Table presents rankings of the public library functions according to the opinions of all participants in the study. We found that a majority of the participants think that a public library should be a place for study and research. Other functions noted were, in descending order, provision of reference services, cultural preservation, providing educational videos and reading books and being a cultural centre. Furthermore, it should be noted that only three-quarters of the futurists assigned any function to libraries in the future, consistently claiming that there will be no need for the public libraries and they will have no function in the future society.

**Table 6.2. Functions of the Library – Comparison between Professional Groups (in percentages)**

| | Library Function | Futurists* | Sociologists | Architects | Urban Planners | Information and Library Science | Library Directors | Total |
|---|---|---|---|---|---|---|---|---|
| 1 | Reading | 44.4 | 100.0 | 100.0 | 71.4 | 88.9 | 95.8 | 81.0 |
| 2 | Reference | 44.4 | 100.0 | 100.0 | 85.7 | 100.0 | 91.7 | 85.7 |
| 3 | Study place | 77.8 | 100.0 | 90.0 | 85.7 | 88.9 | 95.8 | 88.1 |
| 4 | Newspapers | 44.4 | 85.7 | 90.0 | 57.1 | 100.0 | 91.7 | 76.2 |
| 5 | Educational video | 55.6 | 85.7 | 100.0 | 71.4 | 100.0 | 82.3 | 82.3 |
| 6 | Entertainment video | 44.4 | 85.7 | 90.0 | 57.1 | 77.8 | 87.5 | 71.4 |
| 7 | Information center | 66.7 | 85.7 | 80.0 | 28.6 | 88.9 | 75.0 | 71.4 |
| 8 | Communications center | 33.3 | 71.4 | 100.0 | 42.9 | 66.7 | 70.8 | 64.3 |
| 9 | Cultural center | 44.4 | 100.0 | 90.0 | 85.7 | 88.9 | 95.8 | 81.0 |
| 10 | Public clubs | 44.4 | 57.1 | 90.0 | 57.1 | 77.8 | 87.5 | 66.7 |
| 11 | Leisure activities | 55.6 | 85.7 | 80.0 | 71.4 | 100.0 | 100.0 | 70.6 |
| 12 | Meeting of distinctive groups | 33.3 | 71.4 | 60.0 | 42.9 | 88.9 | 66.7 | 59.5 |
| 13 | Attraction for visitors | 22.2 | 57.1 | 50.0 | 28.6 | 55.6 | 66.7 | 42.9 |
| 14 | Cultural preservation | 66.7 | 100.0 | 90.0 | 100.0 | 77.8 | 70.8 | 85.7 |
| 15 | Archive | 66.7 | 85.7 | 70.0 | 85.7 | 33.3 | 54.2 | 66.7 |

*Note*: *Approximately one-quarter of the futurists refused to answer the question regarding functions, claiming that the library has no future.

### *Functions of the Public Library – Comparison of the Interview Groups*

Examination of table reveals that differences exist between the perceptions that members of different professions have regarding public libraries. All (i.e. 100%) of the sociologists and architects think that the libraries' traditional functions, providing books for reading and reference, are most important, compared to only 44.4% of the futurists who indicated that these would be among the public library functions in the future. The sociologists added that the library also functions to preserve the culture and serve as a cultural centre that offers lecturers, cultural events, etc.

People interviewed from the field of information and library science responded that the most important functions are to supply reference materials as well as being a place for recreation and leisure. In contrast, the urban planners gave greater weight to the role of cultural preservation, while the futurists apparently considered the public library's functions less important for future societies.

To determine if there are significant differences between the different professional groups on the question of public library functions, $X^2$ (chi square) analysis was done. This analysis found that there were significant differences regarding several functions: Regarding the library's function as a provider of reading books, it was found that all of the sociologists, architects and interviewees from the field of information and library science thought that this is an important function, in comparison to the futurists who thought otherwise: $X^2 = 12.56$, $p < .05$. Regarding the function of the library as a supplier of reference books and encyclopaedias, we found that all of the people interviewed from the field of information and library science, architects and sociologist thought that this function is important, unlike the futurists: $X^2 = 16.85$, $p < .01$.

Regarding the library's function as a place to read newspapers and magazines, we found that all of the people interviewed from the field of information and library science and most of the architects think that this is an important function, unlike the futurists: $X^2 = 10.61$, $p < .05$. Regarding the provision of video and audio recordings and recorded music for purposes of study and education, there was a significant difference between the people interviewed in the field of information and library science and the architects, in comparison to the futurists: $X^2 = 9.54$, $p < .05$. Regarding the role of the public library as a communications and Internet centre, we found a significant difference between the architects and the futurists and urban planners: $X^2 = 10.89$, $p < .05$.

On this question, we did not find a significant difference between the people interviewed from the field of information and library science and the sociologists. Regarding the function of the public library as a centre for culture and leisure, performances, etc., a significant difference was found between the sociologists, architects, urban planners and interviewees from the field of information and library science, in comparison to the futurists: $X^2 = 10.43$, $p < .05$.

## *Functions of the Public Library in the Opinion of Library Directors*

From the data in Table 6.2 it is possible to see that all of the library directors who participated in this study included serving as a place for leisure time activities in the library functions. Three additional functions: providing reading books, a place for study and research and serving as a cultural centre were also noted by 95.8% of the library directors. About 92% of library directors included the provision of local and international newspapers and reference books in their list of library functions. The library directors expressed less support for several of the functions, including serving as a place for unique groups to meet, an attractive place for tourists, the functioning to preserve the culture and being a centre for Internet communications. When comparing the responses of library directors in Israel to those from abroad, we did not find any significant differences for any of the functions presented. It should be noted that there were library directors who added functions that were not included among the options presented on the questionnaire. In particular, they emphasized instructional functions. In their opinion, the public library plays an active role in education, instruction and nurturing reading.

## Public Library Functions: or has the External Change been Accompanied by a Change of Content

After we examined the functions of the library, in the opinion of all interview groups, as well as the library directors, we attempted to learn what was actually happening inside the libraries, which services they are providing in the new buildings that were opened in the last decade and which of these services were not provided previously, in the old building.

## The Public Library and its Services to the Public: The Desirable versus Actual

From the library directors, we attempted to learn what is

actually happening within the libraries, what services they provide in comparison to the services that are, in their opinion, desirable. Table 6.3 presents the desired functions compared to the actual functions, those that are actually being provided by the libraries.

**Table 6.3. Library Functions (Desirable) Compared to Services Actually Provided (Actual)**

| Library Functions | Desirable % | Actual % | Wilcoxon |
|---|---|---|---|
| Place for leisure activity | 100.0 | 78.2 | 0.02* |
| Reading books | 95.8 | 95.8 | 1.00 |
| Plays for study or research | 95.8 | 71.7 | 0.16 |
| Cultural centre | 95.8 | 79.2 | 0.04* |
| Reference books | 91.7 | 91.7 | 1.00 |
| Local and international newspapers | 91.7 | 79.2 | 0.18 |
| Video and audio – for pleasure | 87.5 | 79.2 | 0.32 |
| Public clubs | 87.5 | 75.0 | 0.08* |
| Video and audio – educational | 83.3 | 75.0 | 0.41 |
| Public information centre | 75.0 | 62.5 | 0.18 |
| Public communication centre – Internet | 70.8 | 75.0 | 0.56 |
| Cultural preservation | 70.8 | 66.7 | 0.32 |
| Meeting place for distinctive groups | 66.7 | 58.3 | 0.32 |
| Attractive place for visitors | 66.7 | 62.5 | 0.56 |
| Archive for storing existing collections | 54.2 | 45.8 | 0.32 |

*Note:* * $p<.05$

## The Services that are Actually being Provided

From Table 6.3, it emerges that two of the services were indicated by most of the library directors, more than 90%, are traditional library services: providing books for reading and reference books. Slightly less than 80% of the library directors indicated that their libraries supply local and international newspapers, video and audio recordings for pleasure and that their library is a cultural centre for lectures, exhibitions, etc. or serves as a locale for leisure activities. Fewer than half of the libraries included in the study also serve as an archive.

It should be noted that most of the libraries claimed that the library is egalitarian and democratic, yet the Table 6.3 shows that only 58.3% of the libraries provide services for distinctive groups with special needs in their community. Again, there were librarians that chose to add services which, in their opinion, are important, but were not included in the possibilities listed on the questionnaire: virtual library services, the ability to access library databases without necessarily being present in the library but rather over the Internet, developing early childhood reading, purchasing and maintaining a large collection including antique books and museums, access to electronic data for the business community, special services for adolescents, and renting library rooms/halls. Table shows a sweeping difference between desirable and the actual.

The library directors think that the library ought to fill many important functions but in actual practice, the libraries offer the public fewer services than their directors believe would be desirable. Regarding traditional library functions – the provision of reading books for lending and serving as a reference room – there is a correlation between the services that libraries are supposed to provide the public and what they actually provide.

For all of the other possible library functions included on the list, except providing Internet, more library directors indicated that the possibility was part of a library's desirable functions than actually provide that service to the public in their library.

All of the library directors (100%) believe that one of the library's functions is to serve as a cultural centre for leisure time activities, yet only 78.2% open their doors for leisure time activities. Similarly, 95.8% think that the library building should serve as a home for cultural events such as lectures, exhibitions, performances, thereby serving as a municipal culture centre, but only 79.2% allow this type of activity. Likewise, 87.5% of the library directors indicated it would be desirable for the library to serve as a place for holding club meetings for the general public, yet only 75% of the libraries actually offer clubs.

## The Differences between the Desirable and the Actual

To highlight the discrepancy between the desirable library functions and the actual services provided by the libraries a nonparametric, Wilcoxon analysis was conducted. This analysis reveals significant differences for three library functions, as follows: the library as a cultural centre, holding club meetings in the library and the public library as the place for leisure time activities. These three functions express the social need for meetings in a cultural locale, such as the public library. All three of these functions are desired more than they are actually provided.

## New Services in the New Building

Having examined the opinions of library directors, the functions of public libraries and the services provided by the libraries, we examined whether new library services, which were not provided in the previous building, are being provided in the new building. In other words, has the public library changed only its external appearance or also its contents? Does a new, larger building make it possible to provide services that were not offered in the old the building? The library directors were asked to indicate which of the services, currently provided by their library, were not offered by their library in its old building. Of the 24 library directors who participated in the study, only 19 answered this question.

**Table 6.4. New Services in the New Building (Percentages)**

| New Services the Library Offers the Public | Percentage |
|---|---|
| Cultural Centre | 47.4 |
| Local and international newspapers | 42.1 |
| Video and audio recordings – for pleasure | 42.1 |
| Public communication centre – Internet | 42.1 |
| Attractive place for visitors | 36.8 |
| Video and audio recordings – educational | 31.6 |
| Public clubs 31.6 Place for leisure activity | 31.6 |
| Place for study or research | 26.3 |
| Public information centre | 26.3 |

*Table Contd...*

| | |
|---|---|
| Meeting place for distinctive groups | 21.1 |
| Cultural preservation | 21.0 |
| Archive for storing existing collections | 15.8 |
| Reading books | 0 |
| Reference books | 0 |

Table 6.4 presents the distribution of the library director answers regarding *new* services in their library, in descending order (by percentage). A new library building makes it possible to offer several new services that were not available in the library's old building. Approximately one-half of the libraries reported that the library now serves as a cultural centre for lectures, art exhibits, performances, meetings with authors, and other events.

Approximately 40% report that they now have a place for reading local and international newspapers and magazines, that they can provide video and audio recordings for pleasure and that they can serve as an Internet communications centre. Approximately one-third of the respondents indicated additional new services: an attractive place for visitors, video and audio recordings for educational purposes, public clubs and a place for leisure activity while slightly more than 20% noted that the new library they manage serves as a meeting place for unique groups, and a similar percentage said that cultural preservation is one of their library's new functions, which was not possible in the old building. Only 15% reported that the library now serves as an archive for existing collection. In this section, too, some library directors noted additional, new functions that were not included on the list of possible library functions: virtual services and expanded programmes for children.

It should be noted that there was no difference in the responses of library directors in Israel and abroad on this subject. The responses from the library directors received clearly indicate that a new, more spacious library building does allow the library to offer more services, not necessarily traditional library services, but rather leisure activities: clubs, exhibitions (rare book displays), performances, theatre, space to read newspapers and magazines.

## DISCUSSION

### Large Buildings–are there More Users

The first research question asked whether the change in library buildings has implications for their popularity. The research findings clearly show that all of the new, large, magnificent buildings that have been built as public libraries receive at least twice as many visitors as their predecessors and there has also been a very significant increase in the percentage of library users and regular clients. Research conducted among public libraries in Israel found a direct connection between the image of the library and its use, both in terms of the number of users and the number of books borrowed.

The present study shows that these new buildings have apparently improved the reputation of the library and thereby increased use. This finding is very important because many libraries around the world report a general decrease in the number of readers, the number of books borrowed and the number of regular clients. By contrast, it is worth noting the research conducted by Westin and Finger, which claims that the number of users increases in every place where a new library was built, regardless of size. Their claim is that any change in the library influences the library's environment and usage. Therefore, they recommend constant revitalization of the library's image. Yet another perspective is presented by McCabe who claims that the number of users increases because a wider variety of services are offered and it is the larger building that makes the services possible.

### Library Functions in a Virtual Age

Most interviewees considered it important for the library to be at the centre of the social and cultural life of the city. Another function mentioned by most of the interviewees, in most of the groups, was the function of gathering, organizing and storing information, as well as making it accessible. All of the people interviewed from the fields of information and library science emphasized the role of the library in the field of cultural activity and in facilitating social meetings. All of the architects consider the library a place for leisure time entertainment. Most of the members of this group referred to the library as a democratic, egalitarian place where social gaps, especially the digital divide, can be narrowed.

They also noted the role of the library in preserving culture, whether through books or other media. Most of the urban planners emphasized the role of the library in preserving existing collections and culture. Sociologists and futurists did not place special emphasis on any one function. The literature deals with the concept of the public library as "the people's university," but in this study only seven of the 42 people interviewed mentioned this function.

Furthermore, when we presented the library as a place for unique populations in society, this function was given a low ranking. Sannwald claims that libraries are becoming a place of social interaction, and research conducted in the United States found that the most important function of the library is to provide access to technology for people of modest means. Westin and Finger stress that the public library should live up to its name: public and free and therefore, by its very nature, serve as a bridge between knowledge and all strata of the population. The library's traditional services were mentioned by the experts in information and library science and the architects. The latter also added the library's function as a communications centre that provides access to the Internet All of the library directors positioned serving as a place for leisure time entertainment as the most important library function, followed by serving as a place for study, circulation and a cultural centre.

## Services Offered by Public Libraries: Or has the External Change been Accompanied by a Change of Content

The second research question examined whether the external change was accompanied by a change of content. Did the large buildings allow changes in or additions to the services provided by the library? If so, is it possible to identify a change that transformed the library from an institution focuses on providing traditional library services into a significant cultural centre for society and the community, as emerges from the opinions of the interviewees? As noted in the literature review, public libraries have shown, throughout their history, the ability to adjust and adapt to the needs of the environment. Although they began as a municipal service to intellectuals by providing reference materials, they quickly opened their doors to the general public, lending books and offering guidance, to make knowledge accessible to all. Over the years, collections have become more varied and services have been added or changed. Knowledge is now available both on paper and on digital media, and the library attempts to provide a response in both the cultural and social realms.

This service actually began in the late 19th century, when the public library entered the field of leisure by offering popular reading books and folklore evenings. The leisure field expanded and libraries also began to offer lectures, clubs, exhibitions and meeting places for different groups. It is interesting to note that the 1972 UNESCO Manifesto states, "The public library is a natural cultural centre for the community, bringing together as it does people. Space and equipment are therefore necessary for exhibitions, discussions, lectures, musical performances and films" yet the next UNESCO Manifesto, published in 1994, does not mention the library's cultural and social function. The current study clearly shows that the emphasis in library functions and services to the public is shifting to the cultural and social realms. All of the library directors believe the public library should serve as a place for leisure entertainment and almost all (95.8%) believe the library building should serve as a municipal cultural centre.

On this issue, all of the architects and a majority of the other interviewees repeated that the library had to serve as "a meeting place with a cultural experience." Most of the people interviewed thought that the public library should be "a cultural shopping mall" that serves as a source of knowledge offered to the general public. Sociologists and architects emphasized the guidance and instructional services for finding the necessary materials, while it was actually the futurists who placed heavier emphasis on cultural preservation. From library directors' responses, it emerges that the most widely accepted services provided by libraries are traditional services, such as providing reading and reference materials. We also found that in almost all cases the desirable functions exceeded the actual services available. In three cases there were significant differences between the desirable than the actual: the library as a cultural centre, the library as a place for leisure activities and the library as a place that allows public clubs. These differences reflect the changes in library services in the society of the future.

All of the library directors believe that the most important function of the library is to be a place of leisure-time activity, and approximately 96% believe the library should serve as a cultural centre. Indeed, most of the libraries do provide this service. Approximately one-half of the library directors report that the library as a "cultural centre" is a new service that was not provided previously in their old library and that the move to a new building has made this possible. This finding confirms the second research assumption that where monumental library buildings are built, the library becomes a social and cultural centre.

Additional services that have been added after the move to a new building include supplying local and international newspapers, Internet communications centre, collections of local and international newspapers and viewing and borrowing movies for pleasure.

## CONCLUSIONS

The current study regards the future of public libraries in the world that is changing before our eyes. The names of library institutions have changed during recent years. In many places the word "library" has been replaced with "mediatech" or "bibliotech", after the style of "hi-tech," to express the combination of books, digital media and high technology. What is their place in society and where are they headed? This confusion intensifies in light of the facts on the ground, which show a significant decrease in reading and borrowing books, the traditional functions of the library.

In contrast to these reports, the current study reveals a dramatic increase in the number of people visiting new, large libraries and a very significant increase in the number of regular clients who come to the library to receive services other than traditional library services. The research findings show that libraries are becoming a cultural centre and a place for social life, cultural meetings and leisure-time entertainment. This research also shows that a new, magnificent building becomes an attraction in its own right and greatly increases the percentage of the population that uses the library.

It is certainly possible that the number of users increases, because of the wider range of services possible because the building is larger. Expanded building size makes it possible to hold cultural events, introduce additional, special materials that could not have been accommodated in the smaller building and, obviously, a bigger library can house a larger, more varied collection that is attractive to many different population sectors. The size of the public library building makes it possible to be attentive to the public's needs and offer a wide range of services: continued traditional services, access to information on a variety of media, holding varied cultural activities, a welcoming, pleasant meeting place and "a shrine of the book" where humanity's cultural legacy is preserved.

The picture outlined by this study shows that the library will be necessary in the society of the future, less for reading and more to meet the public's need for a relatively quiet, refined place for social gatherings with a cultural character. Indeed, the present research shows that the new buildings have allowed libraries to become *cultural centres* and offer services that have not been possible in the past or were offered only on a more limited scale.

# 7

# Research Libraries, Risk and Systemic Change

## INTRODUCTION

In 2008, OCLC Research engaged an organization experienced in conducting risk assessments for corporate, governmental and educational clients with the objective of identifying the most significant risks facing research libraries. We thought that the techniques used to examine risks facing an individual enterprise could be productively deployed to arrive at a measured assessment of risks facing a distributed industry or enterprise— in this case, United States research libraries.

For this group of related organizations, rather than any individual library, we wanted to examine the following:

* In a rapidly evolving information environment, what are the greatest risks to research libraries?
  - Individually—as local service providers
  - Collectively— as a distributed enterprise
* Which of these risks is susceptible to mitigation?
  - Feasibility— is it a controllable risk?
  - Impact—is it worth the investment to mitigate?
* Where can collective action make a difference?

We recognized that the research library within an academic setting is unlike the independent individual organizations that usually undergo this kind of risk assessment process. The research library is not independent of the mission of its home institution. It is not entirely free to set and change goals and objectives. It is a cost center within the academy not a revenue-generating entity. It is often the recipient of specific directions and constraints dictated by the university in which it delivers its services. Because of these differences the range of responses that research library managers can muster to address acknowledged challenges and risks is considerably circumscribed relative to their counterparts in private industry.

Risk assessment within a private company is usually based on interviews with senior managers and board members with the process having two distinct stages. In the first stage, identified risks are characterized, rated, ranked and evaluated based on their likelihood and estimated impact. In the second stage, the resulting risks are assigned to individual managers who take responsibility for action plans that mitigate each specific risk. In the first stage of this investigation our consultants interviewed library directors and summarized the reported perceptions of the source and intensity of risks. Then we in OCLC Research considered the distribution and implications of these risks and explored which might be mitigated by collaborative action and collective resources. No effort was made to assign responsibility for risk management to traditional library operating units, since few of the risks appeared susceptible to local institutional control.

Despite differences between the business and academic sectors, we found the methodology to identify, characterize and rank risks effective. It revealed a convergence of perceived risks. It yielded a shared perspective on a landscape of challenges facing US research libraries. It may support movement towards cooperative mitigation of critical risks. We hope that our descriptive categorization of risk clusters will provide libraries with a common vocabulary for identifying, evaluating and responding to shared challenges. Finally, we believe that assimilating, ranking and analysing these risks will provide a sound basis for OCLC Research to formulate a collaborative action agenda in partnership with the research library community.

## METHODOLOGY

The risk assessment entailed interviews of 15 library directors from members of the *Association of Research Libraries*

(ARL) in the United States with whom OCLC Research works via their participation in the RLG Partnership. The participating library directors were distributed across the ranked ARL membership.

An interview questionnaire was provided in advance to each interviewee and included a section to identify risks and their level based on a predefined risk category. Throughout this process risk was defined as the possibility that an event will occur and adversely affect the achievement of the library's objectives. The risk categories provided consisted of general themes common across industries as well as some library specific categories. Figure 7.1 shows the categories that were used by the interviewees when contemplating current risks. This is a comprehensive typology intended to encourage the interviewees to consider the fullest possible range of risks that research libraries might be facing. Many are not applicable to the research library within the academy and interviewees used this to prompt their reflections.

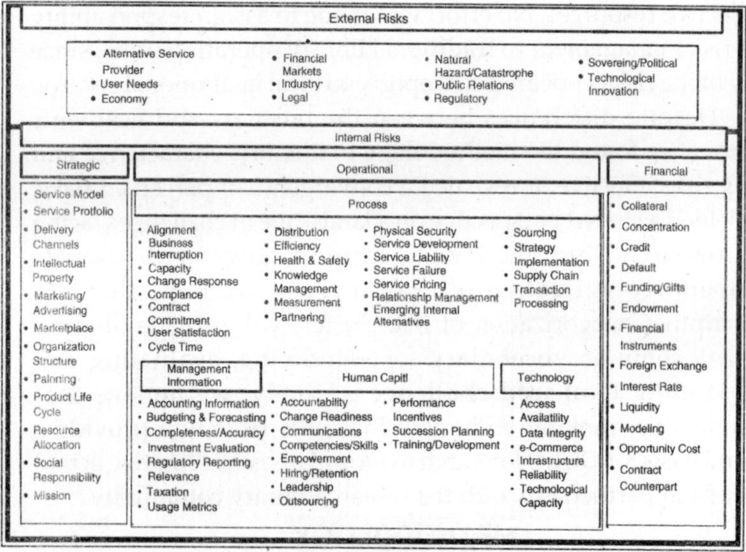


**Fig 7.1.** Categories Used by Interviewees in Contemplating Current Risks

The interviewees were asked to rank their inventory of risks and provide supporting reasons for their rankings, as well as specific examples. The questionnaire was used only to facilitate discussion during the interview. Interviewees were then asked to assess the impact and likelihood of the risks they had identified. The grading scale used in making an assessment is shown in Table 7.1.

**Table 7.1. Grading Scale Used in Assessing Risk**

| | **Impact** |
|---|---|
| Catastrophic | * Organization would not likely survive in present form |
| | * Sustained, serious loss in user share |
| | * Loss of library value where the cost of future library investment outweighs the recovery |
| Major | * Major impact on library—serious damage to library's ability to service users |
| | * Serious diminution in library value and use with adverse publicity |
| Moderate | * Significant impact on library—would affect users |
| | * Use and/or library value will be affected in the short term |
| Minor | * Impact on internal organization only |
| | * There is a minor potential impact on use and library values |
| Insignificant | * Insignificant impact on internal organization |
| | * No potential impact on use |
| | * No impact on library value |
| | **Likelihood** |
| Almost certain | * Event is expected to occur in most circumstances Likely |
| | * Event will probably occur in most circumstances Possible |
| | * Event might occur at some time—moderate probability |
| Unlikely | * Event could occur at some time—low probability Rare |
| | * Event may occur only in exceptional circumstances |

The risks identified by the interviewees were consolidated in a risk register and an average risk rating was calculated. This average rating took into account the frequency with which the risk was mentioned, the impact assigned and the likelihood forecast across all the interviews. Based on these three factors, an overall risk rating was computed and a designation of high, medium or low was applied to each risk.

The resulting synthesis is a basis for assessment of the overall significance of these risks and the degree to which they threaten the academic research library enterprise as it is currently organized. It is important to note that this risk assessment is a snapshot amid continual changes in the challenges faced by research libraries, such as new technology, regulatory requirements, organizational restructuring, new leadership personnel, etc. It is also important to acknowledge that in research libraries, as in all industries, a risk and challenge may be the shadow of an opportunity. The risks enumerated in this report were assessed against the prevailing library business model, and hence represent greater or lesser threats to the current institutionally-organized model of library service rather than threats to the survivability of the research library enterprise as a whole.

## GENERAL OBSERVATIONS

* The plurality of risks (30%) is associated with concerns about an uncertain library value proposition.
* The second largest class, and second priority in terms of medium to high risks, is related to staffing and human resources.
* Risks associated with legacy technology are all high.
* The high risks are chiefly operational in nature and the results of general organizational weaknesses.
* The high risks represent circumstances that require continuous monitoring and are mostly controllable—that is, either the occurrence or the impact can be managed. This confirmed for us that there is an opportunity to collectively consider these risks so that research libraries can appropriately calibrate local and group responses.
* We expected to see serious concerns emerge about the custody of intellectual property that supports the research enterprise. Interestingly enough they did not.

Libraries do not seem to perceive an immediate threat to core operations or services from this.

Twenty-six key risks were identified by all participants, ten (38%) were judged to have a high potential impact and likelihood; three (11%) were considered to have a low impact and likelihood. Overall there were three times as many risks considered to be high versus low. This provides some measure of the pressure and uncertainties under which research library directors are currently operating: the heat is on and it's intense.

## RISK CLUSTERS AND REGISTER

The full register of categorized risks is shown in Table 7.2. Risks identified in the assessment effort are grouped in thematic clusters defined by OCLC Research. Individual risks within each cluster are presented in a sequence that Research staff found to be helpful in illuminating patterns and dependencies within each group.

| | |
|---|---|
| Value Proposition | ... A Reduced Sense of Library Relevance from below, above and within |
| Human Resources | ... Uncertainities about Adequate Preparation, Adaptability, Capacity for Leadership in Face of Change |
| Durable Goods | ... Changing Value of Library Collections and Space; Prices go up, Value goes down – Accounting doesn't Acknowledge the Change |
| Legacy Technology | ... Managing and Maintaining Legacy Systems is a Challegne; Replacement Parts are Hard fo find |
| Intellectual Property | ... Losing Some Traditional Assets to Commercial Providers(*e.g.*, Google Books) and Failing to Assume Clear Ownership Stake in others (*e.g.*, Local Scholarly Outputs) |

**Fig 7.2.** Risk Clusters

**Table 7.2. Register of Categorized Risks**

**Value Proposition: A Reduced Sense of Library Relevance from Below, Above, within**

| No. | Risk | Risk Rating |
|---|---|---|
| 1 | Availability of online and other resources (*e.g.*, Google) may weaken the visibility and necessity of the library. | High |
| 2 | User base erodes because library value proposition is not effectively communicated. | High |
| 3 | Library user satisfaction deteriorates due to lack of understanding of changing user needs. | Medium |

*Table Contd...*

| | | |
|---|---|---|
| 4 | Operations are not managed effectively because library metrics are not established, tracked or utilized and management's accounting and budgeting reporting is not relevant, timely or useful. | Medium |
| 5 | Changes in academic leadership and administration result in changes in perceived value and strategic function of research libraries. | Medium |
| 6 | Strategic planning in the library is not aligned with university goals and objectives. | Medium |
| 7 | Library funding or budget decreases as a result of increased internal competition within the university. | Medium |
| 8 | Decreased institutional support for library fund-raising; lack of focus on capital campaigns or endowment opportunities. | Medium |

**Human Resources: Uncertainties about Adequate Preparation, Adaptability, Leadership in Face of Change**

| No. | Risk | Risk Rating |
|---|---|---|
| 9 | Recruitment and retention of resources is difficult due to competitive environment and reduction in pool of qualified candidates. | High |
| 10 | Difficulty identifying candidates for evolving library management roles. | High |
| 11 | Human resources are not allocated appropriately within the library or university to provide the training, development, cross-training and re-training required to manage change in the current environment. | High |
| 12 | Current human resources lack skill set for future needs (changing technology, etc.). | High |
| 13 | Library workforce fails to embrace implementation of organizational change as a personal and professional responsibility. | Low |
| 14 | Conservative nature of library inhibits timely adaptation to changed circumstances. | High |

*Table Contd...*

**Durable Goods: Changing Value of Library Collections and Space (Prices Go Up, Value goes Down; Accounting doesn't Acknowledge the Change)**

| No. | Risk | Risk Rating |
|---|---|---|
| 15 | Increased challenges with building and maintaining collections as a result of rising costs, limited budgets, and turbulence in foreign exchange rates. | Medium |
| 16 | Library physical storage space is not appropriately managed or optimized, placing constraints on collection growth. | Low |
| 17 | Lack of investments in deteriorating physical space leads to declining user satisfaction with library as place. | Medium |
| 18 | Loss of library assets, content or access due to natural hazard. | Medium |

**Legacy Technology: Managing and Maintaining Legacy Systems is a Challenge; Replacement Parts are Hard to Find**

| No. | Risk | Risk Rating |
|---|---|---|
| 19 | Library cannot adjust fast enough to keep up with rapidly changing technology and user needs. | High |
| 20 | Increased inefficiencies and expenses due to lack of functionality of legacy systems and IT support. | High |
| 21 | Due diligence and sustainability assessment of local or third party services and initiatives is not completed, tracked or analysed. | High |
| 22 | Digital content is lost as a result of not being properly managed and preserved. | Medium |

**Intellectual Property: Losing Some Traditional Assets to Commercial Providers (*e.g.*, Google Books) and Not Assuming Clear Ownership of others (*e.g.*, Local Scholarly Outputs)**

| No. | Risk | Risk Rating |
|---|---|---|
| 23 | Potential exists for increased cost burden to research libraries as access to content previously owned and distributed by libraries (research outputs, digitized | Medium |

*Table Contd...*

| | | |
|---|---|---|
| | collections) is increasingly controlled by commercial agents and online service providers. | |
| 24 | Collection development strategy fails to address changing nature of scholarly record; appraisal and selection processes are out of step with proliferation of new content. | Medium |
| 25 | Public-private partnerships with external organizations (*e.g.*, Google) are not properly evaluated, balancing costs with potential benefits. | Medium |
| | **Uncategorized** | |
| 26 | Increased administrative burden due to changes to the library funding model. | Low |

## RISK CLUSTER OBSERVATIONS

Interviewees offered some illustrative observations about the changing library value proposition, which we paraphrase here.

A notable tautology emerges, in which a weakened value proposition becomes a self-fulfilling prophecy:

* Alternative service providers in the network are providing a more compelling research environment and support tools.
* Our current value proposition can't compete with the alternative service provider.
* Our users have noticed this.
* We're continuing to rely on the old success metrics.
* The university has noticed.
* We haven't responded (with an aligned strategic plan).
* Our internal competitors for dollars are winning.
* We can't get other funders to help.

Interviewee observations about staffing and human resources conveyed a mix of frustration and resignation:

* I can't attract people to support the old (or new) tasks.
* I'm not certain where to find the next generation of leaders, I only know they won't look like me.
* The current staff isn't qualified or motivated to support new library functions.

There is considerable uncertainty about the value of continuing investments in the traditional "durable goods" of research libraries—collections and facilities—and the technologies that support them:

* I'm not able to acquire additional print collections due to price increases—and am not certain that they are worth the investment.
* I don't have the space for these collections, and I'm not sure they're worth the effort to find it.
* I can't attract users to my sofas and workspaces.
* My physical collections and facilities are still at risk—but does it matter?
* Our infrastructure is ill adapted to new needs—built around old workflows and collections.
* It's also inefficient.
* We're hesitant to embrace alternatives—should we migrate now?
* We haven't invested in systems to manage or preserve a different kind of research collection.

## INTENSITY OF RISKS

When these risks are arrayed on a graph that accounts for their perceived impact and forecast likelihood a visual heat map emerges highlighting risks that require significant mitigation.

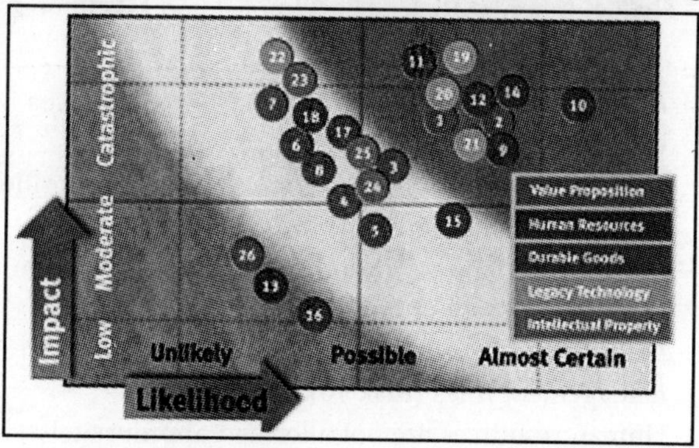


**Fig 7.3**. Sensitivity Analysis: Risk Groups

Notably, risks that were rated as potentially catastrophic and almost certain are dominated by human resource and legacy technology concerns. These are, of course, the challenges that libraries must address if the current organizational model is to be preserved. However, one might conclude that a future research library model will be less dependent on local human resources and systems. Risks considered possible but of limited impact include mismanagement of library space and low motivation levels among library staff.

## MITIGATION

An inventory of the high risks prior to any mitigation is shown in figure. These are the high risks that are perceived by library directors to constitute an immediate and debilitating threat to the future of the research library (Fig. 7.4).

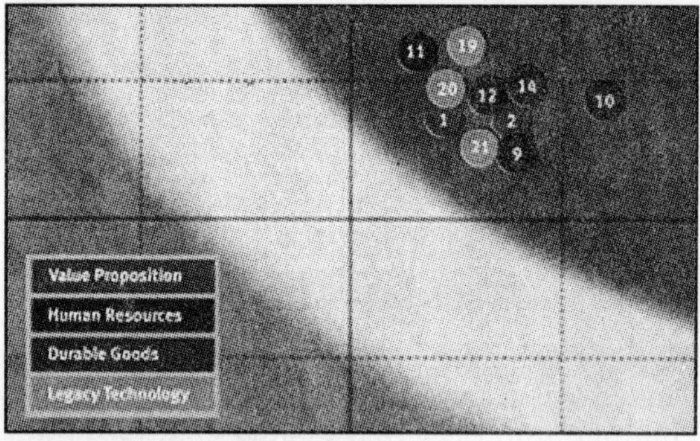


**Fig 7.4**. Inherent Risks: High Impact and Likelihood

*Notes:*

* Availability of online information resources weakens visibility and value of library (Risk 1).
* User base erodes because library value proposition is not effectively communicated (Risk 2).
* Recruitment and retention of resources is difficult due to reduction in pool of qualified candidates (Risk 9).
* Difficulty identifying candidates for evolving library management roles (Risk 10).
* Human resources are not allocated appropriately to manage change in the current environment (Risk 11).
* Current human resources lack skill set for future needs (changing technology, etc.; Risk 12).

* Conservative nature of library inhibits timely adaptation to changed circumstances (Risk 14).
* Library cannot adjust fast enough to keep up with rapidly changing technology and user needs (Risk 19).
* Increased inefficiencies and expenses due to lack of functionality of legacy systems and IT support (Risk 20).
* Due diligence and sustainability assessment of local or third party services is not completed, tracked or analysed (Risk 21).

Two of these relate to the changed value proposition resulting from the ascendancy of external information hubs like Google and the resultant defection of the library user base. We do not regard these as risks that individual libraries can reasonably hope to mitigate—rather, they demand joint action at the group and network level. We think the inattention (or lack of responsiveness) to changing user expectations is an area that demands further reflection and will reward immediate collective action. We think these risks are best addressed through cooperative—rather than local—actions.

Many of the risks rated as high (impact and certainty) pertain to:

* Human resources and organizational culture, including a lack of attention to cross-training and reallocation of existing staff
* Lack of critical skill sets for managing data sets, engaging directly with research faculty, or retooling technological infrastructure
* An organizational culture that inhibits innovation
* difficulty in attracting and retaining staff in a competitive environment where fewer credentialed library professionals are available
* Uncertainties about the appropriate qualifications for library managers who may require skills developed in other sectors.

We believe that a significant number of these can be effectively managed on a local or group level to reduce the impact or incidence of specific risk events. While some of the risks identified are beyond the immediate control of research libraries, at least half of them can likely be mitigated through some combination of local and cooperative actions.

We note that there are a handful of risks that, while not ranked as immediate or catastrophic threats, are associated with the changing value of the library's traditional assets:

* Long-term investments in redundant print collections create a counterweight to innovation in online service development
* Legacy library management systems don't adequately support the transition to digital content
* Inadequate attention is given to benchmarking or assessing the efficiency or value of current services.

If these underlying risks were addressed, a significant reallocation in library resources might be achieved, resulting in a service profile that is more visible and valuable to the research library clientele. In other words, some changes that are disruptive to the traditional organization of library operations at research institutions may ultimately revitalize the library value proposition. These represent opportunities for a new generation of library leadership.

While many of the high risks identified in this study are inherent in the surrounding information environment, legacy library technology is notone of them; rather it represents an obstacle to effecting meaningful change in the library's operations and value proposition. It is not obvious that investment in renovating the library's traditional technology platform—upgrading or migrating from one local system to another—will substantially reduce the systemic risks facing research libraries. This is an area where less, rather than more, library investment may be needed.

## STRATEGIES FOR MITIGATION

We think that several of the risks considered to have both high likelihood and significant impact will be effectively and perhaps inevitably managed via changes that are already emerging in the current research library landscape.

We believe that increased reliance on shared infrastructurealong with increased outsourcing and regional consolidation of services will enable more rapid deployment of the services that research library users want and need moving the following risks into a more acceptable range of impact and occurrence:

* Library cannot adjust fast enough to keep up with rapidly changing technology and user needs (Risk 19).
* Increased inefficiencies and expenses due to lack of functionality of legacy systems and IT support (Risk 20).
* Due diligence and sustainability assessment of local or third party services is not completed, tracked or analysed (Risk 21).

If research libraries restructured workflowsit would enable strategic re-deployment of resources that could significantly mitigate the human resource skill set challenges that were perceived as high risks, particularly:

* Difficulty identifying candidates for evolving library management roles (Risk 10).
* Human resources are not allocated appropriately to manage change in the current environment (Risk 11).
* Current human resources lack skill set for future needs (changing technology, etc.; (Risk 12).

We believe these mitigations can diminish some high risks as shown in Fig. 7.5.

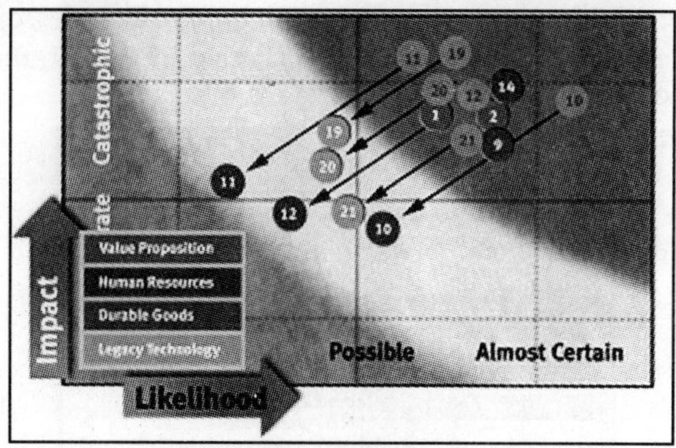


**Fig 7.5**. Proposed High Risk Mitigation Strategy and Sequence.

*Notes:*

* Availability of online information resources weakens visibility and value of library (Risk 1).

* User base erodes because library value proposition is not effectively communicated (Risk 2).
* Recruitment and retention of resources is difficult due to reduction in pool of qualified candidates (Risk 9).
* Difficulty identifying candidates for evolving library management roles (Risk 10).
* Human resources are not allocated appropriately to manage change in the current environment (Risk 11).
* Current human resources lack skill set for future needs (changing technology, etc.; Risk 12).
* Conservative nature of library inhibits timely adaptation to changed circumstances (Risk 14).
* Library cannot adjust fast enough to keep up with rapidly changing technology and user needs (Risk 19).
* Increased inefficiencies and expenses due to lack of functionality of legacy systems and IT support (Risk 20).
* Due diligence and sustainability assessment of local or third party services is not completed, tracked or analysed (Risk 21).

## RESIDUAL RISKS

The risks that remain high after these mitigations may be intractable, or mitigation might require something more or something other than collective action among libraries, or it may be that an adequate response is a change in goals rather than operational change.

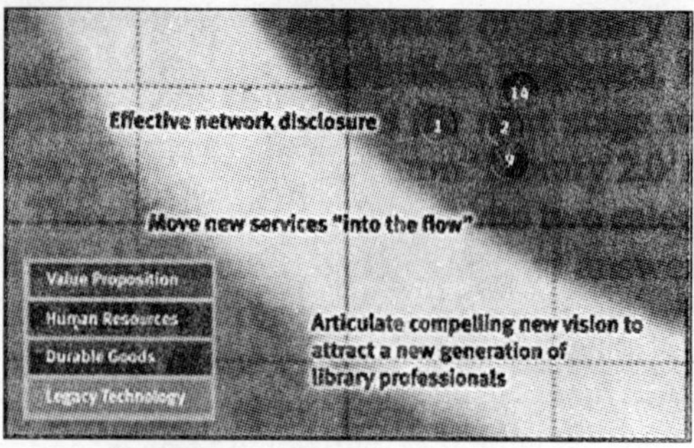


**Fig 7.6.** Residual High Risks

*Notes:*

* Availability of online information resources (Google, etc.)

weakens visibility and value of library (Risk 1).

* User base erodes because library value proposition is not effectively communicated (Risk 2).
* Recruitment and retention of resources is difficult due to reduction in pool of qualified candidates (Risk 9).
* Conservative nature of library inhibits timely adaptation to changed circumstances (Risk 14).

Two of the residual risks seem best addressed by new strategies and services:

* Availability of online information resources (Google, etc.) weakens visibility and value of library (Risk 1).
* User base erodes because library value proposition is not effectively communicated (Risk 2).

If the research library community could disclose its assets in the networked environment more effectively and with an associated set of common service expectations, it might be possible to retain some of the traditional user loyalty even as these services become one of many within the Amazoogle information environment. A more direct approach to the value proposition challenge is to deploy new services within the academy that are in the flow of current networked research practices. Presenting assets and services where the research library academic clientele do their work might renew their view of and reliance on library services.

The other two residual risks are cultural ones:

* Recruitment and retention of resources is difficult due to reduction in pool of qualified candidates (Risk 9).
* Conservative nature of library inhibits timely adaptation to changed circumstances (Risk 14).

The pool of potential library workers might be very different after the library has restructured traditional workflows in favour of a new emphasis on and investment in research support services. That service set would attract a new generation and type of professional that emanates from a variety of disciplines rather than traditional library or information school training. Deploying these new professionals and support services in a parallel organizational structure may be the only way to bypass the obstacles created by the conservative nature of today's library organizations.

## EPILOGUE

In the eighteen months since this work was undertaken, our analysis has been used as the basis for internal planning within OCLC Research as well as facilitated discussion in the broader library community. Initially, our findings were met with resistance and skepticism. Library administrators thought the risks were overstated and particularly resisted the idea that the library value proposition was threatened. More recently there has been a general acceptance that these challenges are real and need to be met with collective effort and a new vision of services. There is some evidence2that research libraries are now confronting these risks and identifying opportunities for cooperative action.

In the absence of organizations within the U.S. library community that can address strategy, operational requirements and implement change on a system-wide basis some bolder institutions are implementing action plans at the local or regional level fueled by the fiscal imperatives of the current dire economic times.

This is heartening but likely to be inadequate. Most institutions continue to direct resources in traditional ways towards operations that are marginal to institutional and national research priorities, towards processes and services that are ignored or undervalued by their clients and towards staff activities that are driven more by legacy professional concerns than user needs.

To properly respond to the risks identified here, research libraries need to come together around an action agenda aimed at improvement of the research enterprise they serve. Incremental revision of traditional operational models will only hasten the movement of important new research services to other entities within the academy, leaving the library with only the vestigial values of its book-determined legacy. It will look the same but everything will have changed.

# 8

# System Design Methodologies

As suggested, look at different design methodologies, or design flows, for multi-processor systems. Design methodologies have evolved together with manufacturing technology, design complexity, and design automation. Improvements in technology have increased design complexity to the point that designers are no longer capable of making complex designs manually. To solve this problem, design automation tools, also known as *computer-aided design* (CAD) tools, were introduced.

In order to make CAD tools more efficient and design algorithms more manageable, design-automation researchers as well as tool developers were forced to introduce more stringent design rules, parameterize components and minimize component libraries. As design complexities continued to increase, tool developers created new design abstraction levels and tried to use the same design strategy from the circuit level, to the logic level, to the processor level, and finally to the system level.

## BOTTOM-UP METHODOLOGY

Bottom-up methodology started even before CAD tools were invented. It is still in use in much of the industry today, at least partially, because it follows an intuitive methodology of building parts before assembling the whole product. In a typical bottom-up methodology, designers develop components and then store them in a library for use on the next-higher abstraction level. We have libraries of transistor, logic, RTL, and processor components. Components in each of the libraries are used to build components in the library on the next abstraction level. On the Circuit level, we use transistors and develop circuits and their layouts for the basic logic components such as gates, flip-flops, bus drivers, and others.

These components become standard cells for higher level design and layout tasks. These standard cells, with their functionality, structure, and layout, are stored in the Logic component library for use on the Logic level in figure. On the logic level, we create register-transfer components such as registers, register _les, ALUs, multipliers, and other components for processor micro architecture using Boolean expressions or FSM and FSMD models. After logic synthesis of these RTL components, we perform the placement and routing with standard cells for each component and store them in the RTL component library.

On the Processor level, we start with C code or an Instruction set and generate the structure of *processing elements* (PEs) or *communication elements* (CEs). At this level we also perform floor planning, placement, and routing of these PEs or CEs using the components from RTL library, and store them in Processor library.

On the System level, we start with a *model of computation* (MoC) and generate the system structure consisting of multiple PEs and CEs from the Processor component library. Finally, we perform the system layout by using the component layouts from the Processor library. Note that each component library has functional, structural, and layout models for each component in the library. So by creating components and storing them in libraries, we can then apply them in each successive abstraction level.

The advantage of bottom-up methodology is that abstraction levels are clearly separated, each with its own library. This allows for globally-distributed locations for design on each abstraction level, and for easier management of design on each abstraction level, since each group supplies a component library for the next level of abstraction (Fig. 8.1).

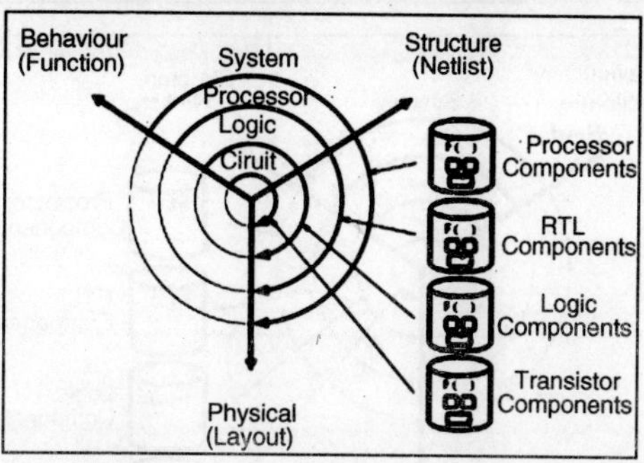


**Fig 8.1.** Bottom-up Methodology

The disadvantage of this approach, however, is that the libraries must include all possible components with all possible parameters and that these must be optimized for the metrics required by any present and possible future applications. This is a very difficult and never-ending task since it is very difficult to anticipate on the lower abstraction level all the needs on the next higher abstraction level.

## TOP-DOWN METHODOLOGY

In contrast to bottom-up methodology, top-down methodology does not attempt a component or system layout until the entire design is finished. A top-down methodology begins with a particular MoC and generates from it a system platform or system structure in which every component has its parameters and required metric values defined, but not its structure or layout. On the next level of abstraction, each PE or CE component is further decomposed into smaller RTL components. For example, in figure, PE and CE components that were generated on the System level are decomposed into RTL components with their parameters and required metrics defined.

In this case, each functional unit, such as the ALU, has all its functions specified, as well as its delay and power requirements. After those are determined, each of the RTL components is further decomposed into logic components or gates. Finally, each logic component is broken down into a transistor net list, in which each transistor layout represents a basic cell (Fig. 8.2).

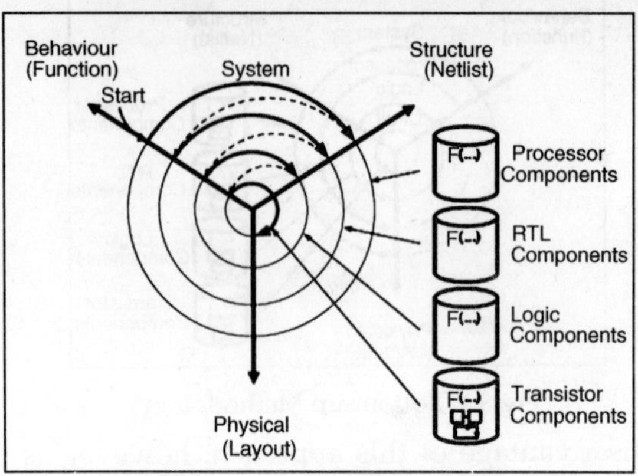


**Fig 8.2.** Top-down Methodology

All such basic cells, for the entire system, are placed on silicon and connected accordingly using placement and routing methods and tools. Such top-down methodologies were in use in design of early computers but today's designs are too complex for such a complete top-down methodology. In general, top-down methodology leaves placement and routing for the last step by avoiding the layouts on other levels of abstraction. Unfortunately, the system and component metrics are not known until the last step and therefore it is very difficult to optimize the whole design.

The design decomposition or synthesis has to be repeated over and over again without designers really knowing whether optimization is going in the right direction. In order to avoid too many design iterations, designers need the concept of metric closure in which different metric values from lower levels of abstraction are used to annotate design on higher level of abstraction. In this case designers can estimate optimized metric values on the lower level of abstraction during the next design iteration on the higher levels of abstractions. Unfortunately, metric closures are difficult to achieve since metric estimations are as difficult as performing real designs.

## MEET-IN-THE-MIDDLE METHODOLOGY

Most designers today use some kind of meet-in-the-middle methodology in order to take advantage of the benefits of both bottom-up and top-down methodologies, while also minimizing their drawbacks. This is convenient because the design standards and CAD tools on the lower levels of abstractions are well understood and developed, but on the processor and system level they are not. While there are some tools on the processor level, almost none, with exception of general simulation tools, exist on the system level (Fig. 8.3 and Fig. 8.4).

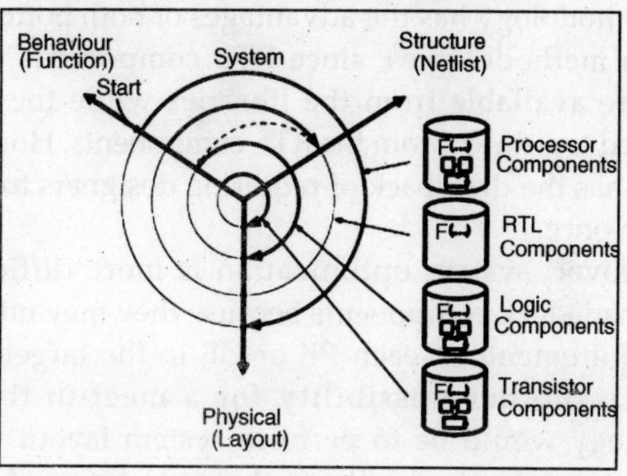


**Fig 8.3.** Meet-in-the-middle Methodology (Option 1)

A meet-in-the-middle methodology allows a designer to take advantage of the tools available for lower level abstractions while also reducing design layouts on higher abstraction levels. In general, a meet-in-the middle methodology applies a top-down methodology to higher abstraction levels and a bottom-up methodology to lower abstraction levels. The main distinguishing feature of this approach is how these styles meet. As shown in figure, a meet-in-the-middle methodology could start with a MoC and synthesize the system platform with virtual PEs and CEs which are after that synthesized with RTL components from the RTL library.

These PEs and CEs also include commercially available IPs which are also supplied as net lists of RTL components. Therefore, all PEs and CEs are decomposed into RTL components from the library. Each RTL component has its own structure and layout layout generated through some bottom-up methodology in the library. These RTL component layouts are combined through floor planning, and routing into the layout of the multi-core platform. For example, ALU components in such a library would be limited to lengths of 8, 16, 32, 64 bits, and nothing in between.

Therefore, with such a meet-in-the-middle methodology, we do physical design or layout three times: once for standard cells, a second time for RTL components and a third time for the entire system platform, using the layout of these RTL components. This mixed methodology has the advantages of both bottom-up and top-down methodologies, since RTL components with their metrics are available from the libraries while the system is synthesized top-down from the RTL components. However, this approach has the drawback of requiring designers to do layout more than once.

Moreover, system optimization is more difficult using already-made RTL components because they may not be tuned to the requirements of each PE or CE in the targeted system platform. Another possibility for a meet-in-the-middle methodology would be to perform system layout with logic components or standard cells, as shown in figure. As with the first meet-in-the-middle methodology we described, this one starts with a MoC and synthesizes the system platform with virtual PEs and CEs.

Those PEs and CEs are then synthesized with RTL components, which themselves are further synthesized with logic components. Commercially available IPs that are described on the RTL level are also synthesized with RTL and logic synthesis tools that generate logic components net lists. Therefore, every IP component, as well as the synthesized PEs and CEs, are decomposed into logic components from the Logic component library. Since each logic component has a layout as a standard cell, they are finally combined through floor planning and routing into the layout of a multi-core platform.

In this case, we do physical design or layout only twice: once for generating standard cells and a second time for the entire system platform, using the standard cells layouts. This mixed methodology has an advantage in that only the standard cell layout has to be upgraded with the introduction of a new fabrication technology.

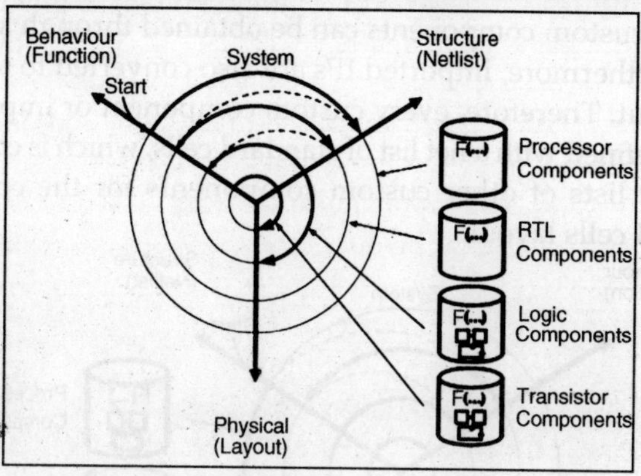


**Fig 8.4.** Meet-in-the-middle Methodology (Option 2)

The RTL component layouts, which are much more complex and in higher numbers do not need to be upgraded. An additional benefit is that the whole design is flattened to standard cells and the layout is performed only once. However, a system layout using standard cells is more complex than it would be with RTL components, and the design metrics are less predictable and controllable since standard cells for each RTL component may not be all in one place. Furthermore, using such inaccurate metrics makes it difficult to perform any system optimization on higher abstraction levels.

## PLATFORM METHODOLOGY

The three design methodologies presented in the previous sections represent ideal cases of three different design concepts. In reality, design methodologies differ from company to company and even between different groups in the same company. They are also very much product oriented. In this case, system design usually starts with an already-defined platform, usually one defined by a well-known platform supplier or defined locally inside the company as shown in Fig. 8.5.

Such platforms may have already some standard components, such as memories and standard processors with well-defined layouts. The system platform may also be upgraded with the addition of custom components that will be synthesized with processor and RTL synthesis tools, after which the layout of these custom components can be obtained through standard cells. Furthermore, imported IPs are also converted to standard cell layout. Therefore, every custom component or imported IP can be defined with a net list of standard cells, which is combined with net lists of other custom components for the combined standard cells layout.

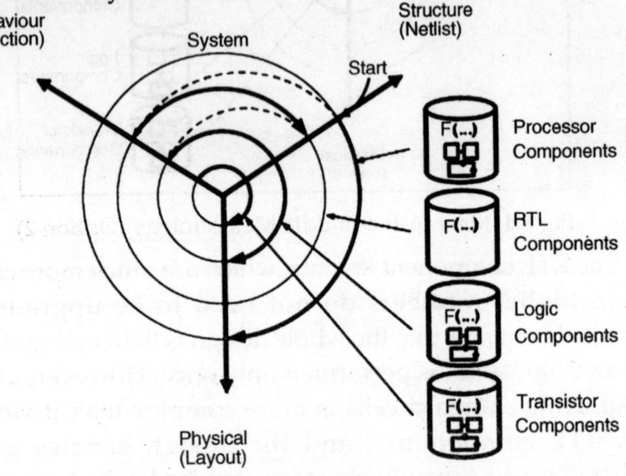


**Fig 8.5.** Plateform Methodology

Such standard cell layout is then combined on the System level with layouts of standard processor and memory components into the system platform layout. When using such a platform, we perform physical design or layout three times: once for standard cells, then we use standard cells for the layout of custom components, and finally we use processor component layouts for the final platform layout.

In order to simplify platform design, some platforms have system layout for all standard processor components finalized with some space left open for the standard cell layout of custom components. When using such a platform, therefore, we perform layout only two times: once for standard cells and second time we use standard cells for the layout of custom components. This mixed methodology has advantages from both bottom-up and top-down methodologies since standard processor components are available from the libraries and custom components can be inserted for application optimization.

However, this approach has the weakness of requiring us to do layout more than once. Also, custom components have to be adapted to reflect the structure and layout requirements of the given platform.

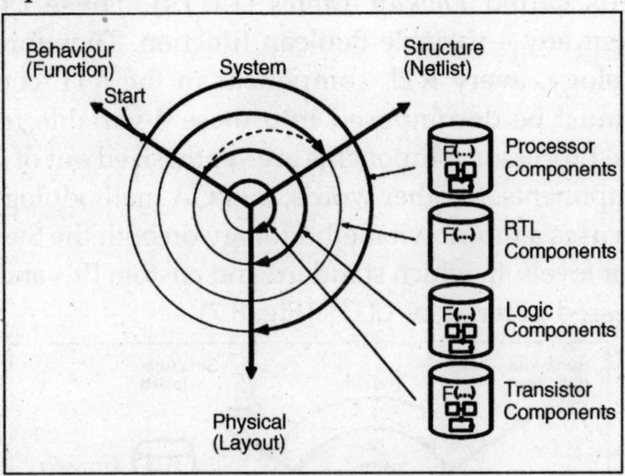


**Fig 8.6.** System Methodology

The platform methodology can be upgraded to a system-level methodology by introduction of standard architecture cells and retargetable compilers (Fig. 8.6). An architecture cell contains a parametrizable programmable processor such as one shown in figure. The parameters include number, type and size of components, component connectivity, and the number of pipeline stages in the functional units, controller and the data path. Such a standard architecture cells can be pre-synthesized with standard cells and inserted into the library of Processor components or generated on demand. A typical system-level methodology based on such architecture cells is shown in figure.

It starts with a MoC and generates the platform architecture consisting of standard or custom architecture cells. Since all the architecture cells have the layout model in the library the final system layout is obtained by combining the layouts of architecture cells. This methodology has advantage of dealing only with two highest abstraction layers. Therefore, it is well-suited for application experts with minimal knowledge of system and processor design. However, it requires a retargetable compiler to cover different architecture cells.

## FPGA METHODOLOGY

*Field-Programmable-Gate-Array* (FPGA) methodology is based on the FPGA substrate, which consists of a multitude of 4-bit ROMcells called *Lookup Tables* (LUTs). These LUT scan implement any 4-variable Boolean function. Therefore, in this methodology, every RTL component in the RTL component library must be decomposed into these 4-variable functions. Then, the Processor components are synthesized out of available RTL components. In other words, a FPGA methodology shown in figure uses a top-down methodology on both the System and Processor levels, in which standard and custom PEs and CEs are all expressed in terms of LUTs (Fig. 8.7).

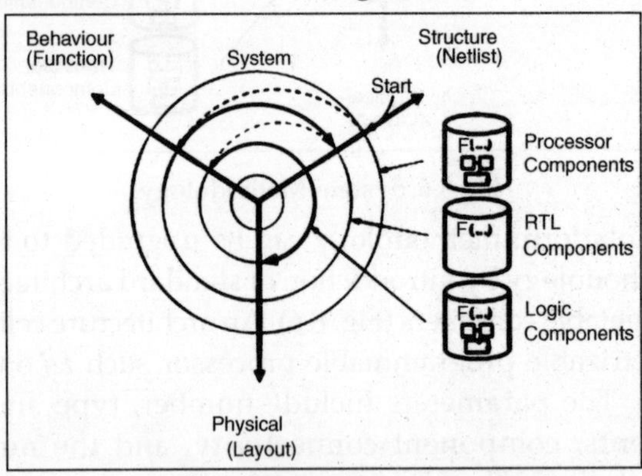


**Fig 8.7.** FPGA Methodology

A system design starts by mapping an application onto a given platform and then synthesizing custom components down to RTL components which are defined in terms of LUTs. Standard processors components in the Processor library are already defined in terms of LUTs. Once all components in the platform are defined, we flatten the whole design to LUTs and BRAMs and perform the placement and routing with the tools provided by FPGA suppliers

This type of top-down system design has the same weaknesses as any top down methodology in that it is difficult to optimize the whole design by flattening the whole design just to basic LUT cells. Furthermore, designers do not know how the

FPGA supplier-provided layout tools will map and connect all the LUTs and BRAMs.

## SYSTEM-LEVEL SYNTHESIS

In the previous sections we described several basic strategies in system design. However, system design flow has been changing alongside fabrication technologies and automation tools over the last 50 years. The changes started with lower levels of abstraction, which are well understood today. However, the higher levels of abstraction are still under investigation and discussion. As suggested, describe briefly the synthesis process from a behavioural description to a structural description on system and processor levels.

As shown in Fig 8.8, system-level synthesis starts with an application written in some MoC such as a set of sequential and parallel processes communicating through message-passing channels. Such a MoC must execute on a platform of multiple standard and custom processors connected through an arbitrary network. This type of platform can be defined partially or completely after estimating some characteristics of the application in terms of performance, cost, power, utilization, configurability, and other considerations. Platform definition can be done manually or automatically. Once the platform is defined, an application must be partitioned and each partition assigned to a processor or IP in the platform.

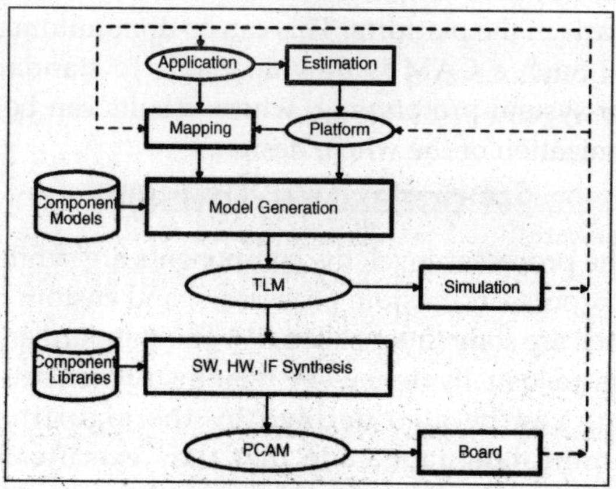


**Fig 8.8.** System-Level Synthesis

In order to verify that the application executes on the platform and satisfies all the requirements, we need to generate a simulatable and possibly verifiable model such as a timed *Transaction-Level Model* (TLM). After simulation, the design can be optimized if it does not satisfy the requirements by changing the platform, the application code, or the algorithms used in that code. We can also change the mapping of the application to the platform. For example, we can minimize external communication by grouping heavily communicating processes and assigning the whole group to one processor. It is also possible to assign performance demanding processes to different processors or specialized IPs, or to pipeline performance-demanding processes if possible.

After we obtain a satisfactory application code, platform, and mapping, we can synthesize each component. Three types of components are needed: custom SW, HW, or IF components. SW components are for scheduling of processes such as different types of RTOS, and for communication and interfacing across the platform. HW components are various custom processors and custom hardware units. We also need communication components such as bridges and transducers for protocol conversion, and interface components such as bus arbiters and interrupt controllers. Having synthesized these platform components, we need to generate a CAM model that contains binaries for downloading to processors and RTL descriptions for the HW parts in the platform. This can be done automatically or manually. Such a CAM is downloadable to standard FPGA boards for system prototyping, whose results can be used for final optimization of the whole design.

## PROCESSOR SYNTHESIS

On the processor level, the components are synthesized as standard processors, custom processors, and custom hardware units, which are sometimes called IPs. The standard and custom processors are usually defined by their instruction sets. Custom processors can be also defined by the algorithm or the programming language code that they execute. They are programmable so that new algorithms and the code can be added or existing one modified. Custom hardware units or IP are usually not programmable.

They are used as accelerators to execute special functions for a particular application, such as multimedia applications. As shown in Fig. 8.9 the synthesis process starts with a given Specification in a programming language, which is compiled into some Tool model such as CDFG or a FSMD or a three-address code. This formal model can be used for Estimation of the future processor architecture and its metrics. It can be also used for some partial or complete allocation, binding, and scheduling. Processor synthesis, sometimes called High-Level Synthesis (HLS), takes the formal model and performs Allocation, Binding and Scheduling. The Allocation task selects necessary and sufficient components from the RTL component library and defines their connectivity.

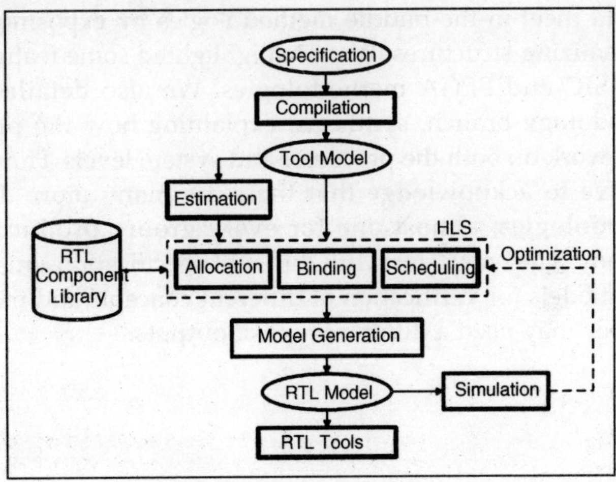


**Fig 8.9.** Processor Synthesis

The Binding task defines binding of variables to registers, register _les, and memories, operations to specific functional units and register-to-register transfers to specific buses. Scheduling assigns operations and register transfers to clock cycles. These three tasks compete with each other, so a completely optimized design is not easy to achieve. That is why estimation and pre-HLS comes handy. Pre-allocation helps in partial or full definition of processor architecture. This way we can avoid the clock-cycle estimates; since many or all of the register-to-register delays are known ahead of time, there is no need to wait until the end of HLS to find out the clock cycle time. Pre-binding may bind frequently-used variables to fast registers, register _les, or a scratch-pad memory to avoid lengthily delays caused by loading and storing to the main memory. Pre-scheduling can assign key inner loops to high speed, pipelined functional units or it can pre-schedule such loops to specific paths in a pipelined data path. Once HLS is finished we need to generate a RTL Model of the processor that can be synthesized with standard RTL synthesis tools.

## CONCLUSION

We explained the differences between top-down, bottom-up, and meet-in-the-middle methodologies by exposing their taxonomizing structures. We also highlighted some features of key ASIC and FPGA methodologies. We also detailed one methodology branch, synthesis, explaining how the process might work on both the processor and system levels. However, we have to acknowledge that there are many more design methodologies, almost one for every group, product, and company. They may start with different specifications, may use other models for verification of different concepts and metrics, and they may need a different type of outputs.

# 9

# Application of Data Mining Techniques for Library System

## INTRODUCTION

At the beginning of each adjustment in a library, librarians or library managers need to think about which kind of books are going to purchase or what kind of magazines have to be ordered in the coming renewal period of the year. The purpose of project is to provide statistics and analysis software. It will offer librarians or managers sufficient information to make right decisions. The statistical data or chart produced by the programme will easily make librarians sense what changes need to be made. We are going to research the reader's behaviour from these statistical data or charts and then improve or modify our library service.

The library professionals do not know which books a patron wants, which is offered for their studying, or which patron prefers what class of book. The library may offer a book that no patron wants to borrow, or the offered books may not have enough readers. Librarians should make a decision so that this kind of book may never be or seldom ordered in the future. On the other hand, librarians have to use a lot of their budget for much used books to provide the reader more services. Librarians will be helped by this programme. This kind of feedback can be researched and can present some trends. This will be important information for further improvement of the library. Data Mining in a Library System will be a product after we digitalize the library. Librarians may get a lot of worthwhile information immediately such as the students' studying trend, the top 10 of circulation in the library, the hottest field of studying by using this system. Not only librarians want this but also patrons need it. This is also a knowledge management strategy system for the current library. Actually, the system will enhance the librarian's efficiency in controlling library resources. Librarians could imagine the future library from it.

The uncertainties of the Internet challenge the modern workplace but also promise unexpected opportunities. Converting uncertainties to opportunities requires human efforts to enhance the capabilities of technology to benefit professional endeavour. In the library profession, practices of unstructured and unrestricted information dissemination and retrieval from the World Wide Web (WWW) not only create an information explosion but make uncertain the future of the profession as well. Facing the need to adapt to the new climate of the information world, academic librarians are charged to extend their services from the reference desk to the virtual environment on the WWW.

To meet the challenge, new information technologies that can assist in organizing and retrieving information are constantly being investigated by academic libraries. Web mining is one of these new technologies that deserves special attention because of its capability to discover and analyse useful information from the Web.

## WHAT ARE DATA MINING AND WEB MINING

Data mining is one of the hottest topics and buzz word in information technology. It automatically and exhaustively explores very large datasets, consequently uncovering otherwise hidden relationships among data.This technology has been successfully applied in science, health, marketing and finance to aid new discoveries and strengthen markets. In addition, data mining techniques are being applied to discover and organize information from the Web.Data mining itself is in the second generation of artificial intelligence; the core concept of data mining is focused on machine learning.This machine-learning ability allows modification of search criteria automatically before the next execution, once particular patterns or trends have been discovered in the data searched.It is important to understand that data mining is a discovery-oriented data analysis technology and not a single product or a system. It is a highly focused data transformation framework.

This transformation process uses a series of analytical techniques, such as clustering, association and classification.These techniques are taken from the field of mathematics, cybernetics and genetics, and can be used independently or cooperatively. The function is to extract high quality information to identify facts and draw conclusions based on relationships or patterns among the data. Most important, data mining can ask a processing engine to "show answers to questions we do not know how to ask". For example, bank customers' data are kept in different databases, thus, they are isolated from each other.

Data mining technology can search all the different databases together, and provide a better customer view so that the bank can concentrate more on potentially good customers.The rationale is that when asking for specific relationships, more important relationships might be missed. Asking to find relationships that we do not know exist will yield more meaningful data or business knowledge.The combination of these two areas, data mining and the WWW, is known as Web mining.

When data mining is applied to the Web, it can perform several functions including:

* Resource discovery the discovery of locations of unfamiliar files on the network;
* Information extraction the acquisition of useful information from the WWW;
* Generalization the discovery of information patterns from said resources

There are two primary dimensions of Web mining:

* Web content mining and
* Web usage mining.

### Web Content Mining

Web content mining is the "process of information or resource discovery from millions of sources across the World Wide Web ".There are two approaches in Web content mining: the agent-based and database approaches. The agent-based approach involves artificial intelligence systems that can "act autonomously or semi-autonomously on behalf of a particular user, to discover and organize Web-based information ". Some intelligent Web agents can use a user profile to search for relevant information, then organize and interpret the discovered information. Some use various information retrieval techniques and the characteristics of open hypertext documents to organize and filter retrieved information.

Another kind of agent is programmed to learn user preferences and use those preferences to discover information sources for those particular users. The database approach focuses on "integrating and organizing the heterogeneous and semi-structured data on the Web into more structured and high-level collections of resources." These organized resources can then be accessed and analysed. These metadata, or generalizations, are then organized into structured collections and can be analysed.

### WEB USAGE MINING

The other dimension of data mining is Web usage mining. This is the process of discovering user access patterns, as data are automatically collected in daily access logs. Recently, referrer logs, which collect information about referring pages for each reference and user registration, also have been included. Web usage mining is crucial in establishing user profiles for a better structured Web site. As the manner in which the Web is used continues to expand, there is a continual need to figure out new kinds of knowledge about user behaviour that needs to be mined for.

## TEN STEPS OF DATA MINING

The following are ten steps of Data Mining for extracting hidden knowledge from data:

## IDENTIFY THE OBJECTIVE

The purpose of Step 1 is creating a list of analyses to perform, questions to investigate, and hypotheses to test. The first of thing is to be clear on what you hope to achieve with your analysis. It includes some advanced planning about what type and level of information you intend to capture from the database. Make sure whether or not the objective is measurable. This advance planning can save you time and money in your data mining efforts.

## SELECT THE DATA

The next step is to select the data to meet this objective. In this step, the data is organized for analysis and to produce an effective representation.

The following are some examples for a quick checklist:

* Is the data adequate to describe the phenomena, the data mining analysis is attempting to model?
* Is there a common field in your data that can be used for linking it to other database?
* Are internal and external information available for the analysis?
* Is the data stable—will the data being mined be the same and available after the analysis?
* Is there redundancy in the data sets when they are merged?
* How current and relevant are the data to the business objective?
* Is there lifestyle or demographic data available?

## PREPARE THE DATA

Once you've organized the data, you must decide which features to convert into usable formats. The purpose of this step is to produce a "data mining-ready" data set.

* Establish strategies for handling missing data, extraneous noise, and outliers
* Identify redundant variables in the dataset and decide which fields to exclude
* Determine the distribution frequencies of the data

For example, it may be efficient to have an account establish date in the format of YY-MM-DD, but it may be necessary to transform this field to one total account number days like NNNN. You can postpone some of these decisions until you select a data mining tool. For example, if you need a neural network or polynomial network you may have to transform some of your fields.

## EVALUATE THE DATA

Evaluate the structure of your data in order to choose the appropriate tools:

* What is the ratio of categorical/binary attributes in the database?
* What is the nature and structure of the database?
* What is the overall condition of the dataset?
* What is the distribution of the data set?

Balance the objective evaluation of the structure of your data against your users' need to understand the findings. For example, neural networks generally work best on data sets with a vast number of numeric attributes.

## FORMAT THE SOLUTION

In conjunction with the evaluation of data and business objective determine the format of the solution.

You may think about:

* What is the optimum format of the solution—decision tree, rules, C code, graph, or SQL syntax?
* What are the available format options from the data mining process?
* What is the goal of the solution, classification, and segmentation?
* What does the end-client need-graphs, reports, code?

## SELECT THE TOOLS

This step is to select an appropriate data mining tool for the business objectives and data structure.

While selecting a data mining tool, we may consider:

* Is the data set heavily categorical?
* What platforms do your tools support?

* Are the tools ODBC-compliant and incorporated with an end-user interface?
* What data formats can the tools import/export?

A data mining tool should help you understand the results of its analysis and the kind of solutions the tool generates. No single tool is able to provide the answer to your data mining project. Some tools integrate several technologies into a suite of statistical analysis programmes, a neural network, and a symbolic classifier.

## CONSTRUCT THE MODEL

At this stage the data mining process begins. This is the process of searching for patterns in a data set and the generation of classification rules, decision trees, clustering, scores, weight, and evaluation and comparison of error rates. Usually the first step is to use a random number seed to split the data into a training set and a test set and construct and evaluate a model.

Resolve these issues:

* What are the model error rates? Are they at acceptable levels? Can they be improved?
* What extraneous attributes did you find? Can those noisy and redundant be purged?
* Is additional data or a different methodology necessary to improve model performance?
* Will you have to train and test a new data set?

## VALIDATE THE FINDINGS

This step involves testing a model. It is important after achieving your data mining analysis that you share and discuss the results of the analysis with the administrator, designer, analysts, managers, and engineers.

Ensure that the findings are correct and appropriate to the objectives:

* Are the findings available and do they make sense?
* Does the process have to return to any previous steps to improve results?
* Can other data mining tools be used to produce the same findings?

## DELIVER THE FINDINGS

This step provides a final report to the business unit or client. The report should document the entire data mining process such as data preparation, tools used, test results, source code, and rules. Thus, you will know if the findings meet the objective, if additional data can improve the analysis, what strategic insight you dig out and how it is applicable, and what proposals can result from the data mining analysis.

## INTEGRATE THE SOLUTIONS

Finally, you share the findings with all interested end-users in the appropriate business units. This process involves incorporating the results of the analysis into the company's business procedures. Although data mining tools automatically invoke database analysis, they can make some mistaken findings and erroneous conclusions if you're not careful.

# ADVANTAGES OF DATA MINING

Data mining uses advanced technology for gleaning valuable insights from database that enable the business user to make the right business decisions. It turns up data that gives business companies just a little edge, but the payoff for this small edge is large. One obtains the competitive advantages required to grow in today's competitive environment. Data mining is simple in theory, but it can get quite involved in practice. That means that users will probably need some help getting set up. Many data mining software solutions are available for small and large businesses in most industries and these tools are constantly improving. The accuracy of mining will make a difference in the bottom line of business. A META Group survey revealed that Fortune 500 firms were using data mining for three general purposes: 64 per cent for strategic planning, 49 per cent for competitive intelligence, and 46 per cent to increase their market share.

So far, the following have been the traditional applications of data mining technology by industry sectors:

* Retailers Database marketing, advertising effectiveness, inventory and category management.
* Banking and Insurance Financial modeling, fraud detection, market and industry profiling, database marketing, customer segmentation.
* Brokerage/Stock Exchange
* Telecommunication call detail record analysis, optimal use of capital equipment, targeted marketing.
* Government Collections, workload selection, logistics, and intelligence gathering.
* Manufacturing Production quality control, supply-chain and inventory control

Data mining provides companies extremely valuable insight that has, to date, been closely guarded as corporate stealth technology to protect competitive advantage. However, there is sometimes a breakthrough when trying something new. Some mistakes will be made. Mistakes can be remedied with statistical expertise, but the technology is becoming more useful for more users.

Data mining is also not designed to fix all business problems or tell you what the real problem is, but it gives a company a sense which can be used to help make intelligent business decisions. Most of all, data mining is an ongoing process that involves a lot of analysis and refining along the way, so think of it as a worthy investment. And like any investment, even if your data-mining portfolio only uncovers small golden nuggets at first, those nuggets properly managed yield a lot of value.

## DATA MINING TECHNIQUES ENHANCE LIBRARY SYSTEM

Suppose a library system has the following goals:

* Increase books borrowing rate.
* Attract more users to borrow books.
* Assist library professionals in making policy on the acquisition of duplicate copies and new publications.

The relationship between Data Mining and Library Management can be shown as in Fig. 9.1.

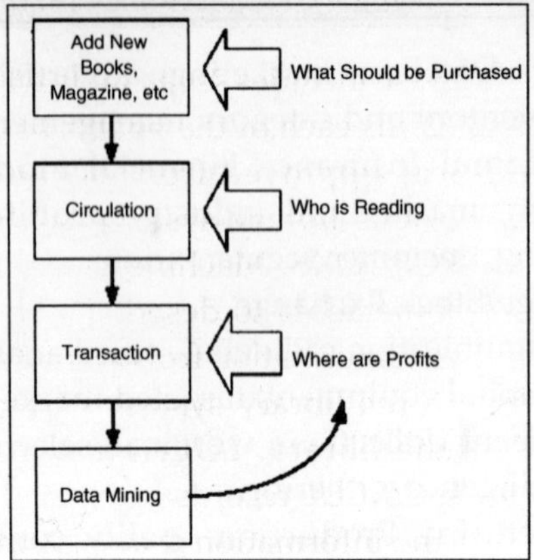


**Fig 9.1.** The Cyclical Relationship between Data Mining and Library Management

## EXAMPLE

Consider a library whose books database includes the data of 2000 volumes of books, and the borrowing history of 5000 users who have borrowed books from library. From this database, we have developed a report system to represent the relationship between books and students. And then we use the data mining association rule to analyse the books of the same cluster borrowed by the students. A report chart of books will be produced, so that the library professionals will find references to the books for making a decision. Additionally, the library collection may be used more effectively.

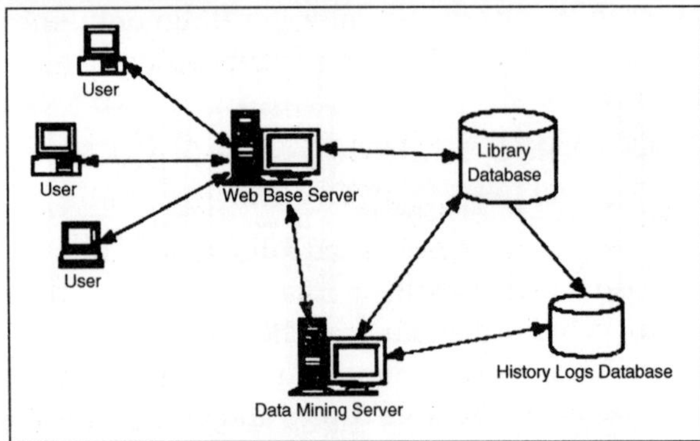


**Fig 9.2.** The Prototype of a Library Architecture

The library database includes seven tables. The first of them is *BOOKS* which contains each of the books' basic information. The table *BOOKS* was improved from *MARCBOOKS* which comes from the previous library system. It kept most of the columns from MARCBOOKS. Machine-readable Cataloguing (MARC) is a kind of metadata to describe a book. *USERS* has part of a student's basic information from the registration system and coordinates with the library system. *COPY* describes the actual volumes in the library. *LOCATION* reports the real location of each book. *CIRCUL* records each circulation of a book. *RESERVATION* has the information that is stored when a user holds a book. Figure 9.2 shows the schema of these tables. Between each table, there is a key column that sometimes is a primary key in one of them. For instance, the relation key between *BOOKS* and *COPY* is ISBN.

The data mining system is under statistics in a library system. It is an advantageous part of the library system. The process between the main page of data mining and its four functions is shown in Fig. 9.3. On the main page of data mining, the administrator has four functions to execute (Fig. 9.4). The first function is backup the *CIRCUL*. The second one is the list of top ten books. The third one is to execute rule. The final one is rule manager.

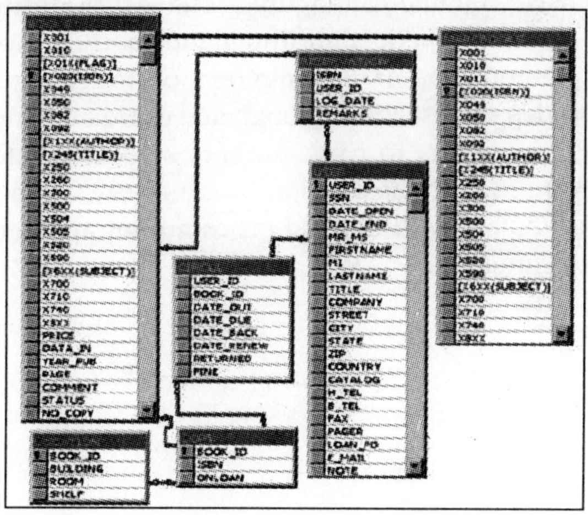


**Fig 9.3.** The Schema of the Library Database

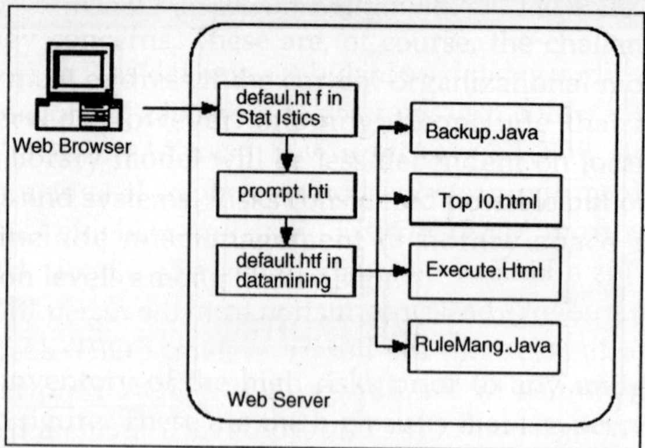


**Fig 9.4.** The Main Process of the Data Mining System

## CONCLUSION

It is unlikely that libraries will continue to satisfy users' information needs using the traditional catalogs as the primary access mechanisms. To be certain, online catalogs provide good access to books, films, microfiche, audio tapes, and other materials traditionally kept in libraries. However, few, if any, libraries have succeeded in using their online catalogs to provide adequate access to a significant number of digital materials. In an era where information costs rapidly increase while budgets remain flat, libraries must find alternatives to slow, awkward, and expensive manual cataloguing. The Artificial Intelligence methods such as genetic algorithms and machine learning, or statistics method support data mining tools to accomplish tasks. These methods are fast and thorough and exploit the tremendous power of computers to find nuggets of useful information embedded in mountains of data. In the future, advanced data mining technology will depend on computer architecture and database technology.

# 10

# Resource Sharing, Networking and Library Consortia

## INTRODUCTION

In the present era of Information technology, the information needs of the users have been increased so enormously that no single library on its own can meet their information needs. This has necessitated the need for effective linkages and cooperation between libraries and information centers for sharing of available resources and information through networking. The consortia for library can be considered as a major step towards library cooperation in sharing electronic resources. The consortium should take lead role in the development of a national strategy for information provision for research in higher education.

## LIBRARY RESOURCE SHARING AND NETWORKING

The term resource applies to a thing, person or action to which one resorts to in times of need and sharing indicates allotting, apportioning or contributing something that is owned, to benefit others. Resource sharing, therefore, refers to reciprocity, implying a partnership where each member has something useful to contribute to others and which each is willing and able to make available when needed.

Resource sharing is an empty concept, but for the approach permitting resource sharing to work is that which:

* Entails having resources to share

* Having a willingness to share them, and
* Having a plan for accomplishing resource sharing

Resource Sharing is an integral part of modern library services. In the developed countries, no library services can be thought without sharing of resources. In the past, rupee was limited to the interlibrary loan system. In the modern age, with the development of science and technology and innovations of techniques and devices, resource sharing has become easier and fruitful due to the availability of databases, information network, and online sharing facilities. Thus, the resourcesharing system helps one library to access to resources of other libraries.

When resource sharing is agreed upon by participating institutions, then the following aspects must be planned:

* Identify and locate major collections, sources and materials
* Assemble, publish and distribute collective information for all participating bodies
* Workout the basis for sharing, reference service, lending service, copying service, access to materials, delivery service, and lists of holdings
* Establish means of sharing ideas, development and problems in the form of a newsletter
* Plan for new developments in the knowledge of what others are doing
* Developing a National Information Policy

The following are the most important benefits of resource sharing to participating institutions:

* Easy access to materials
* Enables co-operating institutions to extend limited resources
* Allow greater staff specialization
* Improve services to users
* Avoids unnecessary duplication
* Reduces the number of places which will need to go for services
* Improves working relationships between cooperating libraries.

Resource sharing refers to a joint use of resources available on a system or a network by user or peripherals. In the language of information management, when we talk about resource sharing we simply mean collective use of information of all types by various end users from a control coordinating unit or from within a network component at a reduced cost with easy accessibility.

Library cooperation and resource-sharing activity can take place in several forms and can happen at many levels, which include:

* Interlibrary loans/reciprocal borrowing privileges
* Exchange or sharing of expertise, resources, and facilities
* Exchange of publications and photocopies and other reprographic services
* Sharing of bibliographic information
* Cooperative acquisition, cooperative cataloguing, and cooperative collection development preparation of union list of holdings
* Cooperative relationship and network development

The implementation of resource sharing is largely depends on library networking. It gives an easy and wider access to information as members have an expanded information-base and service. A network is a form of arrangement or an administrative structure that links a group of individuals or organizations who have agreed to work together and/or share resources. Information networking entails the sharing of resources so that the information needs of both actual and potential users of information—from the local to national level—of all network participants are met. The network enables the participating bodies to facilitate and expand their users' access to literature and information without corresponding investment in purchase, and processing of information is exchanged through the network on a formal basis. The network may be responsible for coordinating, organizing and providing information and literature support at the national and international level. The main activities and functions of the network are as follows:

*Acquisition of materials:*

* Joint purchasing of materials

* Assignment of specialization in material acquisition
* Coordinated subscription
* Exchange of duplicate holdings

*Technical services:*

* Co-operative cataloguing
* Abstracting and indexing services
* Interlibrary loan
* Reciprocal borrowing privileges
* Reference and/or referral services

*Publication programme/repackaging information:*

* Union catalogue/list of periodicals
* Mutual notification of purchase through lists of new arrivals or acquisition list
* Bibliography development
* Newsletters
* Joint directories of personnel, projects, consultants, resource persons, etc.
* Manuals

*Coordination services:*

* Clearing house functions
* Retrieval and storage function
* Referral center

*Delivery/mailing service:*

* Research, training and other special services
  - User interest surveys
  - Joint research projects
  - In-service personnel training
  - Workshops and meetings
  - Translation services

## RESOURCE SHARING AND NETWORKS INITIATIVES IN BANGLADESH

In Bangladesh several Resource-sharing and networks initiatives was taken by different organizations in different sectors to launch Resource sharing and networking systems.

Some of these are as follows:

* *National Agricultural Information System (NAIS)*: The

Agricultural Information Centre (AIC) was taken an initiative to develop a network of agricultural institution.

* *Social Science Research Council (SSRC)*: Social Science Research Council, Dhaka was taken an initiative to develop a social science information network in Bangladesh.
* *Health Literature, Library, and Information Service (HeLLIS) Network*: The HeLLIS network was developed by SEARO (WHO), New Delhi, India and National Health Library and Documentation Centre (NHLDOC), Dhaka. All the health libraries of Bangladesh were brought under this network.
* *Development Information Network on South Asia (DEVINSA)*: The DEVINSA network was organized by CSCD (Committee on Studies for Cooperation for Development in South Asia) through the Marga Institute, Colombo, Sri Lanka. All SAARC countries, except Bhutan, were the participants of this network.
* *Information Network on Rural Development (INRD)*: Centre on Integrated Rural Development for Asia and the Pacific (CIRDAP), Dhaka was taken an initiative to develop a regional network on rural development.
* *Women Information Network (WIN)*: Centre on Integrated Rural Development for Asia and the Pacific (CIRDAP), Dhaka was taken another initiative to develop a network on women information.
* *Bangladesh Development Support Information and Communication (BDSIC) Network*: Bangladesh Academy for Rural Development (BARD), Comilla was taken an initiative to launch a network of rural development institutions in Bangladesh
* *National Science and Technology Information Policy (NASTIP)*: Under this policy, a four-tier science and technology information networking system has been recommended.
* *The Association of Management Development Institutes in South Asia (AMDISA) Library Network*: The Association

of Management Development Institutes in South Asia was launched a library network on management development. The Headquarter of this network was located at the Administrative Staff College of India, Hyderabad. One institute in each SAARC country was selected as a focal point. The Institute of Business Administration Library, Dhaka University was selected as the National focal point for this network.

* *University Libraries*: Dhaka University Library took an initiative several years' back to develop a network of the university libraries, initially by preparing a union catalogue of the holdings of the university libraries.
* The University Grants Commission of Bangladesh (UGC), in collaboration with the Asia Foundation, took an initiative to compile a union catalogue of the collections of different universities of Bangladesh and to establish an information network within the universities.
* *Bangladesh National Scientific and Library Information Network (BANSLINK)*: Bangladesh National Scientific and Technical Documentation Centre (BANSDOC) was taken an initiative to build up a Network, known as BANSLINK, to develop a resource-sharing network having dial up connectivity with 15 libraries and information centres of the country.
* *Sustainable Development Network Programme (SDNP)*: SDNP is a UNDP funded programme, which started a union catalog services in 2002 in their virtual library programme. The SDNP virtual library prepared this union catalog of 13 libraries, all of which are using CDS/ISIS software for bibliographic record keeping. The SDNP virtual library union catalog is a webbased Online Public Access Catalog.

Bangladesh being a developing country cannot effort to waste its resources. To avoid this, an effective resource sharing and networking system is necessary.

*At present the following resource sharing and networking systems are working in the country:*

* *Population Information Network (POPIN)*: The National Institute of Population Research and Training (NIPORT) has taken an initiative to establish an information networking system in the field of health, population, family planning and maternal and child health in collaboration and cooperation with the government and non-government organizations, autonomous bodies, voluntary organizations, and international organizations.
* National Health Library and Documentation Centre (NHLDOC), (Ministry of Health, Government of Bangladesh) and International Centre for Diarrhoeal Disease Research, Bangladesh (ICDDR,B) signed in 1976 an agreement to facilitate library cooperation through an interlibrary loan system and agreed to cooperate with each other to avoid duplication of journal subscriptions. Subsequently, some other library named, BIDS, BIRDEM, USAID, Dhaka, Aga Khan Community Health Programme, Dhaka, and the Bangladesh Rural Advancement Committee joined this programme by signing interlibrary loan agreements. The system has been working well.
* *United Nations Library Network in Bangladesh (UN L-Net BD)*: In March 2002 United Nations Information Centre (UNIC) Library has taken an initiative to establish the UN Library Network in Bangladesh (UN L-Net BD). Initially the Network consisted of twenty major libraries of different government, NGOs, including the UN agencies in Bangladesh. At present there are 26 members in this network. It was agreed that UNIC library would act as a focal point and secretariat of the network.

It is not possible for one libraries or information centers to hold the full stock of information resources or to procure all information, which may be in demand by its clientele. Even not a single library or information centers can meet the thrust of knowledge of all the readers from its holdings.

To solve this problem, library cooperation started long ago, such as Inter-library loan, document delivery, library networks etc. At present the more accepted system of resource sharing is library consortia. Consortia approach is one of the many ways of maintaining cooperation and coordination among the libraries and in fact it has emerged as the 'state of the art' in library cooperation in recent years.

The word 'consortia' was originated from the Latin in early 19th century in the sense of partnership. Oxford Advanced Learners Dictionary describes Consortia as 'a group of people, countries, companies, etc. who are working together on a particular project'.

A library Consortia is an association of a group of libraries that agree to share their resources to satisfy the needs of users. Consortia may be formed on a local, regional, national, or international basis; on a functional or format basis; or on a subject basis.

## BENEFITS OF CONSORTIA

The benefits of Consortia are many:

* A comprehensive collection is possible
* Building communication among different libraries
* Avoid duplication of core collection specially for core journals
* Scope of electronic archives
* Easy access to resource sharing on Internet by developing common resources databases
* Effective document delivery systems
* Better scope for developing a union catalogue
* Reduce cost of information
* Time saving
* Improved resource sharing
* More professional services to users
* Help to develop a competitive professionalism among LIS professionals

## INTERNATIONAL EFFORTS FOR LIBRARY CONSORTIA

The development of library consortia is the outcome of the

desire for resource sharing and consortia seem to be getting bigger. The global development of OCLC is prime example. Due to escalating cost of documents, decreasing budgets, inadequate storage area and competent staff, LIS professionals of the world are coming together to form consortia.

There are several International efforts for library consortia are:

* Consortium of University Research Libraries (CURL)
* Consortium of Academic Libraries in Manchester (CALIM)
* Colorado Library Information Network,
* Washington Research Library Consortium (WRLC),
* BIBSYS (Shared University, Research and National Library of Norway)
* Queensland University Libraries Office of Cooperation (QUOLOC)
* China Academic Library and Information System (CALIS), China,
* Takatsu University Library Consortium (YULC), Japan
* Tokyo Western Regional Academic Library Consortium, Japan,
* Yamatesen Ensen Private University Libraries Consortium, Japan
* Korea Resource Sharing Alliance (KORSA), Korea,
* CONsortium on Core Eletronic Resources in Taiwan (CONCERT),
* Ministry of University Affairs (MUA). ThaiLIS.

## INDIAN INITIATIVES FOR LIBRARY CONSORTIA

In India at present there are many consortia being run successfully by different organizations. Some of them are as:

* CSIR e-Journal Consortia,
* INDEST (Indian National Digital Library in Science and Technology) Consortia
* FORSA (Forum for Resource Sharing in Astronomy)
* UGC-INFONET
* IIM Library Consortia,
* ICICI Knowledge Park,

* DAE Library Consortium,
* ICMR Library Consortia,
* HELINET (Rajiv Gandhi University of Health Sciences, Karnataka).

## BANGLADESH INITIATIVES

The information revolution has brought radical changes to the functions and services in all types of libraries. Many libraries in Bangladesh till today are not in a position to afford to procure all documents and subscribe to core journals in major discipline due to financial constraints. As a result, with the aim of ensuring rapid resource sharing among the major libraries and documentation centers in Bangladesh, many library networking and resources sharing efforts were started to help each other.

The objectives of these consortia are for better resource sharing, to reduce information costs, for speedy delivery of documents, to keep abreast of new developments etc. Much emphasis should be given at the national level in Bangladesh for the development of documentary information resources, because it is considered as vital resources to promote the development of economy, science, technology and culture etc. University Grants Commission of Bangladesh (UGC) and Dr. Javed I. Khan of Kent State University have taken an initiative to develop a digital library system for Bangladesh. A 4-member committee was formed by the UGC to draft a concept paper on forming Consortia in Bangladesh, and the committee has already submitted the report to the UGC for their approval.

## CONSIDERATION NEEDED TO FORM CONSORTIA

*The following issues need to consider before building the consortia:*

* Technology infrastructure
* Resources identification
* Budget and funding
* Pricing issues
* Subscription payment issues
* Access related issues
* Licensing and copyright issues

* Archival issues
* Usages and usability issues
* Coordination among partners
* Availability of efficient staff
* Overcoming political objections
* The egos of individuals and institutions
* Adequate professional training on ICT for the LIS professionals
* Sustainability issues

## RECOMMENDATIONS

In this era of global communication, networks and consortia are highly important. A library consortium in the country is needed to achieve cost effectiveness and bridging of the digital divide. To develop library consortia in Bangladesh we have to overcome many hurdles such as inappropriate ICT infrastructure, inadequate funding, limited trained personnel, technological capability, lack of understanding of the concept of consortia. But anything new comes up with new challenges and opportunity, it is up to the individuals to take up the challenge and accept the opportunity.

So, we can recommend the following suggestions for establishment of library consortia in Bangladesh:

* The Government and LIS Professionals bodies should take initiative to conduct some workshops on Consortia.
* The Government and LIS Professionals bodies should start a forum to bring the librarians/ Information professionals and the publishers/vendors together for better communication and interactions.
* The Government should also make attempts to provide the necessary ICT infrastructure such as high-speed links and a stable network to access the e-journals.
* Policy makers, both in national and international levels together with Internet Service Provider (ISP) should have a shared obligation to seek ways to achieve the wide spread use of the internet.

* Bangladesh should have a separate ministry to coordinate the overall development of the library and information system in the country.
* LIS professionals must market their services to the private sector for sponsorship and support.
* The government should encourage and must recognize the role of librarians and information professionals in building an information society for the development of the nation.
* Involvement of management of the parents organization for sustainability

## CONCLUSION

Consortia in Bangladesh are still in table talk and there is a need to study the consortia models and guidelines and methodologies. It is recommended that the concept of Consortia can work well among similar organizations having similar situations such as sufficient additional funds available for the libraries of the consortia members and above all the committed mindsets of the library administrators. On the other side the subscription of e-journals are increasing day by day and the library budgets are shrinking, so it is needed for the library professionals to work together and formulate consortia for subscription to e-journals. Bangladeshi LIS professionals should seriously think and take initiative for consortium movement like western countries for maximum utilization of resources at the reduced cost, time and space.

# 11

# Library Operations and Use

We concentrate on operational features. The reasons for this are partly technical in that the 'physical' data are more complete than the financial and do not incur the problems of currency conversion and inflation that beset the financial aspects. There are also institutional and accounting problems in compiling financial statistics that are genuinely comparable. (Common examples are whether or not libraries are charged for the cost of premises and staff overheads - which may often be absorbed by the parent institution.) So, for these various reasons, the statistics of operational features are more robust and comparable.

## TRENDS

### STAFF

We estimate that about 374,000 staff were employed in libraries, an increase of 3.7% since 2001. This increase in staffing numbers is weighted towards the professional staff whose numbers increased by 4.9% over the period.

The increase in Trained staff occurs mostly in EU States. The number of trained librarians in all sectors of libraries (206,000) is higher than previous estimates for the mid-2000s (175,800 for 1991). However, the number of other support staff is substantially lower than previous estimates. Proportionately the returns for 'Other Staff' are appreciably lower in the CEE than in the EU.

**Table 11.1. Staff FTE * (thousands)**

| | Qualified | Other | Total |
|---|---|---|---|
| 2001 | 196 | 165 | 361 |
| 2002 | 195 | 163 | 357 |
| 2003 | 191 | 164 | 355 |
| 2004 | 195 | 163 | 357 |
| 2005 | 199 | 162 | 361 |
| 2006 | 201 | 159 | 360 |
| 2007 | 206 | 160 | 367 |
| 2008 | 206 | 168 | 374 |

*Note*: * Full Time Equivalent, *i.e.* part time staff count as fractions in proportion to hours worked.

## MATERIALS

The overall position and trends are summarised in Table 11.2:

**Table 11.2. Trends in Materials Provision (millions)**

| Resources | 2001 | 2008 | % change |
|---|---|---|---|
| Book stock | 2,778.0 | 2,944.0 | 6 |
| Audio Visual stock | 104.0 | 127.0 | 22 |
| Periodical subscriptions | 19.5 | 21.3 | 9 |
| Manuscripts | 29.5 | 32/0 | 8 |
| Microforms | 316.0 | 313.0 | -1 |
| **Annual Movements:** | | | |
| Book Additions | 171.0 | 171.0 | = |
| A/V Additions | 9.7 | 12.1 | 25 |
| Inter Library Loans (received) | 15.2 | 29.0 | 91 |

The trends in annual additions to stock appear to vary between sectors. National libraries report a growth in their annual additions in books and audio-visual materials. Public libraries book acquisitions fell between 2001-2005 but have since stabilised, while their audio-visual materials have increased steadily. With a large increase in the population served by

Tertiary Education, so have their book acquisitions grown hugely: but there has been a decline in audio visual additions. Current periodical subscriptions in the tertiary sector have remained surprisingly constant during the period 2001 to 2008. The largest number of subscriptions are in special libraries. The statistics show that holdings of Manuscripts and Microforms continue to be significant. Inter Library Lending has almost doubled: much of this is concentrated in the activity of national libraries - particularly the large scale operations in the UK and Germany - but it is also important in the smaller states.

## USE AND USERS

The count of Registered Members increased in total from 126 million to 139 million - an increase of 10.5 per cent. As this count includes those who use several libraries the proportion it represents out of the total population (484 million) - 29 per cent - is disappointingly low. But the trend is moving upwards. Estimates for Loan Transactions at 3,543 million and Visits at 3,468 million are close and show only a small difference in trend: + 5.2% against - 1.3%. When taken together the ratio for Loan Transactions per Registered Member point to high intensity of use - moving from 26.8 to 25.5.

## MODERNISATION

Several questions were introduced into the survey in order to assess aspects of service development and automation. The response to these was generally poor, though better in the CEE states than elsewhere. Typically they are not yet found in established statistical series. It will take some time before the efforts of LIBECON 2000, ISO and IFLA rectify this position, but a valuable start has been made and the information compiled here is invaluable in pointing to important trends.

Overall total estimates show the following:

* Workstations for users increased more than fourfold from 74,000 in 2001 to 310,000 in 2008. The stock of CD ROMs went up exponentially during the second half of the period, going from an estimated 456,000 in 2001 to 2,500,000 in 2008. These developments are well publicised in the profession and will come as little surprise.

* Less well known are two aspects relating to the automation of traditional materials and services. The Percentage of Catalogue Records Automated is estimated to have gone up from 36 to 46 per cent while the Percentage of Stock on Open Access increased only from 60 to 61 per cent. These figures show some progress but also point to a large deficit of automation development still required to update services and operations.

## SERVICE POINTS

Including all sectors, it is estimated that in 2008 there were 224,000 service points throughout the study area. There has been a considerable contraction since 2001, averaging 7.1%, but this has taken place particularly in the Central and Eastern European countries (CEE) where the proportionate drop was 14% and where the main closures took place in public libraries.

## THE IMPORTANCE OF THE LIBRARY SECTORS

One would expect, even over a lengthy period, to find little change in the relative size of the various library sectors. Estimates in previous surveys showed that, between 1991 and 2005 public libraries and higher education libraries increased their share of total spending on libraries - with the share of other sectors largely unchanged. In this survey we find a very different result - as illustrated in this Table 11.3:

**Table 11.3. Library Sector Shares**

| | By Total Expenditure | | | By Total Staff |
|---|---|---|---|---|
| Sector | Previous Estimate | | Present Estimate | |
| | 1991 * | 2005 | 2008 | 2008 |
| National | 6.0% | 5.9% | 5.4% | 4.1% |
| Higher Education | 15.3% | 16.9% | 19.9% | 16.5% |
| Public | 47.3% | 49.5% | 45.0% | 45.2% |
| Special | 8.6% | 8.6% | 21.3% | 16.7% |
| Other Major | 4.9% | 4.5% | 0.8% | 2.2% |
| School | 17.8% | 14.7% | 7.7% | 15.5% |

*Note*: * EU States only estimated from The Historic Libecon Database

The main reason for these changes is the new methodologies adopted to evaluate the size of the Special Library sector. This springs from two separate initiatives. First, there has been substantial research activity (chiefly but not exclusively in the UK and Germany) to apply statistical sampling techniques. As a result, what many had always suspected has been demonstrated - namely that the various types of library designated under the Special Library label are very much more numerous than had previously assumed in the absence of any systematic statistical evidence. These new estimates are still subject to error which could be substantial - but the work has been conscientiously done. Second, the exercise launched in connection with the revision of ISO 2789 has already had an effect on these statistics in that many countries (but by no means all) have gone along with the LIBECON suggestion to return libraries in the Miscellaneous sub category under Special Libraries rather than under Other Major.

The sub division of Special Libraries into sub categories has also prompted in some countries more analytical estimates. In view of this major change table also includes a column to show how different the sector proportions appear when analysed by the numbers of staff employed rather than by expenditure. (The high proportions for School and Other sectors are influenced by some unusually high returns on staffing from Poland - which may be exaggerated.).

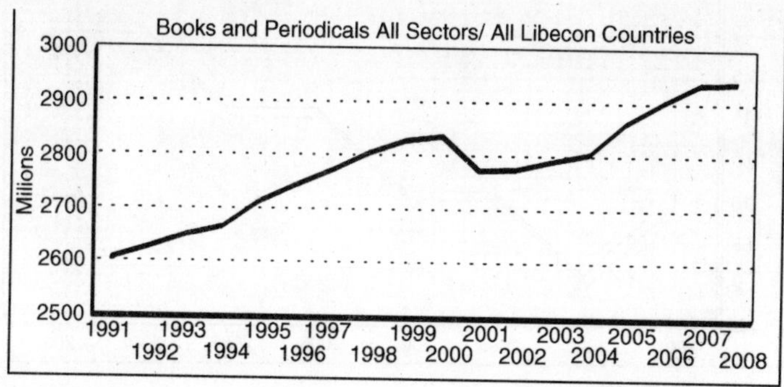


**Fig 11.1.** Book and Peribdicale All Scitirm/All Libecon Countries.

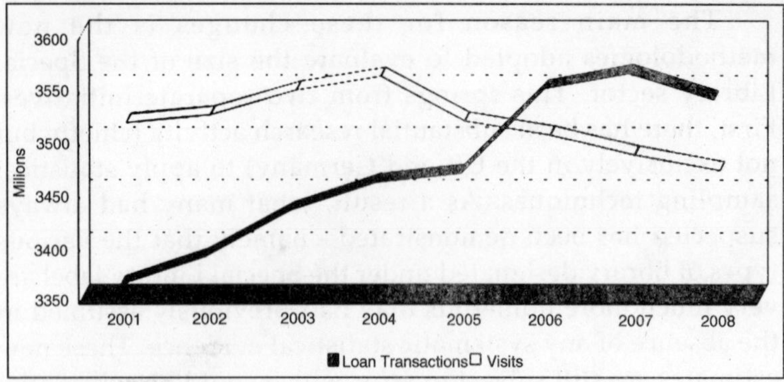


**Fig 11.2.** Visits and Loan Transactions All Sectors/All Libecon Countries

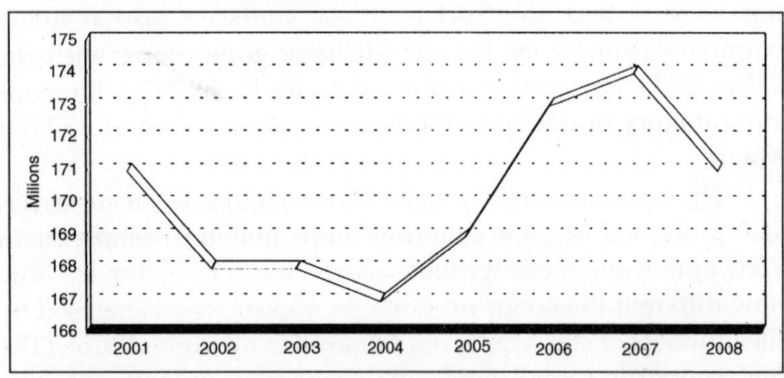


**Fig 11.3.** Book Additions All Sectors/ All Libecon Countries.

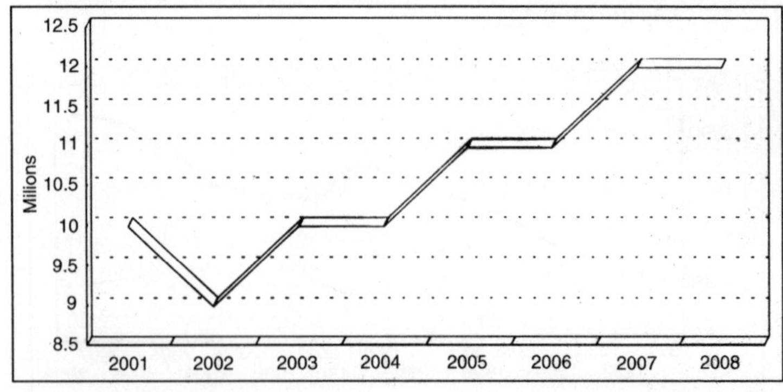


**Fig 11.4.** Audio Visual Additions All Sectors/ All Libecon Countries.

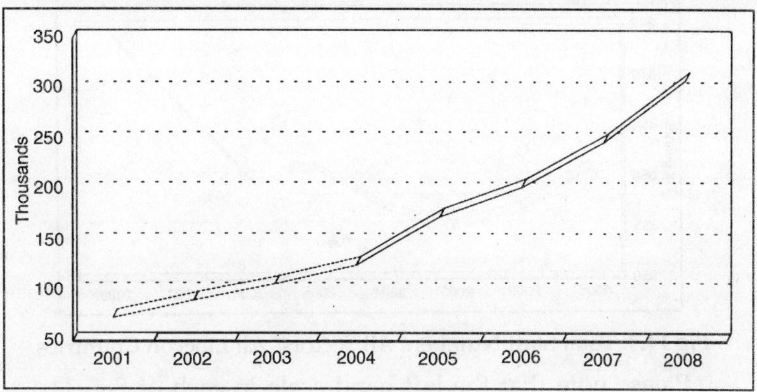


**Fig 11.5.**Workstations Forusers All Sectors/ All Libecon Countries.

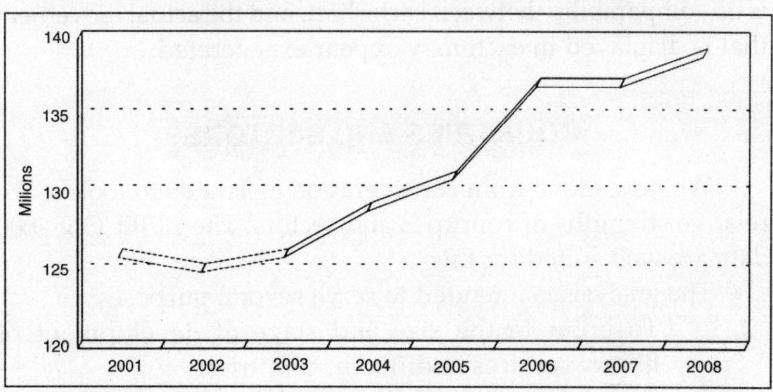


**Fig 11.6.** Registrerd Members All Sectors/ All Libecon Countries.

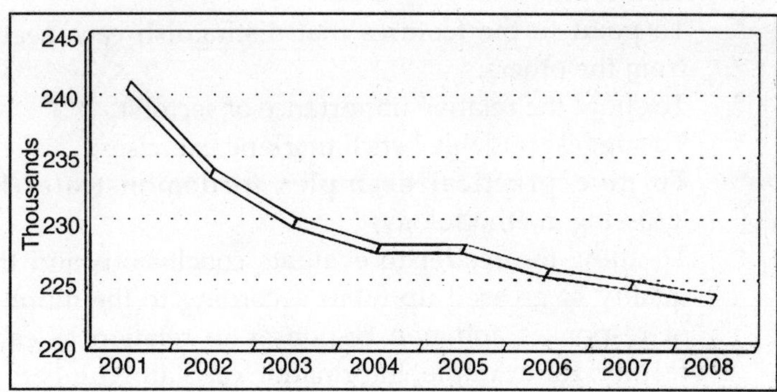


**Fig 11.7.** Service Points All Sectors/ All Libecon Countries.

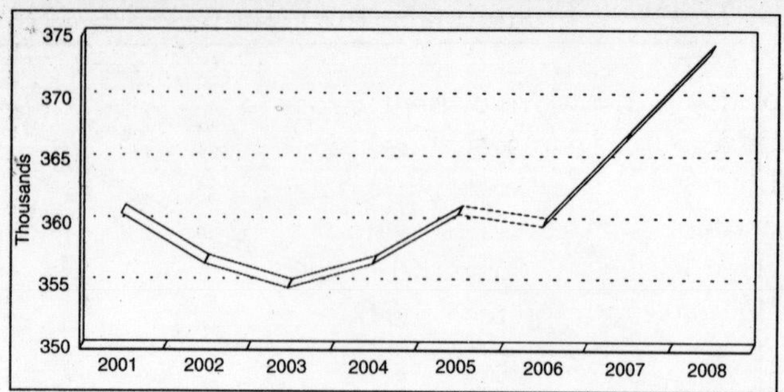


**Fig 11.8.** Total Staff Numbers All Sectors/ All Libecon Countries.

Please note that the left hand scale in each of Fig. 11.1 to 11.8 is scaled to describe the trend shown. For this reason there is no comparability between each chart, and the actual movement that is displayed in each may appear exaggerated.

## COUNTRIES AND SECTORS

We now move from consideration of Trends to look at the relative strengths of countries and sectors. The LIBECON 2000 data are well suited for this.

The analysis is intended to serve several purposes:

* To point to the size and stage of development of library services in different countries;
* To point to the relative importance of sectors within each country;
* To point to the features that distinguish each sector from the others;
* To show the relative importance of sectors;
* To suggest possible bench marking exercises;
* To give practical examples to demonstrate the 'grossing' methodology;
* To allow the reader to evaluate conclusions and the quality of grossed up totals according to the number of responses and non responses in relation to each feature: for example, information on Staff Numbers is fully provided for Public and Tertiary libraries, but it is sparse for Special and School libraries;

* To show in summary form the gaps in data not provided.

For this purpose we present 'Cross Sector Total' tables for the main resource and use features - for the year 2008. The tables shown here mainly give absolute data uncorrected for size of country (population) and their value lies partly in emphasising the differences between large and small states. Each table consists first of the 2008 data entered onto the database for each country. Three dots (...) show that we have no information provided for that feature in that country. The grossed up estimates for All States and for regions and geographical areas. The 'Response%' gives the proportion of the All States grossed up figure that is represented by actual data. Finally percentages are calculated to show, for this feature, the relative strength of each sector overall.

## STAFF NUMBERS

Table 11.4 contains, in a comparative sense, very complete data. It is particularly pleasing to see so many estimates for the Special Library sector - which give rise to an estimate of 16.7% of all staff employed in Special Libraries.

**Table 11.4. Total Staff (FTEs)**

| | National | Tertiary | Public | Special | Other | School | 1998 Total |
|---|---|---|---|---|---|---|---|
| Bulgaria | 329 | ... | ... | ... | ... | ... | |
| Czech Republic | 444 | 608 | 4,344 | ... | 0 | ... | |
| Estonia | 525 | 498 | 1,466 | 157 | 130 | 534 | |
| Hungary | 540 | 960 | 3,881 | 875 | ... | ... | |
| Latvia | 448 | 330 | 1,900 | 194 | 100 | ... | |
| Lithuania | 618 | 646 | 4,116 | 435 | 152 | 1,855 | |
| Poland | 907 | 6,601 | 17,828 | 4,063 | 1,338 | 26,000 | |
| Romania | 351 | ... | 5,014 | ... | 0 | ... | |
| Slovak Rep | 349 | 493 | 1,927 | ... | ... | 105 | |
| Slovenia | ... | 372 | 775 | 243 | 0 | 780 | |

| National | Tertiary | Public | Special | Other | School | 1998 Total | |
|---|---|---|---|---|---|---|---|
| Austria | 308 | 941 | 1,588 | ... | ... | ... | |
| Belgium | 200 | 710 | 3,940 | ... | ... | ... | |
| Denmark | 316 | 894 | 5,199 | 390 | 0 | 1,160 | |
| Ireland | 68 | 750 | 1,300 | 350 | 0 | ... | |
| Finland | 180 | 1,103 | 4,193 | 250 | ... | ... | |
| France | ... | 3,884 | 20,545 | ... | ... | ... | |
| Greece | 486 | ... | 1,834 | 57 | ... | ... | |
| Iceland | ... | ... | ... | ... | 0 | 44 | |
| Italy | 595 | ... | ... | ... | ... | ... | |
| Liechtenstein | ... | ... | ... | ... | 0 | ... | |
| Luxembourg | ... | ... | ... | ... | 0 | ... | |
| Netherlands | 250 | 1,870 | ... | 2,890 | 0 | ... | |
| Norway | 341 | 901 | 1,901 | 443 | 0 | ... | |
| Portugal | 317 | 941 | 1,449 | 1,281 | 91 | ... | |
| Spain | 520 | 4,600 | 5,500 | 3,170 | 1,470 | ... | |
| Sweden | 291 | 1,567 | 5,228 | 328 | ... | ... | |
| Switzerland | 103 | ... | ... | ... | 0 | ... | |
| UK | 2,903 | 13,000 | 25,829 | 18,000 | 0 | 5,200 | |
| Germany | 2,190 | 9,266 | 18,900 | 6,375 | ... | ... | |
| All States | 15,235 | 61,848 | 169,169 | 62,668 | 7,509 | 57,934 | 374,363 |
| CEE | 4,595 | 15,058 | 44,865 | 10,365 | 4,188 | 46,416 | 125,488 |
| EU | 10,184 | 44,401 | 119,091 | 51,124 | 3,321 | 10,796 | 238,917 |
| EFTA | 456 | 2,389 | 5,213 | 1,178 | 0 | 722 | 9,958 |
| Northern Europe | 1,139 | 4,518 | 16,701 | 1,438 | 440 | 4,431 | 28,667 |
| Central Europe | 7,583 | 31,901 | 80,114 | 38,460 | 880 | 6,038 | 164,977 |
| Southern Europe | 1,918 | 10,370 | 27,489 | 12,404 | 2,001 | 1,049 | 55,231 |

*Table Contd...*

| National | Tertiary | Public | Special | Other | School | 1998 Total | |
|---|---|---|---|---|---|---|---|
| Baltic States | 1,591 | 1,474 | 7,482 | 786 | 382 | 2,875 | 14,591 |
| Eastern Europe | 3,004 | 13,584 | 37,383 | 9,579 | 3,806 | 43,541 | 110,897 |
| Response total | 13,580 | 50,934 | 138,658 | 39,502 | 3,281 | 35,678 | 281,633 |
| Response% | 89 | 82 | 82 | 63 | 44 | 62 | 75 |
| Sector proportions | 4.1 | 16.5 | 45.2 | 16.7 | 2 | 15.5 | 100 |

In contrast the estimates for Schools libraries continue to be sparse - and the high figure for Poland is derived from a special survey conducted as long ago as 2001. Almost certainly this has distorted the grossing up estimating so that the sector proportion of 15.5% may prove to be an exaggeration. But the difficulty of obtaining data on Schools libraries has long been UNESCO experience and this gap needs urgent rectification in Europe as in other parts of the world. Complete data for all sectors have been provided by Estonia, Lithuania, Poland, Denmark and the UK. (The absence of positive data from most of them for the 'Other' sector does not indicate incompleteness, rather compliance with the intention of the survey.) Note: In all these tables there is a line to show data provided in actual responses and the percentage this represents of the total estimate. For example, in table National Libraries reported 13,580 staff: this was 89 per cent of the 15,235 estimated total. This total included estimates for Slovenia, France, Iceland, Liechtenstein and Luxembourg.

## BOOK ADDITIONS

Statistics of Book stock and acquisitions are traditionally the other most popular series in countries' statistics - and Table 11.5 demonstrates their anticipated completeness.

**Table 11.5. Book Additions 000s**

| National | Tertiary | Public | Special | Other | School | 1998 Total |
|---|---|---|---|---|---|---|
| Bulgaria | 45 | 103 | 251 | 59 | 133 | 175 |
| Czech Republic | 72 | 246 | 1,816 | ... | 0 | 562 |

*Table Contd...*

| National | Tertiary | Public | Special | Other | School | 1998 Total |
|---|---|---|---|---|---|---|
| Estonia | 38 | 99 | 544 | 28 | 27 | 180 |
| Hungary | 26 | ... | ... | ... | ... | ... |
| Latvia | 25 | 79 | 445 | 1,208 | 46 | ... |
| Lithuania | 75 | 220 | 969 | 52 | 46 | 753 |
| Poland | ... | 1,843 | 3,794 | 343 | 188 | 5,401 |
| Romania | 16 | ... | 984 | ... | 0 | ... |
| Slovak Republic | 45 | 95 | 356 | ... | ... | 199 |
| Slovenia | ... | 110 | 366 | 98 | 0 | 239 |
| Austria | 48 | 457 | ... | ... | ... | ... |
| Belgium | 50 | 393 | 1,602 | ... | ... | ... |
| Denmark | 56 | 242 | 2,242 | 124 | 0 | 1,246 |
| Ireland | 22 | 261 | 650 | ... | 0 | ... |
| Finland | 34 | 436 | 1,569 | 206 | ... | ... |
| France | ... | 1,041 | 6,206 | ... | ... | ... |
| Greece | 74 | ... | 278 | 9 | ... | ... |
| Iceland | ... | ... | 80 | ... | 0 | [illegible]2 |
| Italy | ... | 2,778 | ... | ... | ... | ... |
| Liechtenstein | ... | ... | ... | ... | 0 | .. |
| Luxembourg | ... | ... | ... | ... | 0 | ... |
| Netherlands | ... | ... | ... | ... | 0 | ... |
| Norway | 105 | 339 | 936 | 108 | 0 | 445 |
| Portugal | 33 | 296 | 528 | 195 | 49 | 352 |
| Spain | 199 | 1,228 | 1,836 | 737 | 308 | ... |
| Sweden | 92 | 560 | 1,858 | 54 | ... | ... |
| Switzerland | 33 | ... | ... | ... | 0 | ... |
| UK | 308 | 2,906 | 10,980 | 4,300 | 0 | 9,404 |

*Table Contd...*

| National | Tertiary | Public | Special | Other | School | 1998 Total | |
|---|---|---|---|---|---|---|---|
| Germany | 795 | 3,718 | ... | 1,288 | ... | ... | |
| All States | 3,327 | 20,519 | 62,703 | 15,310 | 1,518 | 67,765 | 171,142 |
| CEE | 553 | 4,210 | 10,542 | 3,344 | 516 | 11,174 | 30,339 |
| EU | 2,633 | 15,413 | 49,625 | 11,681 | 1,002 | 55,402 | 135,756 |
| EFTA | 141 | 896 | 2,536 | 285 | 0 | 1,189 | 5,047 |
| Northern Europe | 290 | 1,596 | 6,686 | 499 | 38 | 3,812 | 12,921 |
| Central Europe | 1,766 | 10,016 | 35,050 | 8,694 | 423 | 35,739 | 91,688 |
| Southern Europe | 719 | 4,697 | 10,424 | 2,774 | 541 | 17,040 | 36,195 |
| Baltic States | 138 | 397 | 1,958 | 1,288 | 119 | 1,182 | 5,082 |
| Eastern Europe | 414 | 3,813 | 8,585 | 2,056 | 397 | 9,991 | 25,256 |
| Response total | 2,191 | 17,447 | 38,292 | 8,808 | 798 | 18,987 | 86,523 |
| Response% | 66 | 85 | 61 | 58 | 53 | 28 | 51 |
| Sector proportions | 1.9 | 12 | 36.6 | 8.9 | 0.9 | 39.6 | 99.9 |

Here there are more data from Schools and less from Special libraries. Of course these data give only the numbers of items acquired and take no account of value. There the financial figures for Tertiary and Special libraries give much higher proportions - in line with very much higher unit prices paid per unit acquired. The low figure for National Libraries will be influenced in some cases by the exclusion of legal deposit acquisitions from this count.

## LOAN TRANSACTIONS

Again the data in Table 11.6 is relatively complete.

**Table11.6. Loan Transactions (000s)**

| National | Tertiary | Public | Special | Other | School | 1998 Total |
|---|---|---|---|---|---|---|
| Bulgaria | 11 | 5,282 | 16,197 | 1,662 | 4,857 | 6,877 |
| Czech | 201 | 2,034 | 62,003 | ... | 0 | ... |

*Table Contd...*

| Republic | | | | | | |
|---|---|---|---|---|---|---|
| **National** | **Tertiary** | **Public** | **Special** | **Other** | **School** | **1998 Total** |
| Estonia | 37 | 1,651 | 15,352 | 1,295 | 490 | 4,444 |
| Hungary | ... | 1,788 | 36,724 | 435 | ... | 8,548 |
| Latvia | 244 | 3,050 | 17,902 | 847 | 2,174 | ... |
| Lithuania | 36 | 6,813 | 21,991 | 2,016 | 20 | 9,690 |
| Poland | 132 | 11,597 | 189,035 | 17,705 | 3,309 | 87,044 |
| Romania | 1,090 | ... | 37,893 | ... | 0 | ... |
| Slovak Republic | 5 | 2,498 | 25,800 | ... | ... | 1,777 |
| Slovenia | ... | 3,565 | 15,600 | 471 | 0 | 5,768 |
| Austria | 345 | 3,643 | 16,066 | ... | ... | ... |
| Belgium | 248 | 1,293 | 68,475 | ... | ... | ... |
| Denmark | ... | 4,789 | 75,514 | 586 | 0 | 29,151 |
| Ireland | ... | 3,049 | 12,485 | ... | 0 | 9,203 |
| Finland | 8 | 7,637 | 100,332 | 510 | ... | ... |
| France | ... | 12,266 | 280,197 | ... | ... | ... |
| Greece | 484 | ... | 1,829 | 57 | ... | ... |
| Iceland | ... | ... | 2,000 | ... | 0 | 441 |
| Italy | 1,081 | 5,556 | ... | ... | ... | ... |
| Liechtenstein | ... | ... | ... | ... | 0 | ... |
| Luxembourg | ... | ... | ... | ... | 0 | ... |
| Netherlands | ... | ... | ... | ... | 0 | ... |
| Norway | ... | 3,051 | 19,029 | 604 | 0 | 4,443 |
| Portugal | 423 | 1,468 | 1,681 | 1,531 | 2 | 773 |
| Spain | ... | 13,817 | 21,417 | 3,714 | 5,356 | ... |
| Sweden | 151 | 5,305 | 80,479 | 469 | ... | 17,000 |
| Switzerland | ... | ... | ... | ... | 0 | ... |

*Table Contd...*

| | | | | | | | |
|---|---|---|---|---|---|---|---|
| UK | 5,781 | 79,742 | 497,889 | 10,000 | 0 | 90,819 | |
| Germany | ... | ... | 324,555 | 5,552 | ... | ... | |
| **National** | **Tertiary** | **Public** | **Special** | **Other** | **School** | **1998 Total** | |
| All States | 21,154 | 254,227 | 2,337,545 | 78,137 | 27,747 | 824,577 | 3,543,387 |
| CEE | 1,984 | 50,511 | 438,496 | 38,660 | 12,715 | 186,244 | 728,610 |
| EU | 18,711 | 195,643 | 1,846,583 | 37,880 | 15,032 | 626,148 | 2,739,997 |
| EFTA | 458 | 8,073 | 52,467 | 1,597 | 0 | 12,185 | 74,780 |
| Northern Europe | 605 | 20,966 | 277,355 | 2,205 | 569 | 59,689 | 361,389 |
| Central Europe | 14,584 | 156,902 | 1,306,743 | 26,026 | 6,340 | 389,244 | 1,899,839 |
| Southern Europe | 3,981 | 25,848 | 314,952 | 11,246 | 8,123 | 189,400 | 553,550 |
| Baltic States | 317 | 11,514 | 55,244 | 4,159 | 2,684 | 18,291 | 92,209 |
| Eastern Europe | 1,668 | 38,997 | 383,251 | 34,502 | 10,031 | 167,953 | 636,402 |
| Response total | 10,277 | 179,894 | 1,940,445 | 47,454 | 16,208 | 275,978 | 2,470,256 |
| Response% | 49 | 71 | 83 | 61 | 58 | 33 | 70 |
| Sector proportions | 0.6 | 7.2 | 66.0 | 2.2 | 0.8 | 23.3 | 100.1 |

This is the measure by which Public library activity is most commonly assessed - and the suggested comparisons with Schools libraries are interesting. The low proportion for Special Libraries corresponds with ways in which they are typically used and is not surprising.

The low figure for the Tertiary sector is probably not a good indicator of use: typically they have heavy use of material on the premises - which, when taken from open shelves, is frequently not included in the statistics of transactions. Ways to overcome this weakness are being actively explored in many places - not least in the context of the revision to ISO 2789. Table

*Table Contd...*

11.7 'Loan Transactions per member of Staff' provides an indication of productivity.

**Table 11.7. Loan Transactions Per Member Of Staff**

| National | Tertiary | Public | Special | Other | School | 1998 Total |
|---|---|---|---|---|---|---|
| Bulgaria | 35 | ... | ... | ... | ... | ... |
| Czech Republic | 452 | 3,346 | 14,274 | ... | ... | ... |
| Estonia | 70 | 3,313 | 10,469 | 8,230 | 3,769 | 8,320 |
| Hungary | ... | 1,863 | 9,462 | 498 | ... | ... |
| Latvia | 545 | 9,242 | 9,422 | 4,368 | 21,740 | ... |
| Lithuania | 58 | 10,547 | 5,343 | 4,635 | 133 | 5,224 |
| Poland | 146 | 1,757 | 10,603 | 4,358 | 2,473 | 3,348 |
| Romania | 3,106 | ... | 7,557 | ... | ... | ... |
| Slovak Republic | 14 | 5,067 | 13,388 | ... | ... | 16,924 |
| Slovenia | ... | 9,584 | 20,129 | 1,938 | ... | 7,395 |
| Austria | 1,119 | 3,873 | 10,116 | ... | ... | ... |
| Belgium | 1,239 | 1,821 | 17,379 | ... | ... | ... |
| Denmark | ... | 5,357 | 14,524 | 1,503 | ... | 25,130 |
| Ireland | ... | 4,065 | 9,604 | ... | ... | ... |
| Finland | 44 | 6,927 | 23,929 | 2,040 | ... | ... |
| France | ... | 3,158 | 13,638 | ... | ... | ... |
| Greece | 996 | ... | 997 | 996 | ... | ... |
| Iceland | ... | ... | ... | ... | ... | 10,071 |
| Italy | 1,817 | ... | ... | ... | ... | ... |
| Liechtenstein | ... | ... | ... | ... | ... | ... |
| Luxembourg | ... | ... | ... | ... | ... | ... |
| Netherlands | ... | ... | ... | ... | ... | ... |
| Norway | ... | 3,387 | 10,008 | 1,362 | ... | ... |

| | | | | | | | |
|---|---|---|---|---|---|---|---|
| Portugal | 1,335 | 1,560 | 1,160 | 1,195 | 22 | ... | |
| Spain | ... | 3,004 | 3,894 | 1,172 | 3,644 | ... | |
| **National** | **Tertiary** | **Public** | **Special** | **Other** | **School** | **1998 Total** | |
| Sweden | 518 | 3,386 | 15,394 | 1,431 | ... | ... | |
| Switzerland | ... | ... | ... | ... | ... | ... | |
| UK | 1,991 | 6,134 | 19,276 | 556 | ... | 17,465 | |
| Germany | ... | ... | 17,172 | 871 | ... | ... | |
| All States | 1,389 | 4,111 | 13,818 | 1,247 | 3,695 | 14,233 | 38,492 |
| CEE | 432 3,354 | 9,774 | 3,730 | 3,036 | 4,012 | 24,338 | |
| EU | 1,837 | 4,406 | 15,506 | 741 | 4,526 | 57,998 | 85,015 |
| EFTA | 1,006 | 3,380 | 10,064 | 1,356 | ... | 16,882 | 32,687 |
| Northern Europe | 531 | 4,640 | 16,607 | 1,533 | 1,292 | 13,471 | 38,076 |
| Central Europe | 1,923 | 4,918 | 16,311 | 677 | 7,205 | 64,466 | 95,500 |
| Southern Europe | 2,076 | 2,493 | 11,457 | 907 | 4,060 | 180,553 | 201,545 |
| Baltic States | 199 | 7,810 | 7,383 | 5,288 | 7,027 | 6,362 | 34,069 |
| Eastern Europe | 555 | 2,871 | 10,252 | 3,602 | 2,636 | 3,857 | 23,773 |
| Response total | ** | ** | ** | ** | ** | ** | ** |
| Response% | ** | ** | ** | ** | ** | ** | ** |
| Sector proportions | 3.6 | 10.7 | 35.9 | 3.2 | 9.6 | 37.0 | 100.0 |

*Table Contd...*

# Bibliography

Arambam Saroj: *Modern Library System,* Kolkata: Kolkata Press Club, 2001.

Bahadur Mutua: *Modern Cataloguing,* Assam: Assam University Press, 2001.

Bareh H.M: *Encyclopaedia of Modern Library System,* Manipur: Mittal Publications, 2001.

Das N.K.: *Modern Cataloguing: Systems and Practices,* New Delhi: Inter - India Publications, 2004.

Dutta P. S.: *Library Work Cumulated,* Assam: Omsons Publications, 2000.

Khanna S.K.: *Encyclopaedia of Library,* Assam: Indian Publishers, 2006.

Lert, F.: *Modern Library Strategies,* Manipur: University Press, 2003.

Nag Sajal: *Handbook of Whole Library,* Mumbai: University Press of Mumbai, 2002.

Sanajaoba N.: *Occupational Outlook,* Guwahati: Akansha Publishing House, 2003.

Sareen H.K.: *Makers of Modern Strategy,* New Delhi: Sterling Publishers Private Ltd, 2000.

Sharma S.C.: *Building Embedded Linux Systems,* Kolkata: Magnum Press, 2000.

Singh A. Lalit: *Staffing the Modern Library,* Mumbai: Mittal Publications, 2004.

Singh Chandrika: *Introducing and Managing Academic Library,* New Delhi: New Delhi Press, 2001.

Singh Lokendra: *Public and its Public Library,* Mumbai: Mittal Publications, 2000.

Stimson, G.: *Advances in Library Administration and Organization,* New Delhi: Inter-India Publications, 2004.

Tarapot Phanjoubam: *Growth, Creativity, and Collaboration in Library System,* New Delhi: Har Anand Publication, 2003.

Tensuba K.C.: *Integrated Library System:* Karnatka: Karnatak University Press, 2005.

Uchtenhagen, A.: *Indian Library System,* New Delhi: Manohar Press, 2002.

Zhimomi Kuhoi K.: *Special Libraries,* New Delhi: Deep and Deep Publications, 2006.

# Index

## H



## I



## K



## M



## N



## P



## R



## S



## T



## U



## V



## W